James Dyer Ball

Cantonese Made Easy

a book of simple sentences in the Cantonese dialect, with free and literal translations, and directions for the rendering of English grammatical forms in Chinese

James Dyer Ball

Cantonese Made Easy
a book of simple sentences in the Cantonese dialect, with free and literal translations, and directions for the rendering of English grammatical forms in Chinese

ISBN/EAN: 9783337284954

Printed in Europe, USA, Canada, Australia, Japan

Cover: Foto ©Andreas Hilbeck / pixelio.de

More available books at **www.hansebooks.com**

CANTONESE MADE EASY:

A BOOK OF SIMPLE SENTENCES IN THE CANTONESE DIALECT, WITH
FREE AND LITERAL TRANSLATIONS, AND DIRECTIONS
FOR THE RENDERING OF ENGLISH GRAM-
MATICAL FORMS IN CHINESE.

SECOND EDITION.
REVISED AND ENLARGED.

By

J. DYER BALL, M.R.A.S., ETC.,

OF HER MAJESTY'S CIVIL SERVICE, HONGKONG.

Author of "*Easy Sentences in the Hakka Dialect with a Vocabulary,*" "*Easy Sentences in the Cantonese Dialect with a Vocabulary,*" "*The Cantonese-made-Easy Vocabulary,*" *and* "*An English-Cantonese Pocket Vocabulary without the Chinese Characters or Tonic Marks,*" *&c.*

HONGKONG:
PRINTED AT THE 'CHINA MAIL' OFFICE.
1888.
[ALL RIGHTS RESERVED.]

CONTENTS.

PREFACES.

	Page.
Preface to the First Edition, ...	I
„ „ Second Edition, ...	IX

INTRODUCTION.

The Cantonese Dialect, ...	XIII
The Correct Pronunciation of Pure Cantonese, ...	XV
The Tones, ...	XVIII
Methods of Describing Tones, ...	XXII
List of Tones, ...	XXIII
Division of the Tones, ...	XXIV
Description of the Tones, ...	XXIV
Marks to Designate the Tones, ...	XXVIII
Tonic Exercises, ...	XXXII
Aspirated and Non-aspirated Words, ...	XXXVIII
Long and Short Vowels, ...	XLII
Pronunciation, ...	XLVI
Syllabary, ...	XLVII

LESSONS.

Abbreviations, ...	1
The Numerals, ...	2
Lesson I.—Domestic, ...	4
„ II.—General, ...	6
„ III.— „	8

		Page.
Lesson IV.—General,	.. ..	10
„ V.— „	.. ..	12
„ VI.—Relationships,	.. ..	14
„ VII.—Opposites,	.. ..	16
„ VIII.—Monetary,	.. ..	18
„ IX.—Commercial,	.. ..	20
„ X.— „	.. ..	22
„ XI.—Medical, ..	.. ..	24
„ XII.—Ecclesiastical,	.. ..	26
„ XIII.—Nautical, ..	.. ..	28
„ XIV.—Judicial, ..	.. ..	30
„ XV.—Educational,	.. ..	32

GRAMMAR.

Nouns,	.. ..	36
Articles,	.. ..	43
Classifiers, &c.,	.. ..	44
Adjectives, ..	.. ..	59
Numeral Adjectives,	.. ..	62
Pronouns, ..	.. ..	68
Adjective Pronouns,	.. ..	73
Verbs,	.. ..	77
Adverbs, ..	.. ..	101
Prepositions,	.. ..	105
Conjunctions,	.. ..	109
Interjections,	.. ..	111
Finals, ..	.. ..	112
Simple Directions,	.. ..	117
Final Directions, ..	.. ..	118

APPENDIX.

Excursus 1. Chinese Grammar, ..	.. ..	1
„ 2. Differences between the Book Language and Colloquial,		1
„ 3. Reasons why Europeans speak Cantonese poorly,	.. ..	3

INDEX.

PREFACE

TO THE FIRST EDITION.

This little book is meant to supply a want. The Author has heard a beginner in Chinese sadly lamenting the difficulty he had in the use of his phrase book to know what the Chinese words really meant. Before him and before many a learner there appear on the opened pages of his book sentences in English and sentences in Chinese. He reads the English and his Chinese teacher reads the Chinese over to him until he learns the sounds. By dint of memory he learns that a certain English sentence is expressed in Chinese by certain Chinese words, which he supposes are the equivalents of the English words; but as soon as he commences to analyse the two sentences—to place them side by side, he finds that there seems to be very little similarity between the two. The one often has more words by far than the other; there are no numbers, no moods, no tenses, or but halting expedients to represent them, which are well nigh unintelligible to him; and the use of his dictionary, at first, affords him but little assistance in his attempts to pick asunder the component parts of a Chinese sentence, for either he does not find the word that is given in his phrase book, or he is embarrassed by the multiplicity of renderings for one word.

ARRANGEMENT OF THIS BOOK.

In some of the first books in Cantonese and English by the veteran sinologists this difficulty was in a great measure met by a literal as well as a free translation being given of the Chinese. The Author has resuscitated this old plan and trusts it will be found of service. In some cases it will be found, however, that it has been well nigh impossible, on account of the idiomatic differences of the two languages, to give a perfectly intelligible and literal rendering of the Chinese; for it sometimes happens, as George MacDonald well remarks, that:—"It is often curious how a literal rendering, even when it gives quite the meaning, will not do, because of the different ranks of the two words in their respective languages." (*Adela Cathcart*, p. 34). Yet with the object of pointing out the connection of the different words

PREFACE.

and their respective places in the sentence, even a poor literal translation will assist the learner far better to grasp the construction of the sentence and the real meaning of the words than a free translation, which must necessarily often be but a paraphrase of the Chinese.

When two or more English words represent one Chinese word the Author has in the literal translation connected them by a hyphen, and the same holds good of the Chinese and English. Any exceptions to this are so plain that there is no necessity to make any note of them.

The fault of most phrase books in Chinese is the multiplying Chinese words in a sentence; especially do such books delight in a redundancy of particles; one is almost sickened by a glance through some of the phrase books in use where 'ko ko', ₍ni ko', ke', and many other particles are brought in at any time and every time to the detriment of the learner's fluency in speaking. The consequence of this fault in that learners pile up the component parts of a sentence until the outcome is something wonderful to hearken to, and more like a foreign language than good Chinese. The Chinese are fonder of expressing themselves in a terse and concise manner than most book-makers represent them as doing. Redundancy of words are cut out of good Chinese colloquial with an unsparing hand: and it would be a good thing for a learner to lay it down as a general rule that if it is possible to express his meaning with few words he should do so; for though to his own ear the addition of words may make the meaning plainer, it has probably a directly contrary effect on a Chinese ear.

Compare :—

⁵Néi ₍lai to' ₍ni shü' k'ap₍ 'péi 'ko ko' ₍shü kwo' ⁴ngo 't'ai kin' ₍la,
and
₍Lai ₍ni shü' 'péi ko' ₍shü ⁵ngo 't'ai ₍la.

There is often also no distinction made in phrase books between the colloquial and book language: immediately after a sentence which would be understood by any woman or child comes one so bookish that if the learner were to attempt to air his newly-acquired knowledge, thus obtained, out of the range of his study or of the ears of his erudite teacher, he would find his talk utterly unintelligible to the mass of his hearers. In short a hotchpotch of anything and everything is thrown together, mixed and pure, Cantonese and provincialisms, and the result is a phrase book.

Many of the simplest and commonest forms of expression are entirely omitted even in books of considerable size where want of space could be no excuse.

There is often also apparent in these books an evident attempt to *put* the English sentence which the compiler chooses into Chinese, ignoring often to a great extent

PREFACE.

the simple fact that the idiom is essentially English; and the result is a sentence composed of Chinese words which is either constructed on an English idiom wholly foreign to the genius of the language, or stilted in order to convey the whole meaning of the English sentence into Chinese; or else the two sentences are not the counterparts of each other, and the learner is misled.

Knowing these defects, the Author has endeavoured to avoid them.

It appeared to him that a compiler should endeavour above everything else to have his Chinese perfect and readable, or *shun*, as a Chinese would term it, and then try his best to render the Chinese into English. Under such conditions there is more likelihood of getting good Chinese into our phrase books than when the opposite plan is tried.

Daily intercourse for nearly a quarter of a century with all classes of Chinese in their daily life, and years of daily contact with all grades of Chinese in the course of his official duties, where no attempts, or but few, are made to adapt themselves to the foreign ear, have placed him, he believes, in an exceptionally favourable position to hear and note the different idioms of good Cantonese. He has endeavoured to embody a number of them in this book, which, if it meets with a favourable reception, might induce him to attempt something more pretentious on a future occasion.

Nothing, he hopes, will be found amongst the fifteen Lessons but pure good colloquial; and from the examples given in that part of the book, as well as in the part which follows, the learner will be able to frame other sentences.

In learning Cantonese, the learner should aim first at acquiring such common idioms and such words as to make himself understood by even the illiterate class, for then all classes will understand him. Starting in this manner he will lay a good solid foundation for his colloquial, which will stand him in good stead all through his stay in China. After this foundation is laid he can easily acquire the mixed colloquial, composed principally of what he has already learned, and partly of book terms; and if he has previously pleased the illiterate ear, qualify himself to please the fastidious ear of the scholar. Though there is no hard and fast line between these two forms of colloquial, as they merge more or less into each other, there is still a distinction. And the learner should keep this distinction in his mind and ask his teacher whether any new phrase he comes across is colloquial or not. Without this precaution he will find himself talking in a most ridiculous style, at one breath as it were using Johnsonian words and pure English.

In most, if not all, phrase books the tones seem to be a thing of secondary importance. If the compiler carefully gives the tones as he finds them in his dictionary he congratulates himself on at least stretching a point. As a general rule

PREFACE.

no attempt is ever made to give the tones as they are spoken, or when the attempt has been made the compiler has had so little idea of the frequency of difference between colloquial and book tones that his attempts to point one or two out have not been of the practical use that they might have been. It is one thing to read a book and utter all the tones correctly, but quite another thing to explain to a Chinese the contents of a few pages thereof, and if the speaker sticks to the same tones in speaking as in reading he will not find that all he says is understood. It is, the Author believes, an ignoring of this fact that often spoils foreigners' Chinese. The awkward thing about ignoring these tones in books for the use of those who wish to learn to speak Chinese is that the learner attempts to say the word in the tone that he sees it marked in his book or dictionary, the consequence being that he systematically mispronounces it; while if the tone were marked properly he would at least attempt to pronounce it properly.

The colloquial tones in this book are given instead of those used in the book language; but an asterisk is placed at such words to show that the word has another tone as well.

It will be noticed that occasionally the tones of one word are different in different connections.

Learners may at once make up their minds to the belief that there are more tones in the Chinese than many of the old scholars will give credit for. The *chung yap* is introduced in this phrase book. The man who pretends to doubt its existence may as well confess at once that he knows nothing about differences in tones; it was well known by one or two of the older sinologists in olden times, but was well-nigh forgotten until unearthed recently. There is more excuse for the scepticism that exists about some of the other tones, though there can be no doubt as to their existence. The Author would call attention to what has never been noticed yet in Cantonese as regards its systematic application to all the tones, and that is what for want of a better term he must call complimental tones. These tones are very distinctly marked in the Swatow dialect, where the latter of two words, the second of which is a repetition of the former, is put in a slightly higher or lower tone according to which series of tones the word occurs in. This, it would almost seem, also happens but to a very infinitesimal degree in Cantonese, though it occurs in conformity to the general rule which differentiates the tones in the Cantonese and Swatow respectively, that is to say that as a certain word in Swatow which is in the lower series of tones, when rendered in Cantonese rises into the higher series, and vice versâ, so the complimental tone which in Swatow would be lower than the original tone in the Cantonese is higher than the original tone sound, and vice versâ. This variation between

PREFACE.

the original and complimental tones in Cantonese is about the interval of half a tone in music.* Each tone of the nine can have this secondary tone. This of course will be considered a moot point at present, as even some Chinese deny their existence. It would appear to be a law of Chinese pronunciation that when two words of identical sound follow each other, the latter of the two falls, or rises into a higher or lower complimental tone. And it is probably the same law or one nearly akin to it that gives rise to the formation of new words in different tones to distinguish them from words of identical sound of which there are not a few in Cantonese, such as 的 'ko and 個 ko' &c.

Instead then of only eight tones in Cantonese it is the fact that there are a dozen well-defined tones at least, and possibly others which are very indefinite and perhaps are only being formed at present. This however need not trouble the beginner. It is well that he should know at the same time that he must not attempt to fit every Chinese word into a sound corresponding to the eight, nine, or ten tones recognised by the dictionaries. Cantonese will not be confined in that way, and much of the poor pronunciation of Chinese by Europeans is on account of their persistent attempts to pronounce all Chinese words as if they must belong to one or other of the eight or nine tones their dictionaries tell them about. Get a good teacher, then copy him exactly no matter what your dictionary may say about the tone of the word; for it is important that the beginner, who wishes to do more than just run a chance of being partially understood, should pay particular attention to these important tones, though at the same time let him not run into the other extreme of hesitating before he utters a word to think what tone it should be in. If he can manage to get fluent in Chinese idioms, an occasional mistake in the tones is not of such vital importance, though to be deprecated.

GRAMMAR.

The Directions for rendering English Grammatical Forms and Idioms into Chinese and vice versâ will, it is hoped, prove of service in enabling the beginner to form a conception of the mode in which English grammatical forms may be rendered in Chinese, a language which at first sight appears to be devoid of all grammar. The construction of the component parts and the building up of the sentence from its component phrases will also appear to a certain extent.

---

* Note to Second Edition.—It will be noted that the Author does not here refer to the Colloquial rising tone at all, though one of his critics so misunderstood and consequently proceeded, owing to the misunderstanding, to contradict the above statement.

PREFACE.

The notes are not exhaustive, but it is hoped that they are of sufficient variety and length to give the learner such an idea of the construction of the colloquial, and of many of its idioms, as to enable him to avoid egregious errors.

So little has been attempted in this way hitherto, that it is with considerable diffidence one makes the attempt of laying down instructions, when hitherto the learner has generally had to bungle on as well as he could himself.

It is hoped, however, that the experience of one who has made the study of Chinese a life work will not prove useless to the beginner.

The study of Chinese is sufficiently difficult to make every little hint a desideratum.

FINAL PARTICLES.

The Final Particles are most useful little words, quite altering the whole force of the sentence when differently applied. These little particles at the end of a sentence are often put to a dreadful martyrdom in beginners' books. The student must not suppose that because they are so plentifully sprinkled over the pages of his book that he cannot close his mouth without enunciating one or two of them as he would punctuate each of his written sentences. They are in fact often left out with advantage; but when left out to make up for their absence the voice lingers often on the last word in the sentence longer than it would otherwise do, and with a peculiar intonation and rising inflection.

Too little attention has been paid to them hitherto. Our dictionaries do not contain all that are in use. A list appears of as many as the compiler has been able to discover up to the present time with their tonal variations; but it is not at all improbable that there are more to be discovered. Nearly half of this list is not to be found in the dictionaries. If the finals used in the different dialects and sub-dialects of Cantonese were included, the list might be made of an enormous length, as, for instance, in the Shun-tak dialect, to mention a few instances amongst many, we have the finals, *tá*, *téi*, *ti*, and others besides those in use in pure Cantonese.

This is, however, not the place to go into a dissertation on the finals, but the hint may be of use if taken advantage of, for there are a great many more shades of meaning to be expressed by a proper use of these little words than most Europeans have ever dreamt of.

CHINESE CHARACTERS.

The Chinese characters are given more as a guide to the teacher than for use by the beginner. If the latter can and will take advice it is this:—Don't

PREFACE.

trouble yourself with the character, or the book language at first. If you will learn the characters, learn them out of the colloquial books for the first year, and then, when you are tolerably proficient in colloquial, a knowledge of the book way of expressing what you have already acquired in colloquial will not be apt to confuse you, or spoil your colloquial.

One thing at a time is enough. If you wish to speak Chinese well, learn to speak it before you learn to read it. A Chinese child learns to speak his native tongue before he learns to read it; and yet we, go-ahead Westerners, think we know better than Dame Nature, and insist on learning two languages (the book language and the colloquial) at the same time—two languages which, be it remembered, are so alike and yet so dissimilar as to create no end of a confusion in the tyro's brain. The result is that we produce but few good speakers of Chinese.

Above all things let him who would speak Chinese not be ashamed to talk whenever he has a chance. Air his Chinese at all times: it will get musty if he does not. What does it matter if he does make mistakes at first? If he finds he is not understood when he puts a thing in one way, then put it in another. He should try to get up a pretty extensive vocabulary of apparent synonyms, and by experience and experiment he will learn what words are best understood by different classes of people, and what are the right words to use. Of course all this implies a great deal of patience; but if a man has no patience he had better not come to far Cathay.

ORTHOGRAPHY.

The orthography is Williams' with the exception of some slight variations where •necessary.

The classes of variants are given below, so that the scholar may find no difficulty in using Williams' Tonic Dictionary or Eitel's Chinese Dictionary.

In this book.	In Williams' and Eitel's.
éi	í (or i in Eitel's.)
ö	éu
wú	ú
wui	ui
yí	í
yü	ü

If the beginner would be a good speaker let him not follow the pronunciations given in Dictionaries, if he finds such to clash with that of his teacher, provided he

PREFACE.

has a good one, but imitate the latter. Let him remember:—

1st. That the dictionaries have been made by Europeans to whom Chinese was not a native tongue, and that consequently they are not free from errors.

2nd. Also let him remember that at the best it is but a halting expedient this attempting to represent Chinese sounds by the letters of an alphabet, which, as we are accustomed to use them in our own language, are never in every case capable of producing the identical Chinese sound.

3rd. Let him also remember that some of the Chinese assistants that Dictionary makers have depended on for their pronunciations were not pure Cantonese speakers.

These several reasons will be sufficient to assure him of the necessity for adhering to the above advice; and when he becomes a proficient in the use of this beautiful (when spoken in its purity) dialect he will see an additional reason in the miserable pronunciation of some Europeans, who have considered their dictionaries wiser then the Chinese themselves, and he may be gratified by being told by the Chinese that his pronunciation is clearer and better in many respects than many a native's.

In conclusion the author may express the hope—a hope that has actuated him throughout the preparation, that this little book will prove a help in the study of a tongue which he has known and spoken from his earliest infancy. Should it prove of assistance to those who unlike him have not been able to avail themselves of the easiest and best mode of learning it, he will be proud that these efforts have proved capable of assisting those who desire to acquire a knowledge of this, one of the finest and oldest dialects in China.

His thanks are again due to Mr. H. A. Giles of H. M.'s Consular Service for again permitting him to make use of his arrangement of sentences and the plan of his book, as far as the first part of it is concerned, which it will be seen he has considerably enlarged upon.

Mr. A. Falconer, of the Government Central School, Hongkong, has also kindly assisted him in correcting proof sheets.

Should mistakes be discovered the author will be obliged by those using the book informing him of them.

———

After having written out the whole of the lessons and while they were in the press, the compiler's attention was called to Mr. Parker's orthography as applied to the Cantonese; and finding that in one instance it supplied a want that he had felt,

PREFACE.

and that in another instance it represented a sound which had not been brought out clearly, his spelling in both these instances was modified in conformity with Mr. Parker's system, though he cannot endorse Mr. Parker's attempts in their entirety (his attempts to rid the orthography from diacritical marks do not always appear to be the best); especially all the conclusions he arrives at as exemplified by his orthography that is to say if he understands what the spelling always refers to, but unfortunately his syllabary is printed without any Chinese characters, so that one scarcely knows what word the new combination of letters always represents. Finding that in certain cases Mr. Parker's was an improvement on the current orthography, other cases have also been referred to Mr. Parker's syllabary, and the author must acknowledge occasional assistance he has derived from such a reference while working by the guidance of his ear to free himself from the, in too many cases, barbarous and incorrect spellings used by the dictionaries. He has been pleased to find on reference to Mr. Parker's syllabary that he also had arrived in the majority of instances at the same conclusions that the author had. This he trusts will give more confidence in the accuracy of those sounds represented by Mr. Parker and himself to those who may be inclined to look with suspicion upon and doubt the propriety of any change, however simple, in the admirable adaptation of Sir William Jones' system of spelling made in his younger days by that venerable and learned sinologist, Dr. Williams.

J. DYER BALL.

HONGKONG, 1883.

PREFACE
TO THE SECOND EDITION.

It is now rather more than four years since the first edition, of five hundred copies, of this book was published. Uncertain of the success of the venture at the time the book was but limited in its scope. The disposal of the first edition and the approval the book has met with has led the author to now issue a second edition of the same work, which, though running on the same lines as the first edition, has been considerably enlarged. The first part of the book, that containing the fifteen lessons, may at first sight appear to be the same in the two editions, but though

PREFACE.

the same number of pages are occupied, it will be found that there are many more sentences in this part of the book than formerly, great care has also been exercised in a careful revision of the lessons, and here the author must acknowledge the great assistance rendered to him by Mr. J. H. Stewart Lockhart, who kindly volunteered to assist him.

In the second or Grammatical portion of the book it will be seen that thirty-six pages are added. A new table of the Classifiers has been drawn up from which it has been attempted to exclude words not rightly entitled to the name of Classifiers, though often so called, and these words have been placed in a list by themselves. A better table of the Personal Pronouns has also been drawn out. An important addition has likewise been the lists of the idiomatic uses of verbs, and other additions it will be seen have been made, all of which the author trusts will make the book more useful. The old matter has also been revised.

A new feature appears in the shape of an Index to the Second part, which will no doubt render reference to passages sought for easier than with the help of the table of contents alone, which is still retained. In the Introduction the tones have been more fully treated.

It has been the author's endeavour in what may be called the Grammatical portion of the book not so much to lay down Grammatical Rules describing the structure of the language irrespective of its analogy to other languages; but it has been his aim so to word these rules as to show the learner the difference between the learner's native language and that he is endeavouring to acquire, for in detecting the points of resemblance and difference between his own language and one foreign to him will the learner be the better able to appreciate the similarity and dissimilarity between the two languages. It is but a waste of time to draw up a Chinese Grammar on the same lines as an English Grammar; such Grammars are useful to those who wish to learn the structure of their own language, but to those who already know something of the Grammar of one language this knowledge is best utilised by being used as a vantage ground. The knowledge already acquired is compared with what it is desired to acquire. The mind instead of being burdened with going over old ground has its powers left free to tabulate the new knowledge under the two heads of "the same as I learnt before, I do not need to trouble about that," and the other head of "this is different from what I learnt before, I must try and remember this."

Any learner who desires to acquire a new language if he wishes to make any progress must consciously or unconsciously thus tabulate his knowledge. If it is not already done for him in the books he uses, his time is taken up with wading

PREFACE.

through a mass of rules and examples to pick out what is new to him. His time is saved and the acquisition of the language rendered easier for him, if it is done before-hand for him.

Exception has been taken by one or two to the use of the literal translation of the Chinese into English on account of its barbarous nature, but its manifest advantages to the beginner are so obvious, not only theoretically but in actual practice in the use of this book, that the Author's predilections in its favour are confirmed. As to its being barbarous, what does barbarous mean? Simply that anything is outside of our pale of civilization and customary mode of expression, &c. A literal translation of any language into English proves more or less barbarous: this is even true with regard to the classic languages of ancient Greece and Rome.

As a hint to the use to which this literal translation may be put the following passage given from an essay by Proctor with regard to the use of literal translations such as the Hamiltonian method, the literal translation employed by the author of the present work being very like that. Mr. Proctor says:—"Take then first * * a passage * * and go carefully over it, word for word as it stands. * * * Next, read it over several words at a time. After this, read the English through alone, and then turn to the original, and read that through. You will find that by this time you can read the original understandingly. Take the passage next * * and turn it into English by a free translation—not too free, but just free enough to be good English. Now follows what in practice I found the most improving part of the whole work. Make a word-for-word translation in the exact order of the words in the original, and note what this tells you of the character of the idiom and also of the mental peculiarities of the nation who * * own the language you are dealing with." (*Miscellaneous Essays*, by R. A. Proctor).

J. DYER BALL.

HONGKONG, 1887.

INTRODUCTION.

THE CANTONESE DIALECT OR LANGUAGE.

An impression appears to have got abroad that Mandarin is the language of China, and that Cantonese and the other languages spoken in China are but dialects of it. The impression is an erroneous one. One might as well say that Spanish was the language of the Iberian Peninsula and that Portuguese, as well as the other Romanic languages spoken elsewhere, were dialects of it. There is no doubt, that, as with Spanish in the Peninsula, Mandarin in some one or other of its various dialects is the language of a large portion of China (say of thirteen out of the eighteen provinces), but no less is Cantonese in some one or other of *its* numerous dialects the language of a great many of the inhabitants of the two provinces of Kwangtung and Kwongsi, (which two provinces have a population roughly stated equal to that of England). It is true that the Mandarin is used as a *lingua franca* in all official courts and Government offices throughout the whole of China, but though more than five hundred years ago for a considerable time in English history French was the Court language of England, yet there was an English language, though it may have been despised by those who knew nothing but French.

One of the unfortunate things about terming these different languages in China dialects is to lead those who know nothing of the subject to suppose that Cantonese is merely a local *patois* differentiated from the Mandarin by dialectic peculiarities, and that those who speak it differ as far from a correct method of speaking their native tongue, as a Somerset man or Yorkshireman, who speaks his native dialect does from an educated Englishman, who by virtue of his education and culture has sunk all the peculiarities of pronunciation, which inevitably point out the illiterate countryman.

In fact the Cantonese is more nearly akin to the ancient language of China spoken about 3,000 years ago than the speech of other parts of China. It is more

INTRODUCTION.

ancient itself than its younger brethren, the other so-called dialects of China, and to prevent any false ideas of its importance the following extract is given from the Preface to Douglas' Dictionary of the Amoy language, the statements in which are equally applicable to Cantonese. It is as follows, viz.:—

"But such words as 'Dialect' or 'Colloquial' give an erroneous conception of its nature. It is not a mere colloquial dialect or patois; it is spoken by the highest ranks just as by the common people, by the most learned just as by the most ignorant; learned men indeed add a few polite or pedantic phrases, but these are mere excrescences, (and even they are pronounced according to the" Cantonese sounds), "while the main body and staple of the spoken language of the most refined and learned classes is the same as that of coolies, labourers, and boatmen.

"Nor does the term 'dialect' convey anything like a correct idea of its distinctive character; it is no mere dialectic variety of some other language; it is a distinct language, one of the many and widely differing languages which divide among them the soil of China. * * *

"A very considerable number of the spoken languages of China have been already more or less studied by European and American residents in the country, such as the Mandarin, the Hakka, the vernaculars of Canton and Amoy, and several others. These are not dialects of one language; they are cognate languages, bearing to each other a relation similar to that which subsists between the Arabic, the Hebrew, the Syriac, the Ethiopic, and the other members of the Semitic family; or again between English, German, Dutch, Danish, Swedish, &c.

"There is another serious objection to the use of the term 'dialect' as applied to these languages, namely that within each of them there exist *real dialects*. For instance, the Mandarin, contains within itself three very marked 'dialects,' the Northern, spoken at Peking; the Southern, spoken at Nanking and Soochow; and the Western, spoken in the Provinces of Szechuen, Hoopeh, &c."

It may be stated that it is as absurd for any one who intends to reside in Hongkong, Canton, or Macao, and who wishes to learn Chinese to take up the study of Mandarin, as it would be for a German, who was about to settle in London to learn French in order to be able to converse with the English.

Cantonese has its "real dialects" some of which are spoken by tens of thousands, or hundreds of thousands of natives, and which if they were spoken by the inhabitants of some insignificant group of islands in the Pacific with only a tithe of the population would be honoured by the name of languages. These "subordinate dialects" of the Cantonese are again subdivided into many little divisions spoken in

INTRODUCTION.

different cities or towns, or groups of cities, towns, and villages where peculiar colloquialisms prevail. Some of these dialects of Cantonese are as follows, viz:—

        The San Wui Dialect.
        „ San Ning „
        „ Höng Shan „
        „ Shun Tak „
        „ Tung Kwún „

THE CORRECT PRONUNCIATION OF PURE CANTONESE.

So far is this minute sub-division carried that even in the city of Canton itself, the seat and centre of pure Cantonese, more than one pronunciation of words is used; the standard, however, being the Sai Kwán wá, or West end speech, to which the learner should endeavour to assimilate his talk. It has been the Author's endeavour to give this pronunciation, or at all events the Cantonese, and the students of this book may take it as a fact that it is Cantonese and pure Cantonese that is given in this book; and that where the author has corrected the orthography of Williams and Eitel it is because this orthography in such cases does not represent pure Cantonese, such for instance as in the spelling of the whole series of words, such as 女 *nui*, 去 *hui*, &c. which these authors give most unfortunately as *nü*, *hü*, &c., such a sound as *nü* being abominable Cantonese—not pure Cantonese at all, but Sai Chiú Dialect or some other wretched dialect, notwithstanding it has the sanction of such sinologues as Williams, Eitel, and Chalmers; and those who know Chinese thoroughly will know that the author is throwing no slur on the masterly scholarship displayed by these men when he says that their pronunciation of Cantonese as shewn by their orthography in many instances is neither pure nor correct.

It is a great pity that Dr. Eitel, in his new Dictionary, has not followed the lead of good speakers of pure Cantonese instead of perpetuating the mistakes of Dr. Williams—mistakes due partly to the implicit following of a Chinese author's ideas of pronunciation and mistakes more excusable in the olden days than at the present time.

To those who are inclined to be suspicious of any change in an established orthography of Chinese by Europeans the fact that the author is not alone in this changing of the mode of representing another class of sounds may give more confidence to their acceptance of it, and to those who know Mr. Parker's wonderfully acute ear for Chinese sounds the following extracts may help to confirm their acceptance of such changes.

INTRODUCTION.

"The only place where a really short e comes in, * * is in the diphthong *ei* (as in feint * *). This, sound is * * actually ignored by Williams in favour of *i*, as in the English *thee*, a Cantonese sound which only exists in one or two colloquial words such as *mi, ni,* &c.," *China Review,* Vol. 8, p. 364.

And again, "but, unfortunately Williams uses *i* to represent both the *ee* and *ei* as in feel and feint," *China Review,* Vol. 8, p. 365.

He again says in a paper on "the Comparative study of Chinese dialects" published in the transactions of the North China Branch of the Royal Asiatic Society. "In Dr. Williams' dictionary again, several classes of vowels existing in theory, according to the standard *in nubibus* encumber the work, when one vowel would have stood in each case for them all. One of the nine regular tones, too, is entirely ignored; and the whole class of colloquial tones called the *pin yam,* which form so striking an element of quasi-inflection in the pure Cantonese dialect, has been completely overlooked. Dr. Eitel, in his corrected edition of the same Dictionary, has introduced the ninth regular tone, but he likewise, instead of adhering steadfastly, (as did Mr. Wade in the case of the Metropolitan Pekingese) to the Metropolitan Cantonese, has, by overlooking these colloquial tones, once more lost the opportunity of firmly establishing another standard dialect."

The opinion of another enthusiastic student of Cantonese, than whom it is difficult to find one showing greater zeal in all matters connected with the language, (the author refers to Mr. J. H. Stewart-Lockhart) likewise says:—"It is much to be regretted that Dr. Eitel's . . Dictionary, though excellent in many ways, has not modified the spelling in Williams'," *China Review,* Vol. X., p. 312.

The matter resolves itself into simply this, whether we are to go on perpetrating mistakes by accepting the orthography of Williams and Eitel *in extenso*—In every minute particular, when it is a well-known fact by those who speak pure Cantonese that this orthography in all its particulars is not pure Cantonese by a long way, but is mixed up with local pronunciations, or whether we are to try to get an English transliteration of Chinese sounds, which shall attempt to approach as near as possible to the standard Cantonese, that spoken in the city of Canton itself. That such attempts may be open to partial failures in some particulars none knows better than the author himself, but because the matter is a difficult one to tackle there is no reason why we should go on in the old ruts. They are getting rather worn out now after half a century of use and it is time that better ways were followed.

A curious argument is sometimes used as a support to a not conforming to a standard,—a real standard and a pure one—namely that it does not much matter as long as they, the Europeans or Americans, who speak Chinese are understood. In

INTRODUCTION.

this argument it is taken for granted that they must be understood, but they are often not.

A good story is told of an Englishman in Russia coming across a Russian, who accosted him in broad Yorkshire to the astonishment of the Britain, the Russian being under the impression that he was conversing in good English, he having availed himself of the services of an Englishman to learn his, the Englishman's, native language, but unfortunately the teacher spoke a dialect, Yorkshire, which is not now considered as pure English.

This is bad enough, but supposing the Russian instead of learning from an Englishman had used books to acquire the language, and that these books had taught him to invariably leave off the initial *h*, as cockneys do; to pronounce the *s*, as if it were a *z*, in imitation of the Somerset dialect; to pronounce the article *the*, as if it were a *t* alone, in imitation of Yorkshire; and to pronounce every word like *bay, day, fay, gay, hay, jay, lay, may, nay, pay, ray, say, way*, as if they were spelled *be, de, fee, gee, he, ge, lea, me, knee, pea, re, see, we*, and other mispronunciations of the same character. What a delightful hotch-potch this would be! This then may give an idea of what results ensue in Chinese from the orthography of some of the books that are now in use by Europeans for learning Chinese.

What would be thought of an argument to the effect that it mattered little to the Russian, as many English dropped their *h* all through the length and breadth of the land, that likewise numbers of genuine Englishmen pronounced the *the* as *t* alone, and that there were not a few that pronounced the *s* as a *z*, and that the other mispronunciations were also in use in English?

And yet the same style of argument is used with regard to these dialectic pronunciations of Cantonese by some book makers.

The following statement by Mr. Parker is conclusive on the point except to those who are prejudiced against any conclusion except their own:—"The argument so frequently used that, in the presence of so many conflicting forms of Cantonese it is unwise to make a special study of one, ought to condemn itself without demonstration to every logical student, apart from the obvious fact that the dialect of a metropolis, as spoken by the most highly educated classes, is *primâ facie* more likely to be a standard and to be more widely known than a dialect spoken by less educated persons in the country, or in a town less thickly populated than the metropolis," *China Review*, Vol. 8, p. 367.

INTRODUCTION.

THE TONES.

As the tones are the initial difficulty in learning Chinese it is well that the beginner should have his attention drawn at the very first to them, Premare says, "The mere sounds are, as it were, the body of the character, and the tones are in like manner the spirit."* This description of the tones, at all events, contains a just appreciation of their importance. And that learned sinalogue seems so thoroughly to understand the subject that his further descriptions of the matter form very good answers to the questions, What are the tones; and are they of any importance? To answer these questions let us take, for instance, the word 先 ₁sín, *before*. The sound is represented by the English spelling, *sin* (pronounced *seen*) and the tone by that little semi-circle, but insignificant as that little semi-circle is, yet a right understanding by a native of the word a European wishes to pronounce is as much conveyed by that little semi-circle as it is by the English letters *s i n*. Neglect that little sign and ignore the tone which it stands for, and the native is at a loss to know what the European means to say.

In other words, Chinese words may be compared to specimens, geological, botanical, or what you like, in a museum, and in this museum, of Chinese ideas, it is necessary not only that the words, the specimens, should be arranged in cases or classes, similar in general characteristics, such as sound, but the differentiation of one from the other, which is already an accomplished fact, shall be represented in a manner to at once appeal to the ear. The methods of so distinguishing them is by the tones. These are the labels to the words to point out clearly what they are.

Tones then are used in this language, so largely monosyllabic that confusion would ensue but for their use. For example, let us take the sound *sin* (pronounced like the English word *seen*) again. That sound, amongst other ideas in the book language, stands in the colloquial for the words, *before*, *ringworm*, and *thread*, but with a separate tone for each word, and written differently in the Chinese character. Now if the word ₁*sin*, meaning *before*, is pronounced in the same way as *sín*², meaning *thread*, it, of course, is no more the word *before*, but becomes the word *thread*, and *vice versâ*, or if it is pronounced ʿ*sin*, it means *ringworm*, and no more *thread* or *before*, or suppose the word is pronounced in some other tone, which does not belong to any word in that sound, no meaning is conveyed, or to use an illustration try to write English without any regard to spelling, and think that *scene* will do for *seen*, or *vice versâ*. It may be imagined how confusing and ludicrous it would be to hear a man talk about *ringworm*

---

* "Meri soni sunt litterarum quasi corpus; accentus autem sunt ipsis loco animæ."

Premare's *Notitia Linguæ Sinicæ*, p. 10.

INTRODUCTION.

when he meant to talk about *thread.* Most ludicrous mistakes are constantly made by those who are just learning the tones, or who will not take the trouble to learn them.

The learner will not have tried to speak Chinese long before he will find every now and then that something he has said falls flat on the ears of his listener, conveying no idea, as his blank or perplexed face will show, in such a case the learner may think himself fortunate if some bystander, guessing at the idea, puts the word or words into the right tone or tones and repeats them, intelligence will now take the place of bewilderment on the listener's face. If the learner is determined to learn the tones he may find, as time goes on, some criterion of his success from noticing if such failures are decreasing.

There are other helps it may be noted here, such as some words being aspirated and others not, and the context also helps to the understanding of the word, but notwithstanding all other helps the tone is of the utmost importance. As Premare rightly says:—"But if the sound simply were pronounced, no regard being had to the tone, or breathing" (the breathing being the aspirate) "it would be impossible to determine its signification; and indeed, it is the want of attention to this subject which occasions Europeans, after protracted labours devoted to the acquisition of this tongue, failing so often to be understood by the Chinese. They are learned, talented and industrious, and yet can only stammer, through their whole lives, while at the same time some stupid Caffrarian, in a very short period, learns to speak as well as the Chinese themselves."*

It is not learning nor talents that are a sure passport to an ability to acquire the tones, but more an ear gifted with, or trained to, a power of distinguishing between musical sounds, or a power of mimicry, a determination to succeed accom-

---

* The quotation in full in Premare is as follows:—"Exemplo ait littera 看 videre; sonus quem ipsi dant sinæ est k'án, spiritus est asper k'au, accentus est rectus k'án, et interdum acutus k'án; atque haec tria, scilicet sonus, spiritus et accentus sunt omnino necessaria. Cum vero sint aliae litterae aliud plane significantes, quae debent eodem modo pronunciari, evidens est quod etiamsi recte dicas k'án, tamen ex circumstantiis, hoc est, ex materia de qua sermo est, et ex his quae praecedunt vel sequuntur, plerumque colligunt sinæ quod vox illa quam profers significat videre. Et quid igitur esset, si duntaxat dicas k'an, nulla habita ratione nec ad spiritum k'an, nec ad accentum k'án atque haec est praecipua causa cur Europaei post tot labores in lingua sinica discenda positos a sinis vix intelligantur. Docti sunt, ingeniosi sunt, attenti sunt, et tamen per totam vitam plerique balbutiunt, interim dum stupidus aliquis cafer (sic) post tempus sat breve tam bene loquitur quam ipsimet sinae."

Premare's *Notitia Linguæ Sinicæ*, p. 10.

INTRODUCTION.

panied with well-directed industrious efforts, which will generally assist a man in his acquisition of the tones, but his success is more rapid and certain if he be blessed with a musical ear and a power of mimicry. A man should not, however, give up the attempt to learn the tones from an idea that he is not thus blessed. It is but few men that have not some idea of musical pitch, or the ability, if they will only try, to closely imitate what others say; and the continual attempt to do the latter, or detect the differences between the tones, will materially increase the ability to do both the one and the other, just as a man who exercises the muscles of his arms and legs, &c. in a properly directed manner is able after months of continual practice to pull an oar in a boat, in perfect time and accord with other rowers, in a manner which would astonish those who do not know what training will do. So training in the tones is bound to produce good results. The pity is that people get it into their heads that they can speak Chinese without knowing the tones. You might almost as well expect to be able to speak French without learning the French pronunciation, though do not be led away by the illustration to suppose that tones are pronunciation.

But still the question remains, What are tones? It is easy enough to say what they are not, for instance they are not pronunciation, emphasis, or accent; but the difficulty consists in explaining to a European something which he knows nothing about, something to which there is nothing akin in his own language, or in the languages, which in the course of his education he has learned, be they dead, Classical languages, or living modern languages, or, if there were, the knowledge of them has been lost.

This being the case it would perhaps have been as well, as Dr. Williams says, if the Chinese name for them, *shing*, had been adopted into our language instead of using a word such as, *tone*, which conveys other ideas to our minds.

It is very much as if a race of mankind, say in the centre of New Guinea, were to be discovered, who had a new sense, that is to say, a sense which the rest of mankind were not endowed with. It would be well nigh impossible to describe this sense to the rest of mankind, who had not seen the effects it produced and what it was, and any attempts at description would be in many cases misleading, for those who heard the description would be inclined to follow the illustrations out in their entirety, and thus misunderstand what was being attempted to be explained to them.

Tones then may be said to be certain positions or inflections of the voice which are used for certain words, each word having its own tone, or in some cases two, which are used at different times. These positions into which the voice is put for words are various in their character. The position is for certain tones a level or sustained modulation, the difference between the tones belonging to this class being

INTRODUCTION.

one of musical pitch. For others it is a rising modulation of the voice, as if when a violin bow were being drawn across a string of the violin the finger of the player should slide from a lower note to a higher;—the difference between the tones belonging to this class being in the amount of rising modulation the voice undergoes. Another class, a diminishing, receding modulation of the voice, the difference between the tones comprised in this class being, as in some of the others, a high or low one. And there is yet another class which has been described as an evanescent modulation, the tones in this class being distinguished from each other by the musical pitch.

If the beginner could only put himself into the same position that a child appears to be in when learning Chinese, there doubtless would be no difficulty at all in the tones. A European child in infancy, given equal facilities, learns Chinese, bristling with difficulties, as it appears to adults, more readily, and, if anything, more correctly than his or her mother tongue. What is the reason of this? The language is, as a general rule, more natural and logical in its construction, or rather the Chinese mind is more natural and logical in its sequence of ideas, and consequently the Chinese language is more logical in the manner of putting ideas; furthermore a monosyllabic language, or at all events with regard to Chinese, one which is to a great extent monosyllabic, it is natural to suppose would be more readily apprehended by a child's mind. Besides these two great advantages there is the further advantage of tone, to which a child is naturally inclined, and it is only by education that an infant learns that tone is unnecessary in a European language. A Chinese child never learns this, and, having originally, in common with its European cousin, copied the exact tone in which it hears a word first pronounced, adheres to this original pronunciation of the tone, assisted materially by the fact that it hears this word pronounced in no other way, or tone, while its cousin, the European child, while acquiring its own language, at first adheres to the original tone in which a word has been first pronounced, and persists in this adherence for some time, as a general rule, till it gets confused by hearing a multiplicity of tones given to the same word and eventually finds it is useless to battle for a language in its infant state when his superiors have long ago decided that the language has outgrown its infantile state, and eventually yields to the force of circumstances and copying the example of his elders forgets that there is such a thing as tone at all.

How is it possible for a European adult to place himself in the same position as regards tones as a child would be in? Clearly he cannot place himself in precisely the same position, as he has already the experience of his own and probably other languages, which at the present day are wanting in tones, to mislead him. Let him however try and get as near the child's position, in this respect, at

INTRODUCTION.

least, as he can. Listen acutely to the tone that his teacher pronounces a word in, repeat it after him and re-repeat it and go on a hundred times—a thousand if necessary, till the exact tone has been got, and do this with every new word. More pains are necessary for the adult than for the child, as to the child the tone is everything while to the adult it is nothing. Repeat the same plan with every new word learned, and surely such infinite pains will not have been spent in vain. Being unfortunately an adult the learner ought also to use his superior abilities and previous knowledge as a vantage ground for further attainments by, for one thing, having a formula, shall we call it? such, for instance as, $_2$sín ⁵sín³ sít$_2$, $_3$sín ⁵sín² sít$_2$, and with each new word finding from enquiry, or better still from the dictionary, the correct tone, then try to say it in exactly the same tone as the same toned word in the formula, but do not be content with supposing that you have it correct, test it with your teacher and bother him with questions as to whether you are perfectly correct or not, and do not be content with anything short of *perfectness*. You may think it is not of much importance and *he* will probably think that you being a European cannot ever learn Chinese perfectly correctly, especially if after several attempts at a word you make very bad shots at it, but other Europeans have learned to speak Chinese, and amongst them have been some, who have approximated very closely to the Chinese in their tones, so close that much of what they said might be supposed to be uttered by Chinese. If others have attained to such an excellence, why should not you? At all events you will not unless you try. And it is well worth the trial, as you will know when you have attained to this excellence.

All this trouble and painstaking when you are in your study, and on the learning of every new word, but when you go out to exercise your hard-acquired knowledge do not cramp yourself by constant thoughts as to the tone of every word in the sentence you utter, any more than you would bend your head down and watch every step you take when walking. Speech must come freely from your mouth, and you must not hesitate over and examine every word mentally before it issues from your lips, or you will never speak freely. A general and his officers do not minutely inspect each soldier to see as they issue out for the attack whether their uniform and accoutrements are all right, that has to be done at drill. Never cease to drill yourself in tones for many a long day after your first start.

METHODS OF DESCRIBING TONES.

Different methods have been used to try and convey to the foreign mind unacquainted with tones an idea of what they are. To depend only upon these descriptions to acquire a knowledge of the tones would be but of little use, as tones

INTRODUCTION.

in their correctness are only to be learned from the native pronunciation of them, but these descriptions may assist the learner, supplemented by hearing them pronounced, to a correct knowledge of what they are, imperfect though such methods may be by themselves alone for conveying a perfectly correct idea of the tones to one who is previously unacquainted with them. One way of describing the tones has been to compare them to the inflections of voice, which are used in certain passages properly read and emphasised, or in speech properly inflected in its utterance. When this explanation is given it must not be supposed that the same words, as a rule, are capable of having different tones applied to them just as in English different words may have a different emphasis, owing simply to the position of the word in the sentence, or the exigencies of the case, such as the emotions the speaker desires to give expression to, by the inflexion of his voice—such are intonation and expression—not Chinese Tones; for Chinese words are capable of intonation of voice and emphasis, which can be thrown into the voice without, though it may seem strange to those unacquainted with the fact, interfering with the *pitch* of the tone, and this brings us to another way in which it has been attempted to make the tonic system intelligible to the foreigner, viz:—by comparing the tones to musical notes.

LIST OF TONES.

The following is a list of the 12 tones in Cantonese, which are all that the beginner need trouble himself about, as the others that may exist in Cantonese are not sufficiently verified yet.

Upper Series.	Middle tones.	Lower Series.
1 上平 Shöng² ₂p'ing.	上'ò 中平 ₍Chung ₂p'ing.	下平 Há² ₂p'ing.
2 上上 Shöng² ²shöng.	上聲變音 Shöng² shing p'in' ₂yam.*	下上 Há² shöng².
3 上去 Shöng² hui³.		下去 Há² hui³.
4 上入 Shöng² yap₂.	中入 ₍Chung yap₂.	下入 Há² yap₂.

"The degree in which these two series" (that is the upper and lower series) "vary from each other is not the same in all the tones; the upper and lower *p'ing shing* being distinctly marked while there is very little perceptible difference between the upper and lower *shöng shing*."

Williams' *Easy Lessons in Chinese*, p. 49.

---

* This is scarcely a correct name for this tone. It is really a 變音 p'in' ₂yam for the 下平 há² ₂p'ing, 下去 há² hui³ and any other of the tones which occasionally rise into it.

INTRODUCTION.

DIVISION OF THE TONES.

These tones are classed together in different ways, such as, those of the Upper and Lower Series, which together make the 8 tones into which the Cantonese as a rule say the words in their language are divided, and which are the only tones appearing in the majority of dictionaries.

These eight tones are divided by the Chinese again into correct and deflected, or 平 ₅p'ing and 仄 chak₃, the first of each series belonging to the former and the others being classed under the deflected, just as in Latin with the nominative and other cases. Of course the three medial tones, if coming under these two divisions, would resolve themselves in the same way, viz:—The 中平 ₅chung ₅p'ing would belong likewise to the correct, while the other two would come under the category of deflected tones.

These eight tones are further divided into the:—

平 ₅p'ing, or Even tones.
上 shöng², or Upper tones.
去 hui³, or Receding tones.
入 yap₃, or Entering tones.

This classification is so simple that there is no need for offering any remarks on it, of course the three other tones can also come under this classification.

DESCRIPTION OF THE TONES.

No better definition can perhaps be given of the 平聲 ₅p'ing ₅shing than is contained in the following words:—"The ₅p'ing ₅shing is precisely the musical monotone, pronounced without elevation or depression, being the natural unconstrained expression of the voice. * * Thus in the sentences:—

I am going to town; *I hope it will not rain*; *You must look and see*;

if the last word in each is sounded in somewhat of a dissatisfied or commanding tone, higher than the other words, the previous part of the sentence will naturally fall in the ₅p'ing ₅shing, In questions, uttered in a pleasant inviting tone, the words preceding the last naturally fall in the upper *p'ing shing*, as,

Will you let me see it? *Will you come too?*

"The negative answer to such questions (spoken by the same voice) would naturally fall into the lower ₅p'ing ₅shing as:—

When I asked him, 'Will you let me see it?' he said, 'No, I'll do no such thing.'

"Here the different cadence of the question and reply illustrate the upper and lower ₅p'ing ₅shing."—Williams' *Easy Lessons in Chinese*, p. 49.

INTRODUCTION.

There is however a second Upper Even Tone into which some words are put. This second, or 中平 ‚chung ‚p'ing, Medial Upper Even Tone, is found in the following words, for example:—

貓 ₀máu, *a cat*, and 鎗 ₀ts'ong, *a gun*.

"It partakes of the nature of a slight shriek," differing not only in musical pitch (being nearer to the 上平 shöng² ‚p'ing, Upper Even Tone, in that respect than to the 下平 há² ‚p'ing, Lower Even Tone,) from the other two Even Tones, but also in the manner of its pronunciation, it having "a certain quickness or jerkiness of pronunciation."—Parker in *Overland China Mail*.

There is an octave's difference between the two Even Tones. That is to say if you pronounce the 上平 shöng² ‚p'ing, Upper Even Tone, as the C which is placed in the third space in the lines in music, you must pronounce the 下平 há² ‚p'ing, Lower Even Tone, as the C which appears in the first leger line below in the treble.

These Lower Even Toned words seem to give a stability and character to the Cantonese; they are full and rich, and a European who has a full toned voice generally speaks Cantonese better than one with a weak piping voice, at all events Cantonese from his lips sounds better than from those of the other man.

There is no doubt this tone, the 中平 ‚chung ‚p'ing, Medial Even Tone, does exist, and the Beginner will do well to keep his ears open for it, though to the average European ear it is so subtle as not to be distinguished, obtuse in this sense as most Europeans have become from speaking a language in which tone is of no account. And here consists the fallacy of learning Chinese by simply learning what the tones of a word are, that is to say learning that a certain word is in the 上平 shöng² ‚p'ing, or Upper Even Tone, for example, instead of first learning to pronounce the word properly, and then bracing yourself up to that pronunciation by comparing it with other words in that same tone and then finally fixing in your memory that it belongs to that tone, the 上平 shöng² ‚p'ing, Upper Even Tone, for supposing you learn first that it belongs to this tone class instead of making a point of pronouncing it properly first, you run away at once with the idea that it is a 上平 shöng² ‚p'ing, Upper Even Tone, and it is possible that it is a 中平 ‚chung ‚p'ing, Medial Even Tone, word. If you have a good ear and good powers of mimicry, great points of advantage in learning Chinese, you run a good chance of learning the word in the right tone, then it is possible you may detect the difference on coming to compare it with other words that are really of the 上平 shöng² ‚p'ing, Upper Even Tone. At all events keep your ear open for these distinctions between the 上平 shöng² ‚p'ing, Upper Even, and 中平 ‚chung ‚p'ing, Medial Even Tones, for no dic-

INTRODUCTION.

tionary yet published gives all the words which should be in the 中平 ,chung ,p'ing, Medial Even Tone, in that Tone. Dr. Eitel puts a few of them into his dictionary. Do not consider such distinctions hypercritical, or a waste of time. The disposition to do so makes some learned Sinalogues commit such egregious errors as to entirely ignore a well marked Tone the 中入 ,chung yap, the Medial Entering Tone, of which we shall speak presently. These distinctions do exist, subtle as they may seem to you, and while not distressing yourself with them too much, at the same time try to train your ear into distinguishing them. There is no reason why you should not try to speak Chinese properly, and if you make the effort you may find that you will succeed better than you thought for at first, and it is possible that eventually you may be able, after a sufficient lengthened course of study, to distinguish some more of these subtle distinctions which are still believed to be lurking about in Cantonese, but which have not yet been brought to book, more's the pity.

"The 上聲 shöng² ,shing," (Rising Tone,) "is a rising inflection of the voice ending higher than it began, such as is heard in the direct question, pronounced in somewhat of a high, shrill tone;—'*it loudly calls, vehement ardent, strong.*' It is also heard in exclamatory words, as, *ah! Can it be!* The last word of the preceding sentences are in the 上聲 shöng² ,shing," (Rising Tone).—Williams' *Easy Lessons in Chinese*, p. 50.

With regard to the difference between the 上上 shöng² ʰshöng, Upper Rising Tone, and 下上 há² ʰshöng, Lower Rising Tone, the following statement will give an idea:—"the Upper Rising Tone gradually ascends, altering its pitch about half a tone while the syllable is being uttered with a steadily waxing intensity of effort, * * the Lower Rising Tone starts from a lower pitch, does not ascend so high as the other and suddenly breaks off with a sort of jerk or circumflex."— Eitel's *Chinese Dictionary in the Cantonese Dialect*, Introduction, p. xxix.

The Third Rising Tone differs from all the other tones in this that every word that is used in this tone belongs originally to another tone and is generally likewise used in this other tone as well. Nearly all the tones contribute words which are occasionally, or often, as the case may be, used in this Third Rising Tone. The words most generally put into this tone are Nouns, "familiar words in Lower Departing Tone (or 下去 há² hui³). It often happens also that words in the Lower Even Tone, or 下平 há² ,p'ing, are put into this Third Rising Tone. Occasionally words in the Upper Departing Tone, or 上去 shöng² hui³ are likewise put into this Tone. It is seldom that words in the two Rising Tones, 上聲 shöng² ,shing, are put into this Tone, but it does happen sometimes. The Upper Even Tone, 上平 shöng² ,p'ing, however, never contributes words to this Third

INTRODUCTION.

Rising Tone. It must be remembered that in reading this changing from the other Tones into this Third Rising Tone never happens, it is only in conversation. It is a little misleading to say, that this Third Rising Tone is adopted when a word ends a sentence. It does undoubtedly do so at times, but the following rules will generally describe their use.

The Third Rising Tone is used when the word stands alone, but when it is used in combination it takes its original tone, as:—渡 'tò (original tone tò²) but when used with 船 ₍shün, *a boat*, it reverts to its original tone, as:—渡船 tò² ₍shün, *a passage boat*.

The third rising tone is also used as a sign of past time—of an action being accomplished, as:—

叫佢嚟 kiú² ʽk'ui ₍lai, *tell him to come.* 嚟咯 'lai* lok₀, *he has come.*
佢嚟囉咩 ʽk'ui 'lai* lo² ₍me? *He has come has he?* 嚟咯 'lai* lok₀, *yes.*

"The 去聲 hui² ₍shing, Departing Tone, is a prolonged tone, diminishing while it is uttered, just as a diminuendo, or an inverted swell, does in music, and sounded somewhat gruffly. The Chinese say that it is 'clear, distinct, its dull, low path is long;' and they call it the *departing* tone, because it goes away like flowing water never to return. It is the converse of the 上聲 shóng² ₍shing, ending lower than it began. The 下去 há² hui², Lower Departing Tone, is nearer a monotone, not so gruff as the 上去 shöng² hui², Upper Departing Tone. The drawling tone of repressed discontent, as when one calls, but is still afraid of offending and ekes out the sound, may perhaps illustrate this tone."—Williams' *Easy Lessons in Chinese*, p. 50.

. There is no difficulty in knowing what words belong to the fourth Tone Class, as all words that end in k, p, and t belong to this class. "They further differ from all the other tones by a peculiar abruptness of enunciation."—Eitel's *Chinese Dictionary in the Cantonese Dialect*, Introduction, p. xxix. There are three well defined tones belonging to this class the 上 shóng², 中 ₍chung, and 下 há², Upper, Middle, and Lower, 入 yap₂, or Entering Tones. There is also some assistance to be derived from the fact that most of the words having long vowels belong to the 中入 ₍chung yap₂, Middle Entering Tone. The others as well as some words with long vowels belong to the 上入 shöng² yap₂, Upper Entering Tone, or 下入 há² yap₂, Lower Entering Tone.

"The correct application of the tones to every word in speaking or reading is the principal difficulty with which the beginner has to contend. In English they are all heard in conversation every day, according to the different humours of people, or their peculiar mode of enunciation ; but in that language, tones of words never affect the meaning of the speaker, except so far as they indicate his feelings;

INTRODUCTION.

and moreover they are applied to sentences rather than to isolated words. In Chinese, on the contrary, the tones are applied to every word, and have nothing to do either with accent or emphasis; in asking or answering, intreating or refusing, railing or flattering, soothing or recriminating, they remain ever the same. The unlettered native knows almost nothing of the learned distinctions into * * tones, but he attends to them closely himself, and detects a mispronunciation as soon as the learned man, while he is much less likely to catch a foreigner's meaning."

MARKS TO DESIGNATE THE TONES.

It must be remembered that Chinese books are not marked with the tones, an educated native knows the right tones of the words, as they occur in the books. It is only when a word is in a tone which is not the common tone of the word that it is marked, and the method by which this is done is to make a little circle at one of the four corners of the character. Each corner has its appropriate tones assigned to it. The left hand lower corner being appropriated to the 平 ₚp'ing, or even tones, the left hand upper to the 上 shöng², or rising tones, the right hand upper to the 去 hui', or receding tones, and the right hand lower corner to the 入 yap₂, or entering tones. These are the only signs that the Chinese use, and this only when it is absolutely necessary that they should be used. It will be seen that there is no distinction in the native signs employed between the different tones which belong to the same class, that is to say a 上 平 shöng² ₚp'ing, Upper Even, and 下 平 há ₚp'ing, Lower Even, are both represented by the same tonal mark. No difficulty, however, arises from this paucity of tone marks, as far as the Chinese are themselves concerned, for as has been already stated these tonic marks are but seldom used, only occurring a few times, if as often as that, in the course of as many pages, and furthermore if those few words which are occasionally used in another tone, it is, as a rule, but one other tone that they are used in, therefore no ambiguity is likely to arise. The case is, however, very different when we come to deal with foreigners, such as Europeans, learning the Chinese language, for here we have those who do not know by conversational practice from infancy upwards, and from an educational course extending over many years the correct tones for each word, and yet again as an additional reason when a foreigner desires to write out the sounds of the Chinese words, transliterating them into his own alphabet, as he best can, he has a number of Chinese words, groups of which are represented by the same spelling in a foreign language; so many words belonging to each group that the foreigner is confused, more especially at the beginning of his course of study, as to which Chinese word

INTRODUCTION.

a combination of English letters is intended to represent. The context will show what many of the words so spelled represent, but in some cases this requires thought, and it is therefore, taking the whole subject into consideration, best that each word so written should be accompanied by a tonal mark, which shall represent accurately, intelligibly and in a manner easily to be apprehended the tone which the word possesses. The above remarks will show the reasons for books prepared for those who wish to learn Chinese bristling with tonic marks, and the man who wishes to learn Chinese thoroughly and properly will find that in the long run he gets on better with such a book, and makes more real progress than he does with another, though the other may be more useful if rightly used to the tourist or to the man who has not the time nor the inclination to learn more than a smattering of Chinese.

We come now to the methods used by foreigners to represent the tones. Some have endeavoured to shew tones by "marking the vowels with different accents." This is a confusing method except to those intimately acquainted with it, as it is the most natural course to utilise such marks to represent the value of the vowels, as is done in our English dictionaries, and use extraordinary signs to represent what is an extraordinary incident of words—to use signs not used by us in English to represent tones which are unknown to us in English,—and moreover such a method of representing the tones has not been employed by foreigners writing books in Cantonese, no types are in existence and if there were it is better to stick to the established usage when that established usage is the better plan. The effect of using the contrary plan is that an awkward arrangement is arrived at of marking over the vowels their quantities or powers as well as the tone of the word, or else nearly all "prosodical marks affecting the vowels" have to be left out and the next step arrived at is to leave out the tonic marks entirely—a process of evolution, or rather of retrogression, eminently unsatisfactory. Another objection is that it would lead beginners to suppose that the tone was connected with the vowel. The vowel no doubt has sometimes something to do with the tone, but not to such an extent as one would naturally infer from such a method of distinguishing the tones.

Another method is that of marking the tones by figures. We have already said that though pretty well adapted for Pekingese with its paucity of tones it would be inconvenient for Cantonese with its twelve or possibly more tones.

Marks of apostrophy have also been used in some of the dialects, but it will be readily seen that there is not sufficient material to use for such a purpose.

In the Hakka as written by the German missionaries there is also another system employed, which consists in putting acute and grave accents at different

INTRODUCTION.

corners of the words, in some cases with a straight short dash underneath the accent as well. Again in Hakka the tones are but few in number, and such arrangements are more easily used than they would be in Cantonese, besides which these marks have never been used in Cantonese, and there is no type available even supposing it were a good plan for Cantonese.

There is yet again another method, which has been employed in Cantonese by Dr. Chalmers, which consists of a combination of one of the above modes with a new plan of using different type, and a leaving out of the tonic marks when the word ends in those consonants which show that it belongs to a certain tone class. This method has not been adopted by anyone else. This method is no doubt very convenient considered from a typographical point of view, but it seems a more regular and systematic way to give every word its tonic mark.

And lastly there is the modification of the native method of representing the tones, which was first used in Bridgman's Chrestomathy, and has continued to be used up to the present day by nearly all who have written books dealing with the Cantonese dialect, amongst whom may be mentioned Williams, Lobschied, Kerr, and Eitel. It is the system adopted in this book. This method has several advantages over the others. All the other methods are strange and unknown to the Chinese. The learner would, in using the others, require to tell his teacher what tone such and such things were meant to represent, and such telling would be of little use with regard to some of the marks that are used in some of the modes employed to represent the tones in Chinese. Of course in the majority of cases the teacher can tell the tone from the character, but in some cases it is well that the teacher should be able to see himself how the tone is marked. In this system likewise every word is marked with its tone, and it occasionally happens that some of the words which by Dr. Chalmers' system are left unmarked go in Colloquial into a rising tone. These marks in this method are as applicable to the Chinese character as to the English spelled word, which represents that character, but figures and accents cannot well be printed along with the Chinese characters. This method is applicable to any dialect in China, and it is a thousand pities that when such an admirable system is in use it has not been availed of by foreigners for all the Chinese dialects, which have been treated of in books instead of different systems being in use for different dialects, thus increasing the difficulty of learning them when the difficulties are sufficiently great without being added to. It unfortunately even happens that in some dialects even more than one system is in use.

This system as has already been stated is an adaptation of the native system, the semi-circle being used for the upper series of tones, and the semi-circle with a

INTRODUCTION. XXXI

INTRODUCTION.

short dash underneath it to represent the lower series, as for example.

上平 shöng² ₍p'ing, Upper Even, as:—₍sía. 下平 há² ₍p'ing, Lower Even, as:—₍lín.
上上 shöng² ʿshóung, Upper Rising, as:—ʿsía. 下上 há² shöng², Lower Rising, as:—ʿlín.
上去 shöng² hui³, Upper Retreating, as:—sin³. 下去 há² hui³, Lower Retreating, as:—lín².
上入 shöug² yap₂, Upper Entering, as:—sü₁. 下入 há² yap₂, Lower Entering, as:—lit₂.

There now remain the three other tones to be dealt with, viz:—the 中平 ₍chung ₍p'ing, Medial Even Tone, the 中入 ₍chung yap₂, Medial Departing Tone, and the Third Rising Tone. The 中平 ₍chung ₍p'ing, Medial Even Tone, is represented by Parker and Eitel by a circle in the 平 ₍p'ing position as ₀máu, being an adoption of a Siamese tone mark, and it is the plan likewise adopted in this book.

The same plan is likewise used for the 中入 ₍chung yap₂, Medial Departing Tone, viz:—a circle, but of course at the 入 yap₂ position, as:—pok₀.

There now remains the Third Rising Tone. This has been represented by the Upper Rising Tone mark, and an asterisk at the Rising Tone position placed at the right hand upper corner of the word.

In this book this asterisk is retained, as it is useful in showing that the word is in a different tone in the colloquial to what it is in the book language. In the first edition of the present work the same mark was likewise used for this Third Rising Tone as for the first, or Upper Rising Tone. This method is unsatisfactory, however, as should by any mishap this asterisk be omitted the word then appears to be in a wrong tone and even without chance of the asterisk being omitted it is apt to be confusing to beginners and for this reason amongst others it is undoubtedly better that each word should have its own tonic mark. It is better that the Tonic Mark should show distinctly the tone of the word, and the asterisk be reserved alone to show that the tone is a different one to the original tone, and not to show what the tone is. Mr. Pearce of Canton recommended to the author the advisability of having a distinctive tonic mark, the trouble was however to know what to have; but at last the author devised the following as a sign of this tone, viz., ʻlai and resolved to adopt it. It has several recommendations. 1st. It is in harmonoy with those already in use. The only difference being that instead of being a semi-circle it has corners. 2nd. It is a mnemonic sign, as being a trifle longer than the semi-circle it helps to fix in the learner's mind the knowledge that this Rising Tone is a longer tone than the other two Rising Tones, beginning lower and ascending higher than either of them. 3rd. It is a distinctive sign and as such attracts attention, preventing the beginner from thinking the

INTRODUCTION.

tone is the same as another tone, and 4th. It is a mark easily procurable in a printing office.

TONIC EXERCISES.

Go through the following Tonic Exercises, taken with slight alterations from Bridgman's Chrestomathy, every day regularly for three months at least.

Let your teacher read each set to you and then repeat them after him. He will read the first line in the First Series to you and then the first line in the Second Series. The meanings of the words are simply given to satisfy any laudable curiosity the learner may have as to the meanings of the words he is repeating so often. In this way it often happens that the meaning of many words are learned without the learner actually setting himself down to learn them.

This drudgery must be gone through most conscientiously and thoroughly, not considering that you have done your duty until you have gone through each set dozens or scores of times every day; for these voice and ear exercises are as important as finger exercises are to the learner on the piano.

"It cannot, however, be too strongly impressed upon learners from the outset that both aspirates and tones are of the utmost importance to one who would learn to speak Chinese intelligibly. * * * * * * * * * * * * * * * * * * * The distinction of tones in Chinese often appears to beginners to make the acquisition of the spoken language almost hopelessly difficult, but this difficulty like many others, is found to yield to persevering effort, and by constantly reading aloud after a teacher, the ear becomes familiar with the difference in the tones of the words pronounced. At the same time it is not desirable to trust to the ear alone in trying to remember what is the tone of a particular word. A child will unconsciously acquire the right tones in speaking, as the Chinese themselves do without any effort of memory, but with the rarest possible exceptions adults, if they wish to speak correctly, will find it necessary to learn what the proper tone of each character is, together with its sound and meaning. Both tones and aspirates are chiefly important in the spoken language, but even in studying the written language, it is necessary to notice that a character often has two sounds, one aspirated and the other unaspirated, or one of one tone and another of another, and its shade of meaning varies accordingly; thus, the word 中 'the middle' is differently pronounced when it means 'to hit the centre.'"—Foster's *Elementary Lessons in Chinese.*

INTRODUCTION.

TONIC EXERCISE IN THE 平 p'ING TONES.

			Shöng[2] ₅p'ing.	₍Chung ₍p'ing.	Há[2] ₍p'ing.	Meaning of the Words.
1.	孖 瘡 床		₍ch'ong	₀ch'ong	₍ch'ong	To wound, tetter,[1] bed.
2.	鄉 香 楊		₍höng	₀höng	₍yöng	A village, clove,[2] to splash.
3.	空 燶 農		₍hung	₀nung	₍nung	Empty, to scorch, to cultivate the ground.
4.	加 假		₍ka	₀ká		To add, false.[3]
5.	高 膏 蠔		₍kò	₀kò	₍hò	High, a plaster[4] (for the stomach), an oyster.
6.	蹣 欄 攔		₍lán	₀lán	₍lán	To crawl, a market, to prevent.
7.	踎 貓 茅		₍mau	₀máu	₍máu	To squat down, a cat, reeds.
8.	尸 詩 匙		₍shí	₀shí	₍shí	A corpse, a hymn, a spoon.
9.	猩 星 形		₍sing	₀seng	₍ying	An ape, a star, form.
10.	丁 疔 庭		₍teng	₀teng	₍t'ing	A nail, a tetter sore,[1] a court.
11.	聽 廳 亭		₍t'eng	₀t'eng	₍t'ing	To hear, a court,[5] a road-side inn.
12.	仃 丁 停		₍ting	₀ting	₍t'ing	Alone, clove,[2] to cease.
13.	丁 耵 婷		₍ting	₀ting	₍t'ing	A nail, jingling, handsome.
14.	當 璫 堂		₍tong	₀tong	₍t'ong	Proper, a hawker's hand gong,[6] a hall.
15.	煎 箋 錢		₍tsín	₀tsín	₍tsín	To fry, note paper,[7] a surname.
16.	淸 靑 刑		₍ts'ing	₀ts'ing	₍ying	Pure, the colour of nature, legal punishments.
17.	倉 艙 藏		₍ts'ong	₀ts'ong	₍ts'ong	A granary, a hold, to store away.
18.	槍 鎗 牆		₍ts'öng	₀ts'öng	₍ts'öng	A spear, a gun, a wall.
19.	貲 資 祠		₍tsz	₀tsz	₍t'z	Wealth, postage,[8] spring sacrifice.
20.	依 意 兒		₍yí	₀yí	₍yí	Depend on, will,[3] an infant.
21.	英 鷹 迎		₍ying	₀ying	₍ying	Superior, the hawk, to receive a guest.
22.	應 英 仍		₍ying	₀ying	₍ying	Suitable, a salad, according to.

Other examples might be given, but these will be sufficient for giving the learner a knowledge of these tones.

1. In 火疔瘡 ʻfo ₀teng ₀chong, tetter.
2. In 丁香 ₀ting ₀höng, cloves.
3. As in the phrase 詐假意 chá⁾ ₀ká yí⁾. This phrase is also pronounced chá⁾ ʻká yí⁾, and also chá⁾ ʻka ₀yí.
4. In 煖臍膏 ʻnün ₍ts'z ₀kò, a certain kind of plaster.
5. In 官廳 ₀kwún ₀téng, a court, and in other connections.
6. In 耵璫 ₀ting ₀tong, a hawker's hand gong.
7. In several phrases, the names of different kinds of paper.
8. In 信資 sun⁾ ₍tsz, postage, and in other connections.

INTRODUCTION.

FIRST SERIES, COMPRISING THE UPPER TONES.

1	2	3	4	Shöng² ₍p'ing.	Shöng² ʻshöng.	Shöng² hui².	Shöng² & ₍Chung yap₎.	Meaning of the Words.
1.	先	綫	屑	₍sin	ʻsin	sin²	sït₌	Before, moss, thread, bits.
2.	威	偉	畏	₍wai	ʻwai	wai²		Dignity, great, awe.
3.	幾	紀	記	₍kéi	ʻkéi	kéi²		Several, to record, to remember.
4.	諸	主	著	₍chü	ʻchü	chü²		All, master, to publish.
5.	修	叟	秀	₍sau	ʻsau	sau²		Adorn, venerable man, elegant.
6.	東	董	凍	篤	₍tung	ʻtung	tung²	tuk₂	East, to rule, cold, real.
7.	英	影	應	益	₍ying	ʻying	ying²	yik₂	Excellent, shadow, answer, beneficial.
8.	賓	稟	殯	畢	₍pan	ʻpan	pan²	pat₂	Guest, petition, court lady, ended.
9.	張	掌	帳	着	₍chöng	ʻchöng	chöng²	chök₂	To draw out, to rule, curtain, to order.
10.	剛	講	絳	角	₍kong	ʻkong	kong²	kok₂	Strong, to speak, to descend, horn.
11.	朝	沼	照		₍chíu	ʻchíu	chíu²		Morning, pool, to illumine.
12.	孤	古	故		₍kwú	ʻkwú	kwú²		Alone, ancient, old.
13.	鴛	婉	怨	乙	₍yün	ʻyün	yün²	yüt₂	Drake, yielding, animosity, curved.
14.	皆	解	介		₍kái	ʻkái	kái²		All, to open, firm or uncorrupted.
15.	登	等	凳	德	₍tang	ʻtang	tang²	tak₂	Ascend, sort, stool, virtue.
16.	師	史	四		₍sz	ʻsz	sz²		Master, history, four.
17.	金	錦	禁	急	₍kam	ʻkam	kam²	kap₂	Metal, embroidery, prohibit, hasty.
18.	交	絞	教		₍káu	ʻkáu	káu²		Intercourse, to strangle, to teach.
19.	栽	宰	載		₍tsoi	ʻtsoi	tsoi²		To plant, to rule, to contain.
20.	雖	髓	歲		₍sui	ʻsui	sui²		Although, marrow, year.
21.	兼	檢	劍	刼	₍kím	ʻkím	kím²	kíp₂	Joined, to examine, sword, to rob.
22.	津	贐	進	卒	₍tsun	ʻtsun	tsun²	tsut₂	A ford, presents, to enter, soldiers.
23.	科	火	貨		₍fo	ʻfo	fo²		Order or sort, fire, cargo.
24.	緘	減	鑒	甲	₍kám	ʻkám	kám²	káp₂	To bind, to diminish, mirror, armour.
25.	翻	反	泛	發	₍fán	ʻfán	fán²	fát₂	To fly, to rebel, to float, to issue.
26.	家	假	嫁		₍ká	ʻká	ká²		Family, price, to marry (a husband).
27.	官	管	貫	括	₍kwún	ʻkwún	kwún²	kwút₂	Officer, tube, to connect, to inclose.
28.	魁	賄	誨		₍fui	ʻfui	fui²		Headmost, a bribe, to teach.
29.	遮	者	蔗		₍che	ʻche	che²		Screen, this, sugar cane.
30.	干	趕	幹	割	₍kòn	ʻkòn	kòn²	kòt₂	A shield, to pursue, business, to cut.
31.	甘	敢	紺	蛤	₍kòm	ʻkòm	kòm²	kòp₂	Sweet, daring, purple, a clam.
32. 33.	} In these two orders no words occur in this series.							

INTRODUCTION.

SECOND SERIES, COMPRISING THE LOWER TONES.

	1	2	3	4	$Há^2$ $_sp'ing.$	$Há^2$ $shöng^2.$	$Há^2$ $hui^2.$	$Há^2$ $yap_2.$	Meaning of the Words.
1.	連	璉	鍊	列	$_slín$	^slín	$lín^2$	$lít_2$	To unite, gem, chain, to separate.
2.	迷	米	袂		$_smai$	^smai	mai^2		To deceive, rice, cuff of the sleeve.
3.	宜	議	貳		$_syí$	$^syí$	$yí^2$		Right, deliberate, the second.
4.	如	語	寓		$_syü$	$^syü$	$yü^2$		As, to converse, to lodge.
5.	留	柳	陋		$_slau$	^slau	lau^2		To detain, willow, base or mean.
6.	容	勇	用	欲	$_syung$	^syung	$yung^2$	yuk_2	Manner, brave, use, to wish.
7.	靈	領	令	力	$_sling$	^sling	$ling^2$	lik_2	Spiritual, the neck, to order, strength.
8.	文	敏	問	勿	$_sman$	^sman	man^2	mat_2	Letters, celerity, to ask, do not.
9.	陽	仰	樣	藥	$_syöng$	^syöng	$yöng^2$	$yök_2$	Light, to look up, pattern, physic.
10.	王	往	旺	鑊	$_swong$	^swong	$wong^2$	wok_2	King, to go, abundance, a pan.
11.	寮	了	料		$_slíu$	^slíu	$líu^2$		A widow, finished, to estimate.
12.	無	母	務		$_smò$	$^smò$	$mò^2$		Without, mother, business.
13.	元	軟	願	月	$_syün$	^syün	$yün^2$	$yüt_2$	Origin, flexible, desire, moon.
14.	鞋	蟹	懈		$_shái$	^shái	$hái^2$		Shoes, crab, lazy.
15.	盟	猛	孟	墨	$_smang$	^smáng	$máng^2$	mak_2	To swear, fierce, first, ink.
16.	詞	似	自		$_sts'z$	$^sts'z$	tsz^2		Sentence, like, self.
17.	吟	衽	任	入	$_syam$	^syam	yam^2	yap_2	To chant, lappet, to sustain, enter.
18.	茅	卯	貌		$_smáu$	^smáu	$máu^2$		Rushes, luxuriant, countenance.
19.	臺	殆	代		$_st'oi$	$^st'oi$	toi^2		Terrace, dangerous, instead of.
20.	嚴	染	驗	業	$_syím$	^syím	$yím^2$	$yíp_2$	Severe, to dye, to examine, occupation.
21.	倫	卵	論	律	$_slun$	^slun	lun^2	lut_2	Relation, egg, discourse, law.
22.	雷	壘	類		$_slui$	^slui	lui^2		Thunder, to involve, species.
23.	鵝	我	臥		$_sngo$	^sngo	ngo^2		Goose, I or we, to sleep.
24.	藍	欖	纜	蠟	$_slám$	^slám	$lám^2$	$láp_2$	Blue, to look, rope, wax.
25.	蘭	懶	爛	辣	$_slán$	^slán	$lán^2$	$lát_2$	Fading, lazy, broken, pungent.
26.	牙	雅	迓		$_sngá$	$^sngá$	$ngá^2$		Teeth, elegant, to receive.
27.	門	滿	悶	末	$_smún$	^smún	$mún^2$	$mút_2$	Door, full, grief, the end.
28.	梅	每	昧		$_smúi$	^smúi	$múi^2$		Plum, each, obscure.
29.	蛇	社	射		$_sshe$	^sshe	she^2		Snake, local deities, to shoot.
30.	寒	旱	翰	渴	$_shòn$	^shòn	$hòn^2$	$hòt_2$	Cold, drought, pencil, hempen cloth.
31.	含	頷	憾	合	$_shòm$	^shòm	$hòm^2$	$hòp_2$	To endure, jaws, indignation, to unite.
32.	彭	棒	硬	額	$_sp'áng$	$^sp'áng$	$ngáng^2$	$ngák_2$	Abundant, a mace, stiff, forehead.
33.	吾	五	悟		$_sng$	^sng	ng^2		My or our, five, to perceive.

INTRODUCTION.

In the following exercise care must be taken that the teacher who reads over the exercise understands that the third word in each series is in the Third Rising Tone and not in its original tone, which may be a 下去 há² hui' or 下平 há² ₅p'ing, &c., as the case may be. The same may be said to a certain extent of the exercise on the 平 ₅p'ing tones (on page 33) where the word given in the 中平 ₅chung ₅p'ing is in certain connections pronounced in the 上平 shöng² ₅p'ing.

TONIC EXERCISE IN THE 上 SHÖNG² TONES.

1	2	3	Shöng² ₅shöng.	Há² ₅shöng.	Third Rising.	Meaning of the Words.
1.	殿	變	漏	ʻau	₅lau	ʻlau*	To fight, a bamboo hamper, dropped.
2.	粉	忿	訓	ʻfan	₅fan	ʻfan*	Flour of any grain, anger, gone to sleep.
3.	訪	朗	房	ʻfong	₅long	ʻfong*	To inquire, lustrous, a room.
4.	虎	婦	壺	ʻfú	₅fú	ʻú*	A tiger, lady, a vase or pot.
5.	喺	蟹	計	ʻhai	₅hái	ʻkai*	To be at, a crab, a plan.
6.	解	械	牌	ʻkái	₅kái	ʻpái*	To explain, to pass anything along, register.
7.	紀	企	棊	ʻkéi	₅k'éi	ʻkéi*	Annals, to stand, chess.
8.	矯	皎	轎	ʻkiú	₅kiú	ʻkiú*	Straight, to bale water, a sedan.
9.	舉	佢	籧	ʻkui	₅k'ui	ʻkui*²	To elevate, he or she, the posts of a certain frame.
10.	寡	褂	挂	ʻkwá	₅kwá	ʻkwá*	Widow, a jacket, hung.
11.	果	莫	過	ʻkwo	₅mo	ʻkwo*	Fruit, stop! passed.
12.	嚟	禮	嚟	ʻlai	₅lai	ʻlai*	To turn, propriety, has come.
13.	欖	攬	纜	ʻlám	₅lám	ʻlám*	Olive, to grasp, rope.
14.	佬	老	爐	ʻlò	₅lò	ʻlò*	A fellow, old, furnace.
15.	兩	兩	梁	ʻlöng	₅löng	ʻlöng*	Tael, two, bridge (of the nose).[1]
16.	蠹	殆	檯	ʻoi	₅t'oi	ʻt'oi*	Foggy, dangerous, table.
17.	稟	眼	銀	ʻpan	₅ngán	ʻngan*	To petition, eye, money.
18.	俾	里	狸	ʻpéi	₅léi	ʻléi*	To give, a mile, a small fox-like animal.
19.	表	了	寮	ʻpíú	₅líú	ʻlíú*	To manifest, finished, a shanty.
20.	保	抱	部	ʻpò	₅p'ò	ʻpò*	To protect, to carry in the arms, a manuscript book.
21.	使	舐	嘣	ʻshai	₅shái	ʻshái*	To use, to lick, dried in the sun.
22.	歹	舵	太	ʻtái	₅t'ái	ʻt'ái*	Bad, rudder, great.
23.	點	斂	簾	ʻtím	₅lím	ʻlím*	A dot, to harvest, bamboo blinds.

1. In the phrase 文 | ₅man ʻkui*.
2. In 鼻梁 p'di² ʻlong*, bridge of the nose, and in some combinations.

INTRODUCTION.

			Shöng².ᶜshöng.	Há².ᶜshöng.	Third Rising.	Meaning of the Words.
24.	頂	挺	錠	ᶜting	ˢting	ʹtiug*	Summit, to pull up, an ingot.
25.	仔	鱭	薺	ᶜtsai	ˢts'ai	ʹts'ai*	Son, a mullet, together.
26.	子	似	柿	ᶜtsz	ˢts'z	ʹts'z*	A son, similar, persimmon.
27.	搵	尹	韻	ᶜwan	ˢwan	ʹwan*	To look for, correct, rhyme.
28.	碗	滿	換	ᶜwún	ˢmún	ʹwún*	A bowl, full, changed.
29.	隱	引	人	ᶜyan	ˢyan	ʹyan*	Small, to entice, man.
30.	朽	有	由	ᶜyau	ˢyau	ʹyau*	Rotten wood, to have, allow.
31.	倚	耳	姨	ᶜyí	ˢyí	ʹyí*	To rely on, ear, sister-in-law.
32.	掩	染	驗	ᶜyím	ˢyím	ʹyím*	To close, to dye, examined, (very seldom used in this tone).
33.	夭	擾	鳶	ᶜyíu	ˢyíu	ʹyíu*	Shortlived, to give trouble, a kite.
34.	抉	養	樣	ᶜyöng	ˢyöng	ʹyöng*	To shake (as a cloth), to rear, pattern.
35.	湧	勇	用	ᶜyung	ˢyung	ʹyung*	Bubbling, brave, commission.¹
36.	婉	遠	院	ᶜyün	ˢyün	ʹyün*	yielding, distant, a college.

The list of *yap* tones, should be studied in the same way as the above.

TONIC EXERCISE IN THE THREE 入 YAP₂ TONES.

			Shöng².yap₂.	ᶜChung yap₂.	Há².yap₂.	Meaning of the Words.
1.	握	鈪	噁	ak₃	ák₀	ngák₂	To grasp, a bangle, contrary to.
2.	洽	鴨	陜	ap₃	áp₀	háp₂	To soak, a duck, a straight passage.
3.	抓	壓	核	at₃	át₀	hat₂	To thrust in, to press down, the kernel of fruits.
4.	舴	責	宅	chák₃	chák₀	chák₂	A small boat, to reprove, a mansion.
5.	執	刻	閘	chap₃	₀cháp	cháp₂	To pick up, to write out, a barrier.
6.	郅	扎	窒	chat₃	chút₀	chat₂	To ascend, a bundle, to stop up the mouth of.
7.	職	隻	直	chik₃	chek₀	chik₂	To govern, one of a pair, straightforward.
8.	竹	捉	濁	chuk₃	chuk₀	chuk₂	Bamboo, to seize, turbid.
9.	忽	法	罰	fat₃	fát₀	fat₂	To dip up, law, to punish.
10.	刻	摑	嚇	hak₃	kwák₀	hák₂	To carve, to slap the face with the hand, to threaten.
11.	急	甲	及	kap₃	káp₀	k'ap₂	Hasty, the plumula, and.
12.	骨	刮	掘	kwat₃	kwát₀	kwat₂	Bone, to scrape, to dig.

1. In 用 錢 ʹyung* ˢtsín, commission.

XXXVIII   INTRODUCTION.

INTRODUCTION.

1	2	3	Shöng² yap₂	Chung yap₂	Há² yap₂	Meaning of the Words.
13.	扐	肋 肋	lak₂	lák₀	lák₂	To bind, the ribs, the ribs.
14.	笠	搚 蠟	lap₂	láp₀	láp₂	A hamper, to lump, wax.
15.	哷	劣 律	lut₂	lüt₀	lut₂	Out of order, infirm, a statute.
16.	乜	抹 襪	mat₂	mát₀	mat₂	What? to wipe, stockings.
17.	搣	咽 臬	mít₂	yít₀	yít₂	To break off, to choke, the judge or ruler of a city.
18.	㦿	鈉 捺	nat₂	nát₀	nát₂	Joyful, to smooth, a dash to the right in writing.
19.	吸	唊 㗇	ngap₂	ngap₀	ngap₂	To talk at random, to tuck in, to beckon.
20.	北	百 白	pak₂	pák₀	pák₂	North, hundred, white.
21.	不	八 魃	pat₂	pát₀	pát₂	Not, eight, the god of draught.
22.	必	鱉 別	pít₂	pít₀	pít₂	Must, a species of pheasant, to separate.
23.	亳	博 薄	pok₂	pok₀	pok₂	Name of a District, spacious, jungle.
24.	濕	焓 十	shap₂	sháp₀	shap₂	Wet, to boil, ten.
25.	失	殺 實	shat₂	shát₀	shat₂	To lose, to behead, firm.
26.	恤	雪 月	sut₂	süt₀	yüt₂	To compassionate, snow, the moon or a month.
27.	嗒	答 踏	tap₂	táp₀	táp₂	To lick, to answer, to step on.
28.	吤	笪 凸	tat₂	tát₀	tát₂	Dab, a spot, projecting.
29.	的	踢 敵	tik₂	t'ek₀	tik₂	Clear, to kick, an opponant.
30.	揉	脚 㝵	tök₂	kök₀	lök₂	To pound on wood, the foot, a little.
31.	則	冊 賊	tsak₂	ch'ák₀	ts'ák₂	Precept, a register, a thief.
32.	喞	插 雜	tsap₂	ch'áp₀	tsáp₂	A heap, to insert, mixed.
33.	七	擦 甲	ts'at₂	ts'át₀	tsát₂	Seven, to brush, a cockroach, as :— 由 甲 kát₂ tsát₂.
34.	卽	瘠 蓆	tsik₂	tsik₀	tsek₂	Immediately, lean, mat.
35.	屈	挖 滑	wat₂	wát₀	wát₂	Bent, to scoop out, smooth.
36.	饁	腌 葉	yíp₂	yíp₀	yíp₂	Provision for journeys, to salt flesh, a leaf.

ASPIRATED AND NON-ASPIRATED WORDS.

Another distinction which calls for the special attention of the learner is the difference between aspirated and non-aspirated words. "It is a very important part of pronunciation, as much so in every respect as the tones, and should be particularly attended to."—Williams' *Easy Leasons in Chinese*, p. 55. "It cannot * * be too strongly impressed upon learners from the outset that * * aspirates * * are of the utmost importance to one who would learn Chinese intelligibly. Carelessness about the difference between aspirated and unaspirated

INTRODUCTION.

words in Chinese, will often render a speaker as absolutely unintelligible in China, as a foreigner in England would be if he should substitute *d* for *t* or *t* for *d*, saying for instance, 'too dry' for 'do try,' or if he should substitute *b* for *p* or *p* for *b*, speaking of 'bears' when he means 'pears' and of 'pears' when he means 'bears.' It is not intended here to assert that the difference between aspirated and unaspirated words is exactly the same as the difference between the English *d* and *t* or *b* and *p* sounds, etc., but the difference is *quite as distinct and great* as this, and it is even more important in speaking Chinese to observe these differences than it is in speaking English."—Foster's *Elementary Lessons in Chinese*, pp. 29 and 30. And yet it is one of the features of Chinese pronunciation which is, one might almost say, systematically ignored by many foreigners learning Chinese, either from a failure to see the distinction, from not understanding the definitions explaining the difference, or from an idea that it can be of no importance. This last idea being probably fostered by the feeling that there is nothing of the kind in English, or in other words instead of the voice passing quietly from the initial consonant to the vowel and the final consonant, a strong breathing out often takes place in English immediately after the initial consonant. To explain the difference between the aspirated and unaspirated pronunciation let us take, for example, the word *tin*. To pronounce this word the following actions take place. First place the tip of the tongue on the palate immediately behind the front teeth, then let it quietly drop while the voice pronounces a something between an English *t* and an English *d*, that is, it has the sound of the English *t* but unaccompanied with any forcible emission of the voice, which generally does accompany the pronunciation of the *t* in English, then after this initial consonant immediately follows the *in* pronounced like *een* in English. Next take an aspirated word spelled in the same way, but with an inverted comma to represent the aspirate in Chinese, as:—*t'in*. Here begin as before by placing the tip of the tongue on the palate behind the front teeth, but immediately the tongue falls and the *t* is pronounced, it is followed by a strong breathing out of the voice, this being the way in which many pronounce the *t* in English. There is, however, some difference amongst different speakers of English as to the way in which they pronounce their consonants: that is to say that there is a dual method of pronouncing two precisely similar combinations of letters of the alphabet by different individuals in English. Some pronouncing them with a more forcible emission of voice, while others let them, as it were, simply fall quietly out of their mouths without any or but slight propulsion. It therefore follows that the usual directions given as to the pronunciation of the aspirated and unaspirated consonants as pronounced in Chinese are misleading to many persons. To many persons the directions should be given to pronounce the

INTRODUCTION.

aspirated consonants in the same way that they do these consonants in English while the unaspirated ones are to be pronounced flatter and more like the other consonants, such as *d* and *b*, which they pronounce without any explosive force of the voice in English.

Now in Chinese it must be distinctly understood it is different. The same consonants are pronounced by the same individuals in two ways, thus manifestly increasing the number of words while economising the spelling according to our English ideas of orthography, or in other words the consonants in Chinese,which are pronounced quietly are also pronounced with a forcible emission of the voice immediately following them which is represented by the inverted comma. Thus ,chá, the ch being pronounced quietly means, *to hold*, while the same sound, but intensified by an explosive force, as, ,ch'á means, *fork*. Just as in English there are two ways of pronouncing the *th* (as for example, *thy* and *thigh*, where the only difference in the sound of the two words consists in the difference between the pronunciation of the first and second *th*); so in Chinese the same English consonants in many cases are used in two different ways, one aspirated and the other followed by the aspirated.

The consonants which have the aspirate after them are the following, viz:—

Ch, k, kw, p, t, and ts.

The learner will find it a good practice to go through the following exercise daily at first, till he finds no difficulty at all with the unaspirated and aspirated words.

渣 差 ,cha *refuse*; ,ch'á, *error*.
齋 差 ,chái, ('tá ,chái, *mass*); ,ch'ái, *police*.
仄 測 chak, *slanting*; ch'ak$_o$, *to fathom*.
責 册 chák$_o$, *to reprove*; ch'ák$_o$, *a register*.
針 沉 ,cham, *a needle*; ,ch'am, *to sink*.
斬 杉 'chám, *to chop off*; ch'ám', *pine*.
眞 塵 ,chan, *true*; ,ch'an, *dust*.
盞 產 'chán, (,tang 'ch'an, .a lamp saucer;) 'ch'án, *to produce*.

踭 橕 ,cháng, *heel*; ch'áng, *to pole*.
閘 插 cháp$_2$, *a gate*; ch'áp$_o$, *to insert*.
扎 察 chát$_o$, *a bundle*; ch'át$_o$, *to examine*.
州 臭 ,chau, *a district*; ch'au', *a bad smell*.
爪 炒 'chau, *claws*, 'ch'au, *to fry in fat*.

遮 車 ,che, *an umbrella*; ,ch'e, *a carriage*.
隻 尺 chek, (a Classifier), ch'ek$_o$ *a foot*.
知 遟 ,chí, *to know*; ,ch'í, *late*.
占 諂 ,chím, *to divine*; 'ch'ím, *to flatter* (book).
氊 躔 ,chín, *felt*; ,ch'ín, *to tread*, (book).
正 稱 ching', *the first*; ,ch'ing, *to style*.
折 設 chit$_o$, *to snap in two*; ch'ít$_o$, *to establish*.
朝 朝 ,chíu, *morning*; ,ch'íu, *the Court*.
阻 初 'cho, *to hinder*; ,ch'o, *the beginning*.
着 棹 chök$_o$, *right*; ch'ök$_o$, *a table*, (book).
章 窓 ,chöng, *a chapter*; ,ch'öng, *a window*.
壯 瘡 chong', *robust*; ,ch'ong, *a boil*.
猪 柱 ,chü, *a pig*; 'ch'ü, *a pillar*.
追 吹 ,chui, *to pursue*; ,ch'ui, *to blow*.

INTRODUCTION.

音 ₂chuk, bamboo; ch'uk₂, domestic animals.
春 ₂chun, to allow; ch'un, spring.
川 ₂chün, a brick; ch'ün, a hill spring.
充 ₂chung, middle; ch'ung, to fill.
出 chut₂, to blame (book); ch'ut₂, to go out.
溪 ₂kai, a fowl; k'ai, a clear hill stream.
楷 ₂kai, a street; 'k'ai, a pattern (book).
金 ₂kam, gold; ₂k'am, a coverlet.
芹 ₂kan, roots; ₂k'an, parsley.
指 ₂kang, soup; ₂k'ang, to oppress.
吸 kap₂, hasty; k'ap₂, to inhale.
咳 kat₂, lucky; k'at₂, to cough.
摳 ₂kau, a pigeon; ₂k'au, to mix.
荳 ₂kau, to unite; ₂k'au, to rely on.
基 ₂kei, a few; ₂k'ei, chess.
展 kik₂, very; k'ek₂, clogs.
鈄 ₂kim, moreover; ₂k'im, tongs.
揵 ₂kin, firm; 'k'in, to lift up (a cover).
鯨 ₂king, capital city; ₂k'ing, a whale.
揭 kit₂, clear; k'it₂, to borrow.
橋 'kiú*, a sedan; ₂k'iú, a bridge.
蓋 'koi, to change; k'oi', a cover.
確 kok₂, each; k'ok₂, really.
却 kok₂, foot; k'ok₂, to stop (book).
匠 'kong, just; ₂k'ong, a sofa.
強 ₂köng, ginger; 'k'öng, by force.
渠 'kui, to dwell; ₂k'ui, a drain.
拳 ₂kün, to squeeze through; ₂k'ün, the fist.
窮 ₂kung, public; ₂k'ung, poor.
栝 kut₂, deficient; k'ut₂, united strength.
誇 ₂kwá, a melon; ₂k'wá, to brag.
規 ₂kwai, home; ₂k'wai, a custom.
裙 'kwan, ruler; ₂kw'an, a skirt.
狂 ₂kwong, light; ₂kw'ong, mad.
琶 'pá, to seize; ₂p'á, a guitar.
批 ₂pai, lame; ₂p'ai, to pare.
牌 'pái, to spread out; ₂p'ai, a shield.
栢 pák₂, hundred; p'ák₂, to clap.

貧 ₂pan, a petition; ₂p'an, poor.
攀 ₂pan, a grade; ₂p'an, to drag.
朋 ₂pang, a fracture; ₂p'ang, a friend.
螃 páng², bang!; ₂p'áng, a land crab.
疋 pat₂, not; p'at₂, a piece (of cloth).
抛 ₂pau, to wrap up; ₂p'au, to cast (anchor).
皮 'pei, to give; ₂p'ei, leather.
擗 pik₂, to urge; p'ek₂, to throw away.
片 ₂pin, the side; p'in², slip (slice).
平 ₂ping, a soldier; ₂p'ing, even.
撇 pit₂, must; p'it₂, a down stroke.
票 piú, a banner; p'iú, a summons.
鴛 ₂po, a wave; ₂p'o, a classifier of trees, &c.
鋪 'po, to boil; ₂p'o, to spread out.
樸 pok₂, intelligent; p'ok₂, to flap.
旁 ₂pong, to help; ₂p'ong, side.
賠 'pui, a cup; ₂p'ui, to indemnify.
盤 ₂pun, to remove; ₂p'un, a basin.
蓬 pung², to run against; ₂p'ung, a sail.
濺 put₂, a coarse dish; p'ut₂, to dash water.
他 ₂tá, to strike; ₂t'á, another.
梯 'tai, to bend down; ₂t'ai, a ladder.
太 tái², a girdle; t'ai², excessive.
泵 ₂tam, to hammer; ₂t'am, a cess-pool.
擔 ₂tám, to carry; ₂t'ám, to covet.
吞 ₂tan, a heap; ₂t'an, to swallow.
攤 'tán, alone; ₂t'án, to spread open.
燈 ₂tang, a lamp; ₂t'ang, rattan.
塔 táp₂, to answer; t'áp₂, a pagoda.
撻 tát₂, to pervade; t'át₂, a dead loss.
偷 ₂tau a dry measure; ₂t'au, to steal.
踢 tek₂, to buy rice; t'ek₂, to kick.
艇 ₂teng, a nail; 't'eng, a boat.
剔 tik₂, clear; t'ik₂, to scrape off.
添 ₂tim, a spot; t'im, to increase.
天 ₂tin, crazy; ₂t'in, the sky.
亭 ₂ting, a jingling sound; ₂t'ing, a pavilion.
帖 tip₂, a plate; t'ip₂, a card.

INTRODUCTION.

跌	鐵	tit₀, *to fall*; tʻit₀, *iron*.	節 切	tsit₀, *averse*; tsʻit₀, *to cut* (in slices).
丟	條	₋tíú, *to throw away*; ₋tʻíú, *a classifier*.	椒 樵	tsíú, *pepper*; ₋tsʻíú, *scattered wood*.
多	拖	₋to, *many*; ₋tʻo, *to lead* (by the hand).	左 錯	ʻtso, *the left*; tsʻoˀ, *wrong*.
刀	桃	₋tò, *a knife*; ʻtʻò, or ₋tʻò, *peach*.	租 粗	₋tsò, *rent*; ₋tsʻò, *coarse*.
代	臺	ʻtoi², *a generation*; ʻtʻoi*, *a table*.	再 咄	tsoiˀ, *again*; ₋tsʻoi! *pshaw!*
度	托	tok₋, *to measure*; tʻok₀, *to carry*.	作 錯	tsok, *to make*; tsʻok, *to tattoo*.
當	湯	₋tong, *proper*; ₋tʻong, *soup*.	葬 倉	tsong³, *to bury*; tsʻong, *a granary*.
剚	妻	tsni, *a dose*; ₋tsʻni, *a wife*.	將 鎗	ʻtsŏng, *shall*; ₀tsʻŏng, *a gun*.
浸	尋	tsum, *to soak*; ₋tsʻum, *to look for*.	聚 取	tsui², *to assemble*; ʻtsʻui, *to take*.
簪	蠶	₋tsám, *a hairpin*; ₋tsʻám, *a silkworm*.	足 速	tsuk, *the foot*; tsʻuk, *hurried*.
贊	飡	tsánˀ, *to praise*; ₋tsʻán, *a meal*.	樽 巡	₋tsun, *a bottle*; ₋tsʻun, *to cruise*.
憎	層	₋tsang, *to hate*; ₋tsʻang, *a layer*.	尊 村	₋tsün, *honourable*; ₋tsʻün, *a village*.
揖	緝	tsap, *a handful*; tsʻap, *to join*.	棕 松	₋tsung, *coir*; ₋tsʻung, *the pine tree*.
疾	七	tsat, *disease*; tsʻat₋, *seven*.	絕 撮	tsüt², *to sunder*; tsʻüt₀, *a pinch*.
走	秋	ʻtsau, *to run*; ₋tsʻau, *autumn*.	子 慈	ʻtsz, *a son*; ₋tsʻz, *mercy*.
姐	邪	ʻtse, *an elder sister*; ₋tsʻe, *depraved*.	堆 推	₋tui, *a heap*; ₋tʻui, *to push away*.
迹	戚	tsik, *a foot-mark*; tsʻik₋, *related to*.	督 禿	tuk, *to lead*; tʻuk₀, *a Buddhist priest*.
尖	簽	₋tsím, *sharp*; ₋tsʻím, *to subscribe*.	敦 湍	₋tun, *angry*; ₋tʻun, *a rapid current*.
煎	千	₋tsín, *to fry*; ₋tsʻín, *a thousand*.	短 團	ʻtün, *short*; ₋tʻün, *a globular mass*.
晶	清	₋tsíng, *crystal*; ₋tsʻíng, *pure*.	東 通	₋tung, *east*; ₋tʻung, *to go through*.
接	妾	tsíp₀, *to receive*; tsʻíp₀, *a concubine*.	奪 脫	tüt², *to take by force*; tʻüt₀, *to strip*.

LONG AND SHORT VOWELS.

Another most important feature in Cantonese is the long and short vowels and diphthongs. The beginner must drill himself in these daily, and make sure that he is pronouncing a word containing a long vowel with the vowel long and one with a short vowel with the vowel short. Dr. Eitel rightly says about these:—
'Another characteristic feature of the Cantonese dialect is the distinction of long and short vowels and diphthongs, which should be specially studied from the beginning, to accustom the ear to the discrimination of these shades, which is indispensable for a ready and correct understanding of the spoken language.'—Introduction *to Cantonese Dictionary*, p. xiii.

To enable the learner to "specially study" these distinctions, tables of many of them are here appended; and the learner should go through them with his

INTRODUCTION.

teacher day by day till perfect, and even then a run through them occasionally will do him good.

握 握 ak, to grasp; ák₀, a bangle.
掩 菡 ,am, to cover; 'ám, an unopened flower.
鶯 甖 ,ang, the nightingale; ,áng, a jar.
洽 鴨 ap, to cover over; áp₀, a duck.
扎 押 at, to thrust in; át₀, to pawn for a time.
仄 責 chak, slanting; chák₀, to reprove.
針 斬 ,cham, a needle; 'chám, to cut in two.
眞 盞 ,chan, true; 'chán, a shallow cup for oil.
箏 爭 ,chang, a harpsichord; ,cháng, to wrangle.
執 閘 chap, to pick up; cháp₀, a barrier.
質 扎 chat, substance; chát₀, a bundle.
分 凡 ,fan, to divide; ,fán, all.
拂 法 fat, to brush away; fát₀, usage.
黑 客 hak, black; hák₀, a guest.
痕 開 ,han, a mark; ,hán, leisure.
鏗 行 ,hang, to knock against; ,háng, to walk.
哈 呷 hap, sleepy; háp₀, to gulp.
喉 巧 ,hau, the throat; 'háu, skilful.
金 監 ,kam, metal; ,kám, a gaol.
根 間 ,kan, root; ,kán, an interval.
羹 逕 ,kang, a thick soup; káng², a by-path.
急 甲 kap, hasty; káp₀, armour for the body.
君 關 ,kwan, the prince; ,kwán, to bar a door.
轟 逛 ,kwang, rumbling; kwáng², to ramble.
骨 刮 kwat, bone; kwát₀, to scrape.
林 籃 ,lam, a grove; 'lám*, a basket.
唥 冷 ,lang, a jingle; 'láng, cold.
笠 立 lap, a pottle; láp₀, to establish.
甪 辣 lat, to let go; lát₀, pungent.
麥 璧 mak, wheat; mák₀, to break in two.
蚊 彎 ,man, mosquito; máu, to pull.
盟 盲 ,mang, an alliance; ,máng, blind.
乜 抹 mat, what; mát₀, to wipe.
腍 男 ,nam, mellow; ,nám, male.

難 ,nan, to handle; ,nán, difficult.
粒 衲 nap, a grain; 'náp*, or náp₀, quilted.
爁 鈉 nat, joyful; nát₀, to smooth.
陌 額 ngak, to swindle; ngak₂, front.
啥 巖 ,ngam, foolish; ,ngám, precipice.
銀 眼 ,ngan, money; 'ngán, eye.
吸 哽 ngap, to talk wildly; ngáp₀, to tuck in.
扤 搻 ngat, to sway; ngát₀, a rank smell.
北 百 pak, north; pák₀, one hundred.
貧 攀 ,p'an, poor; ,p'án, to lead.
崩 峰 ,pang, an emperor's death; páng², bung!

不 八 pat, not; pát₀, eight.
心 三 ,sam, the heart; ,sám, three.
新 散 ,san, new, sán², to scatter.
唧 颯 sap, to enter the mouth; sáp₀, suddenly.
膝 撒 sat, the knee; sát₀, to disperse.
深 衫 ,sham, deep; ,shám, clothes.
身 山 ,shan, body; ,shán, mountain.
生 啥 ,shang, to produce; 'sháng, to scour.
濕 恰 shap, wet; sháp₀, to provoke.
失 殺 shat, to lose; shát₀, to kill.
氹 擔 ,tam, to pound; ,tám, to carry from a pole.

墩 單 ,tan, a heap; ,tán, single.
搭 答 tap, to be rained on; táp₀, to answer.
凸 達 tat, a tenon; tát, intelligent.
鮎 賊 tsak, bream; ts'ák₀, a thief.
浸 簪 tsam², to soak; ,tsám, a hairpin.
親 餐 ,ts'an, related to; ,ts'án, a meal.
戢 雜 tsap, a handful; tsáp₀, mixed.
七 擦 ts'at, seven; ts'át₀, to brush.
雲 還 ,wan, cloud; ,wán, to return.
核 滑 wat, the stony seeds of fruit; wát₂, smooth.

INTRODUCTION.

THE LONG AND SHORT DIPHTHONGS AI AND ÁI.

唉挨 ₀ai, *whew!* ₀ái, *to lean upon.*
擠齋 ₀chai, *to place;* ₀chái, *to abstain.*
費快 fai³, *to spend;* fái³, *quick.*
鷄街 ₀kai, *a fowl;* ₀kái, *a street.*
歸乖 ₀kwai, *home;* ₀kwái, *good (as a child).*
嚟拉 ₀lai, *to come;* ₀lái, *to pull.*
迷埋 ₀mai, *to deceive;* ₀mái, *to hide away.*

篩曬 ₀shai, *sieve;* shái³, *to dry in the sun.*
低帶 ₀tai, *to bend down;* tái³, *a ribbon.*
威壞 ₀wni, *dignity;* wái³, *to spoil.*
泥乃 ₀nai, *clay;* ₀nái, *lady.*
㘉涯 ₀ngai, *to importune;* ₀ngái, *bench.*
跛拜 ₀pai, *lame;* pái³, *to worship.*

EXERCISES ON THE LONG AND SHORT DIPHTHONGS AI ÉI ÁI.

1. 肺非塊 fai³, *the lungs;* ₀féi, *not;* fái³, *a lump.*
2. 係禧鞋 hai², *to be;* ₀héi, *happy;* ₀hái, *a shoe.*
3. 髻幾街 'kai, *coiffure;* ₀kéi, *subtle;* ₀kái, *a street.*
4. 嚟李拉 ₀lai, *to come;* ⁵léi, *a plum;* ₀lái, *to pull.*
5. 米微賣 ⁵mai, *rice;* ₀méi, *minute;* mái², *to sell.*
6. 坭你乃 ₀nai, *mire;* ⁵néi, *you;* ⁵nái, *but.*
7. 㾁俾擺 pai³, *sad;* 'péi, *to give;* 'pái, *to spread out.*
8. 弟地大 tai², *a younger brother;* téi², *earth;* tái², *great.*

THE LONG AND SHORT DIPHTHONGS AU AND ÁU.

區拗 ₀au, *a surname;* 'áu, *to snap in two.*
周找 ₀chau, *universal;* 'cháu, *to exchange.*
喉巧 ₀hau, *the throat;* 'háu, *skilful.*
九絞 'kau, *nine;* 'káu, *to twist.*
流摟 ₀lau, *to flow;* ₀láu, *to drag for in water.*

蹓茅 mau³, *to squat down;* ₀máu, *reeds.*
扭鬧 'nau, *to twist;* náu², *to scold.*
牛咬 ₀ngau, *an ox;* ⁵ngáu, *to bite.*
剖包 p'au³, *to divide;* ₀pau, *to wrap around.*
收筲 ₀shau, *to receive;* ₀sháu, *a basket.*

EXERCISE ON E AND Í (= EE).

車知 ₀che, *a carriage;* ₀chi, *to know.*
唏顯 ₀he, *holloa!* 'hín, *manifest.*
嘅見 ke³, *sign of possessive;* kín³, *to see.*
哩蓮 ₀le, *a final particle;* ₀lín, *the lotus.*
歪面 ₀me, *awry;* mín², *the face.*
哪年 ₀ne, *there!* ₀nín, *year.*

嗯啀 ₀nge, *whine;* ₀ngí, *hesitating.*
啤便 ₀pe, *beer;* pín², *convenient.*
寫先 'se, *to write;* ₀sín, *first.*
賒善 ₀she, *on credit;* shín², *virtuous.*
爹天 ₀te, *dad;* ₀t'ín, *the sky.*
借箭 tse³, *to borrow;* tsín³, *an arrow.*

INTRODUCTION.

EXERCISE ON SHORT AND LONG Í, VIZ., I AND Í.

織 知 chik, *to weare*; ₍chí, *to know*. 　　兵 變 ping, *a soldier*; pin², *to alter*.
抍 顛 fing², *to swing*; ʽhiu, *manifest*. 　　星 仙 ₍sing, *a star*; ₍sin, *genii*.
京 深 ₍king, *a capital*; kit₀, *pure*. 　　聲 詩 shing, *a sound*; ₍shí, *a hymn*.
隙 唎 kwik, *a crack*; kwit₀, *shrill*. 　　定 典 ₍ting, *to fix*; ʽtin, *a canon*.
嚨 憐 ₍ling, *tinkling*; ₍lin, *commiserate*. 　　淨 煎 tsing², *pure*; ₍tsin, *to fry*. ——
明 勉 ₍ming, *clear*; ʽmin, *to force*. 　　拯 㮍 ₍wing, *to throw*; wit,, *creaking*.
拎 臠 ₍ning, *to take*; ʽnin, *a slice*.

Whenever o is only used with an initial consonant or consonants, and without a final consonant both the open o, and close sound ò of the o are used in the Cantonese.

Exceptions:—cho, fo, kwo, and wo, there being no chò, fò, kwò, or wò.

Whenever the o is followed by the final consonants k, n, and ng, then the o is an open one, as:—ok, on, and ong.

Whenever the o is followed by the final consonant m, then it has the close sound of ò, as, òm.

EXERCISE ON LONG AND SHORT O, VIZ., O˙ and Ò.

阻 早 ʽcho, *to hinder*; ʽtso, *early*. 　　鵝 擎 ₍ngo, *a goose*; ₍ngò, *to shake*.
何 毫 ₍ho, *what?* ₍hò, *down (hair)*. 　　波 煲 ₍po, *a wave*; ₍pò, *to boil*.
歌 高 ₍ko, *a song*; ₍kò, *high*. 　　疎 數 sho, *wide apart*; shò², *an account*.
攞 佬 ʽlo, *to fetch*; ʽlò, *a fellow*. 　　鎖 鬚 ʽso, *a lock*; ₍sò, *a beard*.
磨 毛 ₍mo, *to rub*; ₍mò, *hair*. 　　左 做 ʽtso, *left*; tsò², *to do*.

There are other combinations in which the o both long and short are used; but in these other combinations only one kind of o is used with each combination; they do not therefore come into such striking contrast as when appearing simply with initial consonants, and, moreover, the above Exercise is sufficient to give the learner a knowledge of the difference between the two pronunciations.

EXERCISE ON U, Ú AND Ü.

准 寬 專 ʽchun, *to permit*; ₍fun, *to relax*; ₍chün, *single*.
倫 門 亂 ₍lun, *constant*; ₍mun, *door*; lün², *confused*.
順 本 般 shun², *compliant*; ʽpun, *the origin*; ₍shün, *a ship*.

These will be sufficient to show the difference between these sounds.

INTRODUCTION.

EXERCISE ON UI AND ÚÍ.

追灰 ｡chui, *to pursue*; ﬁíi, *ashes*.
水杯 ʻshui, *water*; ｡púi, *a cup*.
最回 tsui³, *to assemble*; ｡wúi, *a time*.

These few examples will show the difference between these two sounds; but the learner must note that the English Dictionaries of Cantonese, which are nearly all based on the *fan wan*, are not to be trusted for giving these sounds; some that should be under ui are classed with those under úi, and again others belonging to these classes are spelled with the ü.

The Chinese, not having an alphabetical language and therefore not being accustomed to such a mode of representing the sounds, have not their ears so acutely trained to distinguish between slight distinctions and differences in sounds as represented by letters of the alphabet, as they are to distinguish differences in the tones, and are consequently not altogether to be trusted in their classifications of sounds. Dictionary makers should take the correct pronunciation of good speakers of a standard dialect (such for example as Canton-city Cantonese, instead of blindly following the guidance of native compilations, which mislead.

PRONUNCIATION.

a like u, e.g.:—san, *as* sun.
á ,, ah, e.g.:—pá, *as* pa.
e ,, e in men, e.g.:—meng.
i ,, i in pin, e.g.:—king, *as* king.
í ,, í in machine, e.g.:—kín, *as* keen.
o ,, o in order, e.g.:—ho, *as* haw.
ò ,, ò in so, e.g.:—mò, *as* (to) mow.
ö nearly like er in her, e.g.:—bö, *as* ho(r).
u ,, u in hur, e.g. shun.
ú like u in fool, e.g.:—wú, *as* woo.
ü ,, French u in l'une, o.g.:—süt.
ai ,, i in while, e.g.:—fai.

ái like i in high, e.g.:—fái, *as* fie.
au ,, ow in low, e.g.:—hau, *as* how.
áu ,, aaow, e.g. háu.
éi ,, ey in they, e.g.:—p'éi, *as* pay.
íu ,, ew in few, e.g.:—shíu.
oi ,, oy in boy, e.g.:—k'oi, *as* coy.
ui nearly as in louis, e.g. shui.
úi like ooee, e.g.:—múi.
sz, run the sounds of the letters *s* and *z* together.
m is the sound of the letter m alone without any vowel and formed with the lips closed.
ng like ng in sing.

There is no b, d, g alone, j, q, v, x or z sounds in Cantonese. The nearest approach to r is in the word for *boot*, which sounds very much like *her*, as an Englishman who scarcely pronounces his *r* would sound it, not as a Scotchman would pronounce it.

INTRODUCTION.

The rest of the letters are pronounced as in English. The only difficulty the learner will find will be in pronouncing them soft enough when unaspirated, (especially is this true with the letters *p*, *k* and *t*,) as we generally pronounce those consonants in English, which are sometimes followed by aspirates in Chinese with sufficient force to render them aspirated, though in some parts of England they are always pronounced unaspirated.

Be very careful about the distinction between the short *a* and the long *á*. Men that have lived many years in China are often so oblivious of the living pronunciation as not to notice that they are led away by the peculiar use of this short *a* to represent a *u*—and in fact pronounce San Ning as spelled, and not as Sun Ning, the correct sound. This is a most common mistake with Europeans, and it is extremely disagreeable and pitiable to hear the persistence with which they will adhere to this egregious mistake, for there is no such sound in Chinese as "san" in sandy.

To correct such and similar tendencies a syllabary is here appended in which, whenever possible to do so, the Chinese sounds have been represented by sounds of the English letters, or by words in English &c., so that between the list given above and this that follows the learner ought, especially with the assistance of his teacher, to arrive at the correct pronunciation.

Let the learner remember that this is of great importance.

SYLLABARY OF CANTONESE.

THE ORTHOGRAPHY ADOPTED IN THIS BOOK REPRESENTED BY SIMILAR SOUNDS IN ENGLISH, &c., WHEN SUCH SOUNDS EXIST, OR BY COMBINATIONS OF THE LETTERS OF THE ENGLISH ALPHABET.

Only the letters not bracketed are to be imitated in sound, but with the sound that they have when in union with those in brackets.

If blanks are left in the syllabary it is in consequence of no equivalent sounds appearing in English, or under such circumstances it is stated that the sound is nearly, or somewhat like such and such a combination of English letters. In such cases the former list and a careful imitation of the Chinese voice ought to assist the beginner, especially with perseverance, to attain to what at first may seem to him almost to necessitate an impossible contortion of his vocal organs.

Even when tolerably sure of his pronunciation the beginner will find it of advantage to check it by this syllabary, as mistakes at first generally result in a tendency to a permanent vicious pronunciation, which when once fixed will be very difficult to change.

INTRODUCTION.

The unaspirated words the learner will notice, by listening to his teacher, are pronounced much softer and without the explodent force which the aspirated words have. The sounds of the consonants when unaspirated must be particularly noticed. They sound much flatter than the English consonants, which are used to represent the nearest approach to their sound. Remember that ch unaspirated is much flatter than ch in English, almost reaching the dj, but never actually that. In order to draw particular attention to this sound of some of the consonants the aspirated ones are followed by an h in the English spelling in this syllabary, though it must be remembered, as said before, that the aspirated consonants often approach nearer to the English sound of the consonants than the unaspirated ones in Chinese.

ch unaspirated sounds almost midway between the English sounds of *dj* and *ch*.

k	,,	,,	,,	,,	*g*	,, *k*.
kw	,,	,,	,,	,,	*gw*	,, *kw*.
p	,,	,,	,,	,,	*b*	,, *p*.
t	,,	,,	,,	,,	*d*	,, *t*.
ts	,,	,,	,,	,,	*ds*	,, *ts*.

These are the only consonants and combinations of consonants which are followed by the aspirate.

A

1 Á *as* ah!
2 Ai *as* i(dle).
3 Ái *as* eye, or aye.
4 Ak *as* Ux (bridge).*
5 Ák *as* a(r)k.
6 Am *as* (h)am.
7 Ám *as* a(r)m.
8 Án *as* A(h)n(hold).
9 Ang *as* (h)ung.
10 Áng *as* ahng.
11 Ap *as* up.
12 Áp *as* (h)a(r)p.
13 At *as* (h)nt.
14 Át *as* (h)a(r)t.
15 Au *as* (h)ow.
16 Áu *as* a(h)oo.

C

17 Chú *as* cha(rm).
18 Ch'á *as* chha(rm).
19 Chai *as* chi(ld).
20 Chái *as* Chi(na).
21 Ch'ái *as* Chbi(na).
22 Chak *as* chuck.
23 Ch'ak *as* chhuck.
24 Chák *as* chahk.
25 Ch'ák *as* chhahk.
26 Cham *as* chum.
27 Ch'am *as* chhum.
28 Chám *as* cha(r)m.
29 Ch'ám *as* chha(r)m.
30 Chan *as* chun.
31 Ch'an *as* chhun.
32 Chán *as* chahn.
33 Ch'án *as* chhahn.
34 Chang *as* ch(h)ung.†
35 Cháng *as* (h)chahng.
36 Ch'áng *as* chhahng.
37 Chap *as* chup.

* Like Uk, that is to say the s in the x not being sounded.
† Not choong, but the word is pronounced as if the h of hung were changed into ch.

INTRODUCTION.

35 Cháp *as* chahp.
²⁴ Ch'áp *as* chhahp.
¶⁸Chat *as* chut(ney).
¶⁷Chát *as* cháht.
¶²Ch'át *as* chhaht.
⁴³Chau *as* chow.
¶⁷Ch'au *as* chhow.
⁴⁵ Chán *as* chabow.
Ch'án *as* chhahoo.
Che *as* che(rry).
Ch'e *as* chhe(rry).
Chek *as* chek.
Ch'ek *as* chhek.
Cheng *as* cheng.
Chí *as* cheese.
Ch'í *as* chhee(se).
Chik *as* chick.
Ch'ik *as* chhick.
Chím *as* cheem.

Ch'ím *as* chheem.
Chín *as* cheen.
Ch'ín *as* chheen.
Ching *as* ching.
Ch'iug *as* chhing.
Chíp *as* cheep.
Chít *as* cheat.
Ch'ít *as* chhee(tah).
Chíú *as* cheeoo.
Ch'íú *as* chheeoo.
Cho *as* chaw.
Ch'o *as* chhaw.
Chok *as* chalk.
Chŏk *as* Ch(h)u(r)k.*
Ch'ŏk *as* Chh(h)n(r)k.*
Chong *as* chong.
Ch'ong *as* chhong.
Chŏng *as* Ch(h)u(r)ug.*
Ch'ŏng *as* Chh(h)u(r)ug.*

Chū *as* chue.
Ch'ū *as* chhue.
Chui *something like* chooee.
Ch'ui *something like* chhooee.
Chuk *something like* chook.
Ch'uk *something like* chhook.
Chuu *as* chu(r)n.
Ch'uu *as* chhu(r)n.
Chūn *as* chune.
Ch'ün *as* chhune, *combination of* ch *and French* une.
Chung *as* choong.
Ch'ung *as* chhoong.
Chut *as* ch(h)u(r)t.
Ch'ut *somewhat like* chut(uey), but purse the lips together.
Chūt *as* Chuet.

E

E *as* e(dible).

F

Fú *as* Fa(ther).
Fai *as* fi(ne).
Fái *as* fi(delity).
Fák *as* Fa(r)q(uhar).
Fan *as* fun.
Fán *as* fahn.
Fang *as* f(h)ung.
Fat *as* fnt.

Fát *as* faht.
Fau *as* fow.
Féi *as* fay.
Fik *as* fick(le).
Fing *as* fing(er).
Fít *as* feet.
Fo *as* fo(rtune).
Fok *as* fok.

Fong *as* fong.
Fú *as* foo(l).
Fui *as* fooee.
Fuk *as* fook.
Fún *as* foon.
Fung *as* fung.
Fút *as* fōōt.

H

Há *as* Ha!
Hai *as* hi(de).
Hái *as* high.

Hak *as* huck(ster).
Hárk *as* ha(r)k.
Ham *as* hum.

Hám *as* ha(r)m.
Hau *as* hun.
Hán *as* hahn.

* This u to be pronounced like the German ŏ.

INTRODUCTION.

Hang *as* hung.
Háng *as* hahng.
Hap *as* hup.
Háp *as* ha(r)p.
Hat *as* hut.
Hau *as* how.
Háu *as* ha(h)ow.
Hé *as* hey.
Héi *as* hay.
Hím *as* heem.
Hín *as* heen.

Hing *as* hing.
Híp *as* heep.
Hít *as* heat.
Híú *as* hew, *or* beeoo.
Ho *as* haw.
Hò *as* Ho!
Hö *as* he(r).
Hoi *as* (slip a) hoy!
Hok *as* hock.
Hòm *something between* ho(r)m *and* hum.

Hòn *as* ho(r)n.
Hong *as* hong.
Höng *as* he(r)ng.
Hòp *something between* ho(r)p *and* hut.
Hot *as* ho(r)t(ïculture).
Huì *nearly* hooee.
Huk *as* hook.
Hün *as* huen.
Hung *as* hung.
Hüt *as* huet.

K

Ká *as* ca(r).
K'á *as* khá.
Kai *as* ki(te).
K'ai *as* khi(te).
Kái *as* c(r)y.
K'ái *as* ch(r)y.
K'ak *as* k(h)uck(old).
Kák *as* kahk.
Kam *as* come.
K'am *as* chome.
Kám *as* Ca(r)m(el).
Kan *as* kun.
K'an *as* khun.
Kán *as* khan.
Kang *as* k(h)ung.
K'ang *as* khung.
Káng *as* cangue.
Kap *as* cup.
K'ap *as* khup.
Káp *as* ca(r)p.
Kat *as* cut.
K'at *as* khut.
Kát *as* ca(r)t.

Kau *as* cow.
K'au *as* khow.
Káu *as* ka(h)ow.
K'áu *as* kha(h)ow.
Ke *as* ca(re).
K'e *as* ca(re).
Kéi *as* kay.
K'éi *as* khay.
Kek *as* keck.
K'ek *as* kheck.
Keng *as* keng.
K'eng *as* kheng.
Kík *as* kick.
K'ík *as* khick.
Kím *as* keem.
K'ím *as* kheem.
Kín *as* keen.
K'ín *as* kheen.
King *as* king.
K'ing *as* khing.
Kíp *as* keep.
Kít *as* keet.
K'ít *as* kheet.

Kíú *as* keeoo.
K'íú *as* kheeoo.
Ko *as* co(r)e.
Kò *as* co(de).
Koi *as* coy.
K'oi *as* khoy.
Kok *as* cock.
K'ok *as* khock.
Kòm *as* co(r)m.
Kon *as* co(r)n.
Kong *as* kong.
K'ong *as* khong.
Kòp *as* co(r)p(se).
Kot *as* con(r)t.
Kök *as* ke(r)k.
K'ök *as* khe(r)k.
Köng *as* kn(r)ng.
K'öng *as* khn(r)ng.
Kuí *nearly like* kooee.
K'uí *nearly like* khooee.
Kuk *as* cook.
K'uk *as* khook.
Kün *as* kune.*

* This has the sound of the French word une with a k prefixed.

INTRODUCTION.

K'ūn as khune.*
Kung as koong.
K'nng as khoong.
Kŭt as kuet.
K'ŭt as khu(e)t.
Kwá as qua(lm).
K'wá as qhua(lm).
Kwai as kwiee.
K'wai as khwiee.
Kwái as qui(etus).
Kwák as kwahk.

Kwan as kwun.
K'wan as khwun.
Kwán as kwahn.
Kwang as kwnng.
Kwáng as kwahng.
K'wáng as khwang.
Kwat as kwut.
Kwát as kwaht.
Kwik as qnick.
Kwing as kwing.
Kwít as kweet.

Kwo as kwoh.
Kwok as kwok.
Kwong as kwong.
K'wong as khwong.
Kwú as kwoo.
K'wú as khwoo.
Kwui as kwooee.
Kwun as kwoon.
Kwut as kwoot.

L

Lá as La!
Lai as (g)li(de).
Lái as lie.
Lak as luck.
Lák as la(r)k.
Lam as Lum(ley).
Lám as Lahm.
Lan as Lun(dy).
Lán as lahn.
Lang as lung.
Láng as lhahng.
Lap as lup.
Láp as lahp.
Lat as Lut(ton).

Lát as laht
Lau as l(h)ow.
Láu as la(h)oo.
Le as l(th)e(re).
Léi as lay.
Leng as leng.
Lik as lick.
Lím as leem.
Lín as lean.
Ling as ling.
Líp as leap.
Lít as lit(re).
Líú as leeoo.
Lo as law.

Lò as Lo!
Lö as ler.†
Loi as (al)loy.
Lok as lock.
Long as long.
Lök as le(r)k.
Löng as le(r)ng.
Lúi somewhat like looee.
Luk as look.
Lun as lea(r)n.
Lūn as l'une.
Lung as lung.
Lut as l(h)u(r)t.
Lüt something like looeet.

M

M as m(a).
Má as ma.
Mai as mi(ne).
Mái as my.‡
Mak as muck.
Mák as mahk.

Man as mun(dane).
Mán as mahn.
Mang as mung.
Máng as mahng.
Mat as mut(ter).
Mát as maht.

Man as mow.
Máu as ma(h)oo.
Me as me(ddle).
Meng as meng.
Méi as may.
Mik as mick.

* This has the sound of the French word une with a k prefixed.
† Only give the faintest ghost of a sound to the er.
‡ An open full sound.

INTRODUCTION.

Mín *as* mean.
Ming *as* ming.
Mít *as* meat.
Míŭ *as* mew.
Mo *as* maw.

Mò *as* mo(de).
Mok *as* mawk.
Mong *as* mong.
Múi *as* mooee.
Muk *as* mook.

Mŭn *as* moon.
Mung *as* moong.
Mŭt *as* moot.

N

Ná *as* nah.
Nai *as* ni(ne).
Nái *as* nigh.
Nak *as* nuk.
Nam *as* numb.
Nám *as* nahm.
Nan *as* nun.
Nán *as* nahn.
Nang *as* nung.,
Nap *as* nup.
Náp *as* nahp.
Nat *as* nut.
Nát *as* naht.
Nau *as* now.
Náu *as* naaow.
Ne *as* Ne(d).
Neng *as* neng.
Ng *as* (si)ng.
Ngá *as* (si)ng-ah !
Ngai *as* (si)ng-i(dle).
Ngái *as* (si)ng-I.
Ngak *as* (si)ng-uk.
Ngák *as* (si)ng-ahk.

Ngam *as* (si)ng-um.
Ngám *as* (si)ng-ahm.
Ngan *as* (si)ng-uu.
Ngán *as* (si)ng-ahn.
Ngang *as* (si)ng-ung.
Ngáng *as* (si)ng-ahng.
Ngap *as* (si)ng-up.
Ngáp *as* (si)ng-ahp.
Ngat *as* (si)ng-ut.
Ngát *as* (si)ng-aht.
Ngau *as* (si)ng-(h)ow.
Ngáu *as* (si)ng-a(h)ow.
Nge *as* (si)ng-(th)e(re).
Ngí *as* (si)ng-ee.
Ngít *as* (si)ng-eat.
Ngo *as* (si)ng-awe.
Ngò *as* (si)ng-oh !
Ngoi *as* (si)ng-(ah)oi.
Ngok *as* (si)ng-(s)ock.
Ngon *as* (si)ng-(h)on(g).
Ngong *as* (si)ng-(h)ong.
Ni, *or* Ní *as* nih, *or* nee.
Néi *as* ney.

Nik *as* nick.
Nim *as* neem.
Nin *as* neen.
Ning *as* ning.
Níp *as* neap.
Nít *as* nent.
Niŭ *as* neeoo.
No *as* no(r).
Nò *as* no.
Noi *as* (au)noy.
Nok *as* knock.
Nong *as* nong.
Nöng *as* nu(rr)ng.
Nui *somewhat like* nooee.
Nuk *as* nook.
Nŭn *as* nune.*
Kung *as* noong.
Nut *as* nu(r)t(ure)

O

O *as* awe.
Ò *as* oh !
Oi *as* (h)oy.

Ok *as* awk(ward).
Òm *as* u(r)m.
Òn *as* o(r)n(ament).

Ong *as* (s)ong.

---

* French une.

INTRODUCTION.

P

Pá *as* pa.
P'á *as* p(h)a.
Pai *as* pi(ne).
P'ai *as* p(h)i(ne).
Pái *as* pie.
P'ái *as* p(h)ie.
Pak *as* Puck.
Pák *as* pa(r)k.
P'ák *as* p(h)a(r)k.
Pan *as* pun.
P'an *as* p(h)un.
Pán *as* pahn.
P'án *as* p(h)ahn.
Pang *as* l(h)ung.
P'ang *as* p(h)ung.*
Páng *as* pahng.
P'áng *as* p(h)ahng.
Pat *as* put.
P'at *as* p(h)nt.
Pát *as* paht.

Pau *as* pow.
P'au *as* p(h)ow.
Pán *as* pa(h)ow.
P'áu *as* p(h)a(h)oo.
Péi *as* pay.
P'éi *as* p(h)ay.
Peng *as* peng.
P'eng *as* p(h)eng.
Pik *as* pick.
P'ik *as* p(h)ick.
I'ín *as* peen.
P'ín *as* p(h)een.
Ping *as* ping.
P'ing *as* p(h)ing.
Pít *as* peat.
P'ít *as* p(h)eat.
Píú *as* pecoo.
P'íú *as* p(h)ecoo.
Po *as* paw.
P'o *as* p(h)aw.

Pò *as* Po.
P'ò *as* P(h)o.
Pok *as* pawk.
P'ok *as* p(h)awk.
Pòm *as* pom.
Pong *as* pong.
P'ong *as* p(h)ong.
Pop *nearly as* Pu(r)p.
P'op *nearly as* p(h)u(r)p.
Púi *as* pooee.
P'úi *as* p(h)ooee.
Puk *as* pook.
P'uk *as* p(h)ook.
Pún *as* poon.
P'ún *as* p(h)oon.
Pung *as* poong.
P'ung *as* p(h)oong.
Pút *as* pnt.
P'út *as* p(h)oot.

S

Sa *as* sah.
Sai *as* cy(der).
Sái *as* sigh.
Sak *as* suck.
Sam *as* some.
Sám *as* sahm.
San *as* sun.
Sán *as* sahn.
Sang *as* (I)sung.
Sap *as* sup.
Sáp *as* sahp.
Sat *as* sut.

Sát *as* saht.
Sau *as* sow.
Se *as* Se(ttle).
Seng *as* seng.
Shn *as* Shah.
Shai *as* shi(ne).
Shái *as* shy.
Shák *as* sha(r)k.
Sham *as* shum.
Shám *as* shahm.
Shan *as* shnn.
Shán *as* shahn.

Shang *as* sh(h)ung.
Sháng *as* shahng.
Shap *as* shup.
Sháp *as* sha(r)p.
Shat *as* shut.
Shát *as* shaht.
Shau *as* sh(h)ow.
Sháu *as* sha(h)oo.
Shé *as* sche(dule).
Sheng *as* sheng.
Shí *as* she.
Shik *as* shik.

---

* That is to say pronounce *hung*, then put a *p* in the place of *h*, retaining the same pronunciation to the rest of the letters as before.

INTRODUCTION.

Shím *as* sheem.
Shín *as* sheen.
Shing *as* shing.
Shíp *as* sheep.
Shít *as* sheet.
Shíú *as* sheeoo.
Sho *as* Shaw.
Shò *as* show.
Shok *as* shock.
Shong *as* shong.
Shök *as* shi(r)k.
Shöng *as* she(r)ng.
Shü *as* chu(t).
Shui *nearly like* shooee.
Shuk *as* shook.

Shūn *as* shune.
Shun *as* shu(r)n.
Shung *as* shoong.
Shut *as* shi(r)t.
Shüt *nearly* shuet.
Sik *as* sick.
Sín *as* seen.
Sing *as* sing.
Síp *as* s(l)eep.
Sít *as* seat.
Siú *as* seeoo.
So *as* swo(rd).
Sò *as* so.
Sö *as* si(r).
Soi *as* soy.

Sok *as* sawk.
Sök *as* se(r)k.
Song *as* song.
Söng *as* su(r)ng.
Suí *nearly like* sooee.
Suk *as* sook.
Sun *as* (con)ce(r)n.
Sün *as* sooeene.
Sung *as* soong.
Sut *as* (con)ce(r)t.
Süt *as* suet; *pronounce the word quickly and run the vowels together.*
Sz *join s and z and sound together.*

T

Tá *as* tah.
T'á *as* t(h)ah.
Tai *as* ti(dy).
T'ai *as* t(h)i(dy).
Tái *as* tie.
T'ái *as* t(h)ie.
Tak *as* tuck.
Tam *as* tum.
T'am *as* t(h)um.
Tám *as* tahm.
T'ám *as* t(h)ahm.
Tan *as* tun.
T'an *as* t(h)un.
Tán *as* tahn.
T'án *as* t(h)ahn.
Tang *as* tong(ue).
T'ang *as* t(h)ong(ue).
Tap *as* tup.
T'ap *as* t(h)up.
Táp *as* tahp.
T'áp *as* t(h)ahp.

Tat *as* tut.
Tát *as* taht.
T'át *as* t(h)aht.
Tau *as* t(h)ow.
T'au *as* t(h)(h)ow.
Te *as* ten(r).
Téi *as* t(h)ey.
Teng *as* teng.
T'eng *as* t(h)eng.
Ti, *or* tí *as* tib, *or* tea.
Tik *as* tick.
T'ik *as* t(h)ick.
Tím *as* team.
T'ím *as* t(h)eam.
Tín *as* teen.
T'ín *as* t(h)een.
Ting *as* t(h)ing.
Típ *as* teep.
T'íp *as* t(h)eep.
Tít *as* teet.
T'ít *as* t(h)eet.

Tíú *as* teeoo.
T'íú *as* t(h)eeoo.
To *as* to(re).
T'o *as* T(h)o(re).
Tò *as* toe.
T'ò *as* t(h)oe.
Toi *as* toy.
T'oi *as* t(h)oy.
Tok *as* talk.
T'ok *as* t(h)alk.
Tök *as* te(r)k.
Tong *as* Tong(a).
T'ong *as* T(h)ong(a).
Tö *as* t(h)u(r).
Töng *as* te(r)ng.
Tsá *as* tsah.
Tsai *as* tsie.
Ts'ai *as* tshie.
Tsak *as* tsuk.
Tsák *as* tshahk.
Tsam *as* tsum.

INTRODUCTION.

Ts'am *as* ts(h)um.
Tsam *as* tsahm.
Ts'am *as* tshahm.
Ts'an *as* tsan.
Tsan *as* tsahn.
Ts'an *as* tshahn.
Tsang *as* ts(h)ung.
Ts'ang *as* ts(h)(h)ung.
Tsap *as* tsup.
Ts'ap *as* tship.
Tsap *as* tsahp.
Tsat *as* tsut.
Ts'at *as* tshnt.
Tsat *as* tsaht.
Ts'at *as* tshaht.
Tsau *as* ts(h)ow.
Ts'au *as* tshow.
Tse *as* ts(th)e(re).
Ts'e *as* tsh(th)e(re).
Tseng *as* tseng.
Tsik *as* tsik.
Ts'ik *as* tshik.
Tsim *as* tseem.
Ts'im *as* tsheem.
Tsin *as* tseen.

Ts'in *as* tsheen.
Tsing *as* tsing.
Ts'ing *as* tshing.
Tsip *as* tseep.
Ts'ip *as* tsheep.
Tsit *as* tseet.
Ts'it *as* tsheet.
Tsiu *as* tseeoo.
Ts'iu *as* tsheeoo.
Tso *as* tsawe.
Ts'o *as* tshawe.
Tsò *as* tso.
Ts'ò *as* tsho.
Tsoi *as* tsoy.
Ts'oi *as* tshoy.
Tsok *as* tsawk.
Ts'ok *as* tshawk.
Tsong *as* tsawng.
Ts'ong *as* tshawng.
Tsöng *as* tsu(rr)ng.
Ts'öng *as* ts(h)u(rr)ng.
Tsui *nearly like* tsooee.
Ts'ui *nearly like* tshooee.
Tsuk *as* tsook.
Ts'uk *as* tshook.

Tsun *as* tsu(r)n.
Ts'un *as* tshu(r)n.
Tsün *as* tsooeene.
Ts'ün *as* ts(h)ooeene.
Tsung *as* tsoong.
Ts'ung *as* tshoong.
Tsut *as* ts(h)u(r)t.
Ts'ut *as* tsoocet.
Ts'üt *as* ts(h)ooeet.
Tsz *as* tsz.
Ts'z *as* tshz.
Tui *nearly like* tooee.
T'ui *nearly like* t(h)ooee.
Tuk *as* took.
T'uk *as* t(h)ook.
Tun *as* tu(r)n.
T'ún *as* t(h)u(r)n.
Tün *as* tune.
T'ün *as* t(h)une.*
Tung *as* toong.
T'ung *as* t(h)oong.
Tüt *nearly like* tooeet.
T'üt *nearly like* t(h)ooeet.

U

Uk *something between* uk *and* ook.

Ung *as* ooong.

W

Wá *as* wah.
Wai *as* wei.
Wái *as* Wye.
Wák *as* wahk.
Wan *as* one.
Wán *as* wahn.
Wang *as* wung.

Wáng *as* wahng.
Wat *as* wut.
Wát *as* waht.
We *as* we(ar).
Wik *as* wick.
Wing *as* wing.
Wit *as* weet.

Wo *as* wa(r).
Wok *as* walk.
Wong *as* wong.
Wu *as* woo.
Wui *as* wooee.
Wun *as* woon.
Wut *as* woot.

* French une.

INTRODUCTION.

Y

Yá as yah.	Ye as y(th)e(re).	Yŏk as yu(r)k.
Yai as yi(dle).	Yí as ye.	Yŏng as yu(r)ng.*
Yák as yahk.	Yik as yik.	Yü as yue.
Yam as yum.	Yim as yeem.	Yui as nearly yooee.
Yan as yun.	Yin as yeen.	Yuk as yook.
Yap as yup.	Ying as ying.	Yun as yu(r)n.*
Yáp as yahp.	Yip as yeep.	Yün as yune.
Yat as yut.	Yit as yeet.	Yung as yoong.
Yau as y(h)ow.	Yiú as yeeoo.	Yüt as yueet.

* It is well nigh impossible to represent the difference between this ŏ and u; but it may be of some assistance to know that the former is pronounced with the lips open, while the lips require to be pursed together in pronouncing the latter.

ABBREVIATIONS USED IN THIS BOOK.

[C.] = Classifier.

[S. of p. t.] = Sign of past time.

Lit. = Literally.

* Indicates that the tone the word is marked in is different from the tone in the book language.

† Indicates that the pronunciation of the word as given in this book is different from that given to it in the book language.

The figures at the end of phrases and sentences denote the Final Particle which is used in the Chinese. The numbers correspond with the numbers of the list of Final Particles towards the end of the book.

THE NUMERALS.

		Complicated form.	Simple form.	Running hand.
1.	1	壹	一	
2.	2	貳	二	
3.	3	叁	三	
4.	4	肆	四	
5.	5	伍	五	
6.	6	陸	六	
7.	7	柒	七	
8.	8	捌	八	
9.	9	玖	九	
10.	10	拾	十	
11.	11	拾壹	十一	
12.	12	拾貳	十二	
13.	13	拾叁	十三	
14.	20	貳拾	二十, or 廿[1]	
15.	21	貳拾壹	二十一, or 廿一	
16.	22	貳拾貳	二十二, or 廿呀二	
17.	30	叁拾	三十, or 卅[1]	
18.	31	叁拾壹	三十一, or 卅呀一	
19.	40	肆拾	四十, or 呀[1]四	
20.	79	柒拾玖	七十九, or 呀九	
21.	84	捌拾肆	八十四, or 呀四	
22.	96	玖拾陸	九十六, or 呀六	
23.	100	壹佰	一百	
24.	101	壹佰零壹	一百零一	
25.	110	壹佰壹拾	一百一十	
26.	111	壹佰壹拾壹	一百一十一	
27.	200	貳佰	二百	
28.	300	叁佰	三百	
29.	1,000	壹仟	一千	
30.	10,000	壹萬	一萬	
31.	100,000	拾萬	十萬	
32.	1,000,000	壹佰萬	一百萬	

1. Note these contracted forms for the tens are not used alone in colloquial, but precede some other word, as, 卅呀錢 *Sá-d² ʿts⁴ín*,* thirty cash. When nothing follows thirty, 三十 ʿSám shap₂ should be used.

LESSON I.—Domestic.

1.	Ning ₍pūi—ch'á ₅lai.	Bring cup tea come.
2.	'Héi—ts'án ₅lá.	Get-up meal.²
3.	K'ú² 'kūn-t'ím³ (or 'tím*) ₅lai.	Call house-coolie (or shop-coolie) come.
4.	⁵Ngo yiú³ 'sai—shān lok₀.	I want wash body.³²
5.	⁵Mò 'shuí po³. [lok₀.	No water.⁶⁰
6.	Shik₋fán² ₅m ₅ts'áng á²? ₅M- koi lok₂, shik₂	Ate rice not yet eh?². Beg-pardon,³² eaten.³²
7.	⁵Yau ₅ngau-yuk₂ ⁴mò ₅ni?	Have beef (lit. ox, or cow's meat) not eh?⁵³
8.	⁵Mò ₅ngau-yuk₂ lok₀.	No beef.³²
9.	⁵Yau ₅yōng-yuk₂ á³.	Have mutton (lit. sheep meat).²
10.	Mín²- ₋páu ₅sün lok₀.	Bread sour.³²
11.	₅O! Hai² ₅me?	Ah! 'tis is-it.³⁹
12.	Ning ₅ti¹ yīt₂ 'shui ₅lai.	Bring some hot water come.
13.	⁵Ngo ₅m oí³ ₍tsau á³.	I not want wine.²
14.	₍ch'ü* méi²-ts'ang ₅fán- ₅lai á³.	Cook not yet back come.²
15.	⁵Yau ₅ngau-⁵nái ⁴mò á?	Have cow's milk not eh?¹
16.	⁵Yau ₅ti lok₀.	Have little.³²
17.	'Hò ₅m 'hò á³.	Good not good eh?²
18.	₅M bai² shap₋₂ fau (or ch'í³) 'hò; ₅m hai² 'kéi 'hò; ₍chung- ₍chung-'téi* chik₂.	Not is ten parts (or very) good (or best) ; not is very good; middling only.⁷
19.	₍Chai (or ₅fong₋² tsoí³) 'ko-shü³ lok₀.	Place (or place on) that place.³²
20.	... hai² kai-'tán* á³.	Those are fowls' eggs.²
21.	...ò lok₀; hai² ch'àn³ ke³.	Not good;³² are stinking.¹⁵
22.	...kái ni? 'Hò ch'ut₂ ₅k'éi ke³ lok₀.	How explain eh?⁵³ Very extraordinary.¹⁵ ³²
23.	...hik₂ má? 'Hò shik₂ á. ₅M koi á³.	Good eat isn't-it?⁹² Good eat.³⁵ Not proper.²
24.	...kai ⁵mò ni? ⁵Yau síu³ kai, ⁵yau ...i 'ni lok₀.	Have fowls not eh?⁵³ Have capons, have hens.³²
25.	...hai² mi²-⁵ye ni? 'Péi ti ⁵ngo ₅lá.	This is what thing eh?⁵³ Give some me.²¹
26.	...se² ⁴néi lok₀. ₍Chung-⁵yau ⁴mò ni?	Many thanks to-you.³² More have no eh?⁵³
27.	...² ⁵yau ₅ti. 'Fo-'t'au* ₅lai lok₀.	Besides have some.³² Cook come.³²
28.	...hai² mi-'yan?* ⁵K'ūi shik₂- yín ₅me?	He is what man? He smokes eh?³⁹
29.	...hí-tak₂ shat₂ lok₀. P'á³ hai² ⁵yau.	Not know certainly.³² Fear (it) is (that he) does.
30.	...sai ch'ut₂ kái ⁴mái sung³ á³.	Boy gone-out street buy viands.²
31.	...ui hai² ⁴mái ₍chū yuk₂, péi² ts'oí³ ni?	He has bought pork, or vegetables eh?⁵³ [come.¹⁵
32.	...hai² T'ong ₅yan; 'hai Fat₂ ₅shán ₅lai ke³.	He is T'ong man; (i.e. Chinese) from Fat shan

* This word is uniformly spelled i in this book, but it must be remembered that it is often ...ed í as well.
... is is a very common contraction of 物, mat₂, in colloquial.

LESSON II.—General.

1.	Come here. Why don't you come?	嚟呢處呀,做乜你唔嚟呢.
2.	Who has come? Who is it?	乜人嚟吖,乜誰吖, or 邊個吖.
3.	No one has come.	冇人嚟吖 (or 冇人呀 or 冇邊個吖).
4.	Who is that?	咽個係乜人呢[1]
5.	I don't know. How should I know?	唔知呀,我點知呀.
6.	He is not a good man. He is a very bad man.	佢係唔好人呀,佢係好惡人嚦.
7.	Tell him to go away.	叫佢扯咯.
8.	He has gone. He went long ago.	佢去嘅咯,去好耐咯.
9.	Close the door, don't fasten it.	掩埋門,咪閂吖.
10.	Open the door. Why did you lock it?	開門呀,做乜你鎖呢.
11.	Tell the Amah to come to me.	叫亞媽嚟見我喇.
12.	Come quickly: the quicker the better.	快啲嚟,越快越好咯.
13.	Where's the coolie; has he come?	管店呢,嚟未曾呀.
14.	Come to-morrow, or it will do to come the day after to-morrow.	聽日[2] 嚟喇,後日嚟都好吖 (or 都做得吖).
15.	There is only a very little.	有少少啫.
16.	It's good is it? He says so.	好孻嗎,佢係噉話.
17.	What does he say? Tell me.	佢話乜野,講過我聽喇.
18.	He says he doesn't wish to come. [with me.	佢話唔想嚟咯.
19.	Explain to him that he must certainly go	解明過佢聽是必要同我去.
20.	How many persons are there old and young?	唔論大細,有幾多人.
21.	More than ten.	有十幾個 or 有十零個有多.
22.	Altogether there are sixty men.	喊埋唥有六十人咯.
23.	Are there any children?	有細佬仔冇呢.
24.	There is a boy.	有個 (or 壹個) 仔咯.
25.	Is that a boy, or a girl?	咽個係仔嚊女呢.
26.	He is in my employ.	佢喺我處打工嘅.
27.	Who is your master?	邊個係你事頭呢.
28.	He is a native of the place, that is a Cantonese.	佢係本地人,卽係城
29.	He is not a fellow-villager of yours.	佢唔係同你同鄉嘅.
30.	Where does he live?	佢喺邊處住呢.
31.	A long way from here.	離呢處有好遠咯.
32.	Do you go by land, or by water?	打路去嚊搭船去呢.

1. Or as in No. 2.
2. 聽日 t'ing yat, very often also means any indefinite time in the future.

LESSON II.—General.

1. ₅Lai ₍ni-shū² á². Tsò²-mat₂ ⁵nếi ₍m ₍lai ₍ni? — Come this place.² Why you not come eh?⁵³
2. ₍Mi-'yan* ₍lai ₍á? ₍Mi-'shui* ₍á? ₍Pin ko² ₍á? — What man come eh?¹ Who eh?¹ Which one eh?¹
3. ⁵Mò ₍yan ₍lai ₍á, or simply ⁵Mò ₍yán ₍á, or ⁵Mò — No man come,¹ or no man,² or no which one.²
4. 'Ko-ko² hai² ₍mi-'yan* ₍ni? [₍pin ko² ₍á. — That is what man eh?⁵³
5. ₍M ₍chí á². ⁵Ngo 'tim ₍chí á²? — Not know.² I how know eh?²
6. ⁵K'ui hai² ₍m-'hò ₍yan á². ⁵K'ui hai² 'hò ok₀ — He is not good man.² He is very wicked man.¹⁴
7. Kúi² ⁵k'ui 'ch'e lok₀. [₍yan ká². — Tell him to-be-off.³⁹
8. ⁵K'ui hui²-'cho lok₀. Hui² 'hò noi² lok₀. — He gone [s. of p. t.].³² Gone very long.³²
9. ⁵Tím ₍mái ₍mún, ⁵mai ₍shán ₍á.] — Close to door, don't fasten it.¹
10. ₍Hoi ₍mún á². Tsò²-mat₂ ⁵nếi ⁵so ₍ni? — Open door.² Why you lock eh?⁵³
11. Kíú² Á²-⁵Má ₍lai kíú² ⁵ngo ₍lá. — Call Amah come see me.²¹
12. Fái²- ₍ti ₍lai: yüt₂ fái² yüt₂ 'hò lok₀. — Quickly come: still quicker still better.³²
13. 'Kúu-tim² ₍ni; ₍lai méi²- ₍ts'ang á²? — House (or shop) coolie eh;⁵³ come not yet eh?²
14. ₍T'ing-yat₂ ₍lai ₍lá, hau² yat₂ ₍lai ₍tò 'hò ₍á² (or ₍tò tsò² tak₂ ₍á). — To-morrow come.²¹ Day after to-morrow also good,¹ (or also do can).¹
15. ⁵Yau 'shíú 'shíú ₍che. — Have little little only.⁷
16. 'Hò lá² ma²? ⁵K'ui hai² 'kòm wá². [₍lá. — Good?²³ ³⁷ He does so say.
17. ⁵K'ui wá² ₍mi-⁵ye? 'Kong kwo² ⁵ngo ₍t'engt — He says what thing? Tell over to-me to-hear.²¹
18. ⁵K'ui wá² ₍m 'söng ₍lai lok₀. — He says not wish come.³²
19. 'Kái ₍ming kwo² ⁵k'ui ₍t'engt shí²-pit₂ yíú² ₍t'ung ⁵ngo hui². — Explain clearly to him to-hear certainly must with me go. [eh?⁵³
20. ₍M lun² tái² sai² ⁵yau 'kéi ₍to ₍yan ₍ni? — No matter (whether) big small have how many men
21. ⁵Yau shap₂ 'kéi ko², or ⁵yan shap₂ ₍lengt ko² lok₀, or shap₂ ko² ⁵yau ₍to. — Have ten odd ones, or have ten plus others,³³ or ten ones have more.
22. Hám²-pá₍ng²¹ ₍láng² ⁵yau lok₂-shap₂ ₍yan lok₀. — In-all have sixty men.³²
23. ⁵Yau sai² (or more often ₍sam) ₍man-'tsai ⁵mò — Have children not eh?⁷³
24. ⁵Yau ko² (or yat₂ ko²) 'tsai lok₀. [₍ni? — Have one boy.³²
25. 'Ko-ko² hai² 'tsai, péi² ⁵nui ₍ni? — That is boy, or girl eh?⁵³
26. ⁵K'ni 'bai ⁵ngo shū² 'tá-₍kung ke². — He at my place works.¹⁵
27. ₍Pin-ko² hai² ⁵néi sz²-'t'au* ₍ni? [₍yan lok₀. — Which one is your master eh?⁷³
28. ⁵K'ni hai² ₍pún téi² ₍yan, tsik₂ hai² 'sheng*† — He is native soil man, that is city man.³²
29. ⁵K'ui ₍m hai² ₍t'ung ⁵néi ₍t'ung 'bòng-ke². — He not is with you same villager.¹⁵
30. ⁵K'ui 'bai ₍pin shū² chū² ₍ní? — He at what place lives eh?⁵³
31. ₍Léi ₍ni shū² ⁵yau 'hò ⁵yün lok₀. — Separated-from this place have very far.³²
32. 'Tá lò² hui², péi² táp₂ ₍shün hui² ₍ni? — By road go, or on ship go eh?⁵³

---

1. This word is pronounced *pá*² when spoken rapidly.

LESSON III.—General.

1. What o'clock is it? 幾點鐘呢.
2. O! it's half-past ten. 啊十點半咯.
3. Come back at four o'clock. 四點翻嚟喇.
4. Tell him to wait. Wait. 叫佢等吓. 等一吓喇
5. Come by and bye. 等吓嚟.
6. He says you must wait. 佢話你要等呀.
7. When are you going out? 你幾時出街呢.
8. It's very hot to-day. 今日好熱啊.
9. It's not very hot. 唔係十分熱嚁.
10. It was rather hot yesterday as well. 昨日都係幾熱吖.
11. To-day is hotter than yesterday. 今日熱過昨日咯.
12. Next month will be cold. 第二個月(係)冷嚁.
13. To-morrow is the end of the month. 聽日月尾嘞.
14. It was very cold last night. 昨晚真正冷嚁.
15. Is this a long, or short month? 呢個月大嗎月小呢.
16. There was a typhoon some days ago. 先幾日打風颶.
17. Is there any wind now? 而家有風冇呢.
18. It's raining now. It's only a slight shower. 呢陣落雨囉 落雨微呎.
19. Bring me an umbrella. There is no need. 攞把遮俾我, 唔使呀.
20. It rains heavily in summer (or hot weather). 天熱落大雨咯.
21. I want to go out in the afternoon. 我下晝要出街.
22. Call the coolies to come and carry the chair. 叫抬轎佬 (or 轎夫) 嚟抬轎.
23. Are there any horses here? 呢處有馬冇呢.
24. I think they are not particularly good. I fancy they are pretty good. 我估唔多好啩, 都幾好啩.
25. The sun is intensely hot to-day. There are no clouds hiding it. 熱頭今日好猛, 冇雲遮住咯.
26. It's too hot. I dare not go out in the day-time. 熱過頭, 我日頭唔敢行街.
27. Call some one to pull the punkah. 叫人嚟扯 (or 搖) 風扇呀.
28. You needn't pull it. You have no strength. 你唔使扯吖, 你冇力吖.
29. It's only a trifling matter. It's no matter. 閒事嚹; 冇相干咯.
30. I'm afraid I shall catch cold. I feel very cold. 我慌冷親呀, 我見好冷呀.
31. I am in a perspiration. It's very hard work to take a walk when it is so hot. 出汗咯, 叫熱行街見好辛苦咯.
32. The climate does not suit me. 呢處水土唔合我咯.

LESSON III.—General.

1. ʽKéi ʽtím ₍chung ₍ni?	What stroke clock eh?[53]
2. ₅O, shnp₂ ʽtím pún' lok₀.[1]	Ah! Ten stroke half.[32]
3. Sz' ʽtím ₍fúu ₎lai ₎lá. [₍lá.	Four o'clock back come.[21]
4. Kíú' ⁵k'uí ʽtang ⁵há. ʽTang yat₂⁵há (or ʽhá*)	Tell him wait little. Wait a little.[21]
5. ʽTang ₍há*₎lai.	Wait a-bit come.
6. ⁵K'ui wá² ⁵néi yíú' ʽtang á'.	He says you must wait.[2]
7. ⁵Néi ʽkéi- shí ch'ut₂ ₍kái ₍ní?	You what time go-out street eh?[53]
8. ₍Kam-yat₂ ʽhò yít₂ o'.	To-day very hot.[56]
9. ₅M hai² shap₂ ₍fan yít₂ ká'.	Not is ten parts hot.[14]
10. Tsok₂-yat₂ ₍tò hai² ʽkéi yít₂ ₍á.	Yesterday also was somewhat hot.[1]
11. ₍Kam yat₂ (*often pronounced* mat₂) yít₂ kwo' tsok₂ yat₂ (*or* ₍ts'am-mat₂) lok₀.	To-day hotter than yesterday.[32]
12. Tai²-yí²-ko' yüt₂ (hai')² ⁵láng lo'.	Next (*or* another) month (will be) cold.[31]
13. ₍T'ing-yat₂ yüt₂ ⁵méi lá'. [ching' ⁵láng lo'.	To-morrow month end.[22]
14. Tsok₂ (*often pronounced* ₍ts'am) ⁵mán ₍chan	Last night truly really cold.[31]
15. ₍Ní-ko' yüt₂ tái², péí² yüt₂ ʽsíú ₍ni?	This month large, or month small eh?[53]
16. ₍Sín ʽkéi yat₂ ʽtá ₍fung-kau².	Before several days strike typhoon.
17. ₎Yí-₍ká ⁵yau ₍fung ⁵mò ₍ní?	Now have wind not eh?[53]
18. ₍Ni 'chan* lok₂ ⁵yü lo'. Lok₂ ⁵yü ₍méi* ₍che.	This time fall rain.[31] Fall rain fine only.[7]
19. ₍Ning ʽpá ₍che ʽpéi ⁵ugo. ₅M ʽshai á'.	Bring [C.] umbrella give me. Not need.[7]
20. ₍T'ín yít₂ lok₂ taí² ⁵yü lok₀.	Weather hot falls great rain.[32]
21. ⁵Ngo há²-chau' yíú' ch'ut₂ ₍kái.	I afternoon want go-out street. [ry chair.
22. Kíú' ₍t'oi ʽkíú* ʽlò (*or* ʽkíú*₍fú) ₅lai ₍t'oi ʽkíú*.	Call carry chair fellows (*or* chair bearers) come car-
23. ₍Ní shü' ⁵yau ⁵má ⁵mò ₍ní?	This place have horse not eh?[53] [I-think.[18]
24. ⁵Ngo ₍kú ₍m ₍to ʽhò kwá'. Tò ʽkéi ʽhò kwá'.	I think not very good probably.[18] Also pretty good
25. Yít₂-'t'au* ₍kam yat₂ ʽhò ⁵máng á', ⁵mò ₍wan ₍che chü² lok₀. [hángʈ ₍kái.	Sun to-day very fierce. No clouds hide.[32]
26. Yít₂ 'kwo*-₍t'au ⁵ngo yat₂-'t'au* ₍m ₍kòm	Hot over-much I daytime not dare walk streets.
27. Kíú' ₍yan ₎lai ʽch'e (*or* ₍mang) ₍fung-shín' á'.	Call man come pull punkah.[2]
28. ⁵Néi ₍m ₅shai ʽch'e ₍á. ⁵Néi ⁵mò lík₂ ₍á.	You not need pull.[1] ₋ You no strength.[1]
29. Hán sz² ₍che; ⁵mò ⁵söng-₍kòn lok₀. [á'.	Trifling matter only;[7] no importance.[32]
30. ⁵Ngo ₍fong ⁵láng ₍ts'au á². ⁵Ngo kín' ʽhò ⁵láng	I fear cold catch,[2] I feel very cold.[2]
31. Ch'ut₂-hòn² lok₀, kòm' yít₂ hángʈ ₍kái kín' ʽhò ₍san-⁵fú lok₀.	Perspire.[32] So hot walk streets feel very distressing.[32]
32. ₍Ni shü' ⁵shui 't'ò ₍m hòp₂ ⁵ngo lo'.	This place water soil not agree me.[32]

1. Let the learner remember that this final *k* is scarcely heard.
2. The verb may, or may not be used, and so in similar sentences throughout the book.

LESSON IV.—General.

1.	What is this?	呢啲係乜野呢.
2.	This is butter.	呢啲係牛油㗎.
3.	Is there any fruit?	有菓子冇呀.
4.	There are only two kinds.	有兩樣嚹.
5.	Are there not several kinds?	唔係有幾樣咩.
6.	No; there are plantains and pine-apples.	冇,有蕉有波羅.
7.	Are there no other kinds?	冇第二樣咩.
8.	There are no other kinds.	冇第二樣咯.
9.	Bring a light. I'll trouble you for a light (for my cigar or pipe).	摞火嚟, 唔該你借個火我.
10.	Where did this letter come from?	呢封信喺邊處嚟呢.
11.	From the Tak kee hong.	喺德記行嚟嘅.
12.	Is there any answer?	有回音冇呀.
13.	There is no answer.	冇回音囉.
14.	Bring me a chair.	摞張椅俾我.
15.	Put it on the table.	擺在檯面.
16.	Nonsense! Why are you so silly?	咪做乜你咁衰吖,嘥,整成個[啲衰樣.¹
17.	I am only jesting. Do you think it strange?	我講笑話啫. 你見怪咩.
18.	Bring me a pen and ink.	摞筆墨嚟俾我喇.
19.	I think there is a pencil up stairs. [see.	樓上 (or 樓) 有支筆𠻹.
20.	Is there anyone down stairs? Go down and	樓下有人冇呢. 落去睇吓.
21.	This house has seven rooms.	呢間屋有七間房呀.
22.	Has it a garden? Where is the gardener?	有花園冇呢, 花王喺邊處.
23.	It has a small garden.	有個細花園呀.
24.	Where is your master? He is out.	事頭呢,出街囉.
25.	How long has he been gone?	佢出街有幾耐呢.
26.	When will he be back?	幾時翻嚟呢.
27.	He didn't say.	佢又冇話幾時翻嚟啊 (or 冇話).
28.	Is your mistress at home?	事頭婆 (or 東家婆²) 喺處唔喺處呢.
29.	She is not here; she went out with my master.	唔喺處. 佢同事頭出街咯.
30.	Go with me to find him. I can't go.	孖我去搵佢喇. 我唔去得吁.
31.	I can't. I'm busy. I have no time.	唔得呀, 有事吖, 唔得閒吁.
32.	Come again to night. Don't come so late.	今晚又嚟喇. 咪咁夜嚟呀.

1. The first of these sentences is what a woman would say; the second, what a man would say.
2. The second is a more polite form, though the first is most commonly used.

LESSON IV.—General.

1. ˛Ni-ˌti hai² ˌmi-⁵ye ˛ni?   This is what thing eh?⁵³
2. ˛Ni-ˌti hai³ˎngau-ˎyau po³.   This is butter (*lit.* cow's oil).⁶⁰
3. ⁵Yau ꞌkwo-ꞌtsz̄ ⁵mò á³?   Have fruit not eh?²
4. ⁴Yau ⁵lŏng yöng² ˌche.   Have two kinds only,⁷ [that there are several kinds?
5. ˌM hai² ⁵yau ꞌkéi yöng² ˌme?   Not is have several kinds is-it-not?³⁹ *or* Is it not
6. ⁴Mò: ⁵yan ˌtsíú, ⁵yau ˌpo-ꞌlo* (*or* ˎlo).   No, have plantains, have pineapples.
7. ⁵Mò tai²-yí² yöng² ˌme?   No second kind eh?³⁹
8. ⁵Mò tai²-yí² yöng² lok̥.   No second kind.³²
9. ˛Ning ꞌfo ˌlai.   ˌM-ˌkoi ⁵néi tse³ ko³ ꞌfo ⁵ngo.   Bring fire come. Trouble you lend a light to-me.
10. ˛Ní ˌfung sun³ ꞌhai ˌpín shü³ ˌlai ˛ni?   This [*C.*] letter from what place come eh?⁵³
11. ꞌHai Tak̥-kéi³ ꞌhong* ˌlai ke³.   From Tak-kéi hong come.¹⁵
12. ⁵Yau ˌwúi-ˎyam ⁵mò á³?   Have answer not eh?²
13. ⁵Mò ˌwúi-ˎyam lo³.   No answer.³¹
14. ˛Ning ˌchöng ꞌyí ꞌpéi ⁵ngo.   Bring [*C.*] chair give me.
15. ˛Chai tsoi² ˌt'oi (*or* 'tꞌoi*) ꞌmín*.   Place on table face.
16. ˌTsꞌoi! Tsò²-mat̥ ⁵néi kòm³ ˌshui ˌá?   Nonsense! Why you so silly eh?¹
    ˌTsꞌai ꞌching ˌshengt ko³ ˛ti ˌshui ꞌyöng.*   Nonsense! Act in that silly way! [strange eh?³⁹
17. ⁵Ngo ꞌkong síú³-wá² chè³.   ⁵Néi kíu³ kwái³   I speak laughing words only.⁸ You perceive
18. ˛Ning pat̥, mak̥ ˌlai ꞌpéi ⁵ngo ˌlá.   [ˌme?   Bring pencil, ink come give me.²¹
19. ˌLau-shöng² (*or* ꞌlau*) ⁵yau ˌchí pat̥ ˌkwá³.   Upstairs have [*C.*] pencil I-think.¹⁹
20. ˌLau-há² ⁵yau ˎyan ⁵mò ˛ni? Lok̥ hui²ꞌꞌ tꞌai   Downstairs have man not eh? Down go see a-bit.
    ⁵há.
21. ˛Ni ˌkán uk̥ ⁵yan tsꞌat̥ ˌkáu ꞌfong* á³.   This [*C.*] house has seven [*C.*] rooms,² [place?
22. ⁵Yau fá-ꞌyún* ⁵mò ˛ni?   Fá ⁵wong ꞌhai   Have flower garden not eh?⁵³ Flower king at what
    ˛pín-shü³?
23. ⁵Yau ko³ sai³ ˌfá-ꞌyün* á³.   Have a small flower garden.²
24. Sz²-ꞌtꞌan* ˛ni? Chꞌut̥ ˛kái lo³.   Master eh?⁵³ Gone-out street.³¹
25. ⁵Kꞌui chꞌut̥ ˌkái ⁵yau ꞌkéi ꞌnoi* ˛ni?   He go-out street have how long eh?⁵³
26. ꞌKéi ˌshí ˌfán ˌlai ˛ni?   [⁵mò wá²).   What time back come eh?⁵³
27. ⁵Kꞌui yau² ⁵mò wá² ꞌkéi ˌshí ˌfán ˌlai o² (*or*   He even not say what time back come (*or* not say).⁵⁷
28. Sz²-ˌtꞌau-ˌpꞌo (*or* ˛tung-ˌká-ꞌpo*) ꞌhai shü³   Mistress at place, not at place eh?⁵³
    ˎm ꞌhai shü³ ˛ni?   [ˌkái lok̥.
29. ˌM ꞌhai shü³; ⁵kꞌui ˌtꞌung sz²-ꞌtꞌan* chꞌut̥   Not at place; she with master go-out street.⁵³
30. ꞌMá ⁵ngo hui³ ˎwan ꞌkꞌui ˌlá. ⁵Ngo ˌm hui³ tak̥   With me go find (*or* look for) him.²¹ I not can go.
31. ˌM tak̥, á³.   ⁵Yau² ˛á. ˌM tak̥ ˌhán ˛á. [˛á.   Not can.² Have business.¹ Not have leisure.¹
32. ˌKam-ꞌmán* yau² ˌlai ˌlá.   ⁵Mai kòm³ ye² ˌlai á³.   To night again come.²¹ Don't so late come.²

LESSON V.—General.

1.	What does he say? [up for money.	佢話乜野呢.
2.	He says he has no money. He says he is hard	冇銀㗎. 銀両緊啊.
3.	Did he say that? Give him some.	佢係咁話咩. 俾啲佢喇
4.	Can you read?	你識字唔識吖.
5.	I can't read. Neither can I write.	唔識咯. 我又唔曉寫字添.
6.	Ask the teacher to come.	請先生嚟喇
7.	What is your surname? (*To an inferior*) What is your surname?	高姓呀. 你姓乜呢.
8.	My surname is Wong.	小姓黃. *or* 姓黃.
9.	Can you speak Chinese?	你會講唐話唔會呢.
10.	I can. What's your name?	會吖. 你叫(做)乜名呢.
11.	My name is A Luk.	我名叫(做)亞六 *or* 我叫做阿六.
12.	He is an Englishman.	佢係英國人呀.
13.	You are a native of the place.	你係本地人咯. 〔旗人.
14.	He is an American.	佢係美國人, *or* (more commonly) 花
15.	How many Chinese are there?	有幾多唐人呀.
16.	Do you like this?	你中意呢啲唔中意呀.
17.	Do you like being here?	你中意喺呢處唔中意呢.
18.	I do. It would be well to be here always.	中意吖. 時時喺處都好呀.
19.	Tell him to go back. He cannot come.	叫佢翻去罅. 佢唔做得嚟.
20.	Seize that man. If you don't, he will run off.	拉响個人吖. 唔係佢就走咯.
21.	What has he been doing? *or* What does he do?	佢做乜野吖.
22.	He is a thief.	佢做賊咯 (*or* 佢係賊咯).
23.	What has he stolen? Is it of value?	佢偷乜野呢. 係值錢嘅唔值呢.
24.	He has not stolen anything yet. [strike with?	唔曾偷倒(到)野呀. 〔打呢.
25.	Has he struck anybody? What did he	有打人冇呢. 係使乜野嚟
26.	With his hand; he is a very dangerous man.	使手咯. 佢好勢兇嘅.
27.	He wanted to snatch that pair of bracelets.	佢想搶個對鈪咯.
28.	Take him to prison. [tan.	拉佢去坐監喇.
29.	Afterwards give him twenty blows with a rat-	後來打佢二十籐.
30.	Only let him go when he has been beaten.	打咗啫好放佢出去咯.
31.	He ought to be sentenced to two weeks' imprisonment.	應該辦佢坐兩個禮拜監呀.
32.	Warn him not to do it again. If he does he will be more severely punished.	警戒佢咪製過 (*or* 咪再製若 係再製就加重嚴辦咯.

1. This is the correct character, but the first represents the correct tone.

LESSON V.—General.

1. ͵K'úi wá² ͵mi-⁵ye ͵ni? — He says what thing eh?⁵³
2. ͵Mò 'ngan* wo². ͵Ngan-'lóng 'kan wo². — No money he says.⁶⁵ Money pressing he-says.⁶⁵
3. ⁵K'úi hai² 'kòm wá² ͵me? 'Péi ͵ti ⁵k'úi ͵lá. — He did so say eh?³⁹ Give some him.²¹
4. ⁵Néi shik͵ tsz² ͵m shik͵ á? — You know characters not know eh?¹
5. ͵M shik͵ ló³. ⁵Ngo yan² ͵m ⁵hiú 'se tsz² ͵t'ím. — Not know.³¹ I besides not understand to-write
6. ͵Ts'engt ͵Sín- ͵shángt ͵lai ♠. — Invite Teacher come.²¹ [character moreover.
7. ͵Kò sing² á²? ⁵Néi sing² ͵mat͵ ͵ni? — Exalted surname eh?² Your surname what eh?⁵³
8. ͵Síu sing² ͵Wong, or Sing² ͵Wong. — Diminutive surname Wong, or Surname Wong.
9. ⁵Néi ⁵wúi ⁵kong ͵T'ong-'wá* ͵m ⁵wúi ͵ui? — You can speak Chinese words not cau eh?⁵³
10. ⁵Wúi ͵á; ⁵néi kíu³ (tsò²) mat͵ 'meng*† ͵ni? — Can;¹ you called what name eh?⁵³
11. ⁵Ngo 'meng*† kíu³ tsò² A³ Luk͵, or ⁵Ngo kíu³ — My name is-called A Luk, or I am-called A Luk.
12. ⁵K'úi hai² ͵Ying kwok₀ ͵yan á³.[tsò² A³ Luk͵. — He is English nation man.²
13. ⁵Néi hai² ͵pún-téi² ͵yan lok₀. — You are native soil man.³²
14. ⁵K'úi hai² ⁵Méi Kwok₀ ͵yan, or ͵Fá͵ k'éi ͵yan. — He is American man, or Flowery Flag man.
15. ⁵Yau ͵kéi ͵to ͵T'ong- ͵yan á³? — Have how many Chinese eh?²
16. ⁵Néi ͵chung-yí³ ͵ni- ͵tí ͵m ͵chung-yí³ á³? — You like this not-like eh?²
17. ⁵Néi ͵chung-yí³ 'hai ͵ni shü³ ͵m ͵chung-yí³ ͵ni? — You like being at this place not like eh?⁵³
18. ͵Chung-yí³ ͵á. ͵Shí- ͵shí 'lai sbü³ tò ⁵hò á³. — Like.¹ Always in (this) place also good.²
19. Kíu³ ⁵k'ni ͵lán hui³ lá³. ⁵K'ni ͵m tsò² tak͵ ͵lai. — Call him back go.²³ He not do can come.
20. Lái 'ko-ko³ ͵yau á. ͵M hai² ⁵k'úi tsau² — Arrest that man.¹ If not he will-just run.³²
21. ⁵K'úi tsò² ͵mi-⁵ye ͵á? ['tsau lok₀. — He does what thing eh?¹
22. ⁵K'úi tsò² ts'ák͵ lok₀. ⁵K'ni hai² ts'ák͵ lok₀. — He is thief.³² [worth eh?⁵³
23. ⁵K'ni t'an ͵mi-⁵ye ͵ni? Hai² chik͵ 'ts'ín* ke³. — He steal what thing eh?⁵³ Is worth money—not
24. ͵M- ͵t'sang ͵t'an 'tò ⁵ye á³. [͵m chik͵ ͵ni? — Not-yet stolen anything.²
25. ⁵Yau 'tá ͵yan ⁵mò ͵ni? Hai² ⁵shai mat͵ ⁵ye — Have strike man not eh?⁵³ Have use what thing
    ͵lai 'tá ͵ni? — in-order-to strike eh?⁵³
26. ⁵Shai 'shau lok₀. ⁵K'úi 'hò shai³- ͵hung ke³. — Use hands.³² He very violent one.
27. ⁵K'ni ⁵söng 'ts'öng ko³ tui³ ák₀ lok₀. — He wished snatch that pair bracelets.²¹
28. ͵Lái ⁵k'ni hui³ 't'so*† ͵kám ͵lá. — Pull him away sit prison.²¹
29. Han²- ͵loi 'tá ⁵k'ni yí² shap͵ ͵t'ang. — Afterwards beat him twenty rattans.
30. 'Tá 'cho [s. of p. t.] che³ 'hò fong³ ⁵k'ni — Beat finished only good loose him out go.³²
    ch'nt͵ hui³ lok₀. [pái³ ͵kám á³.
31. ͵Ying- ͵koi pán² ⁵k'ni 'ts'o*† ⁵löng ko³ ⁵lai — Ought sentenced him sit two [C.] weeks prison²
32. ͵King-kái² ⁵k'ni ⁵mai ͵chai³ kwo³, (or ⁵mai — Warn him not do again (or not again do). If does
    tsoi³ chai³). Yök̊ hai² tsoi³ chai³ tsan² — again do then add more severely punish.³²
    ͵ká 'ch'nng*† ͵yím pán² lok₀.

LESSON VI.—Relationships.

1. Who are you? 你係乜人呢.
2. He is my father. 佢係我老哣咯.
3. Have you a mother? 你有老母冇呢.
4. When did you marry? 你幾時娶親呢.
5. More than ten years ago. 十幾年, or 十年有多囉.
6. Have you any children? 有仔女冇呀.
7. I have several daughters, but no sons. 有幾個女冇仔.
8. How old is the eldest? 至大 (or 至大個, or 嘅) 有幾大呢.
9. She is between ten and twenty. 今年有十幾歲.
10. Is she married? 嫁咀 (or 嫁) 唔曾吖, 出門未呢.
11. How many brothers have you? 你有幾多兄弟呢.
12. One elder brother, one younger. 一個大佬,一個細佬.
13. Have you any sisters? 有姊妹冇呢.
14. I have one elder sister and one younger. 一個亞姐,一個亞妹.
15. Are you married? 你娶老婆未曾呢.
16. Not yet. 未曾 (or 唔曾) 娶咯.
17. I cannot say certainly when I shall marry. 我唔話得定幾時娶親.
18. My wife is in the house. 我女人喺屋趾.
19. I think you will get married next year. 你出年娶老婆咧.
20. Why is your child crying? 做乜你個細佬仔喊呢.
21. He is hungry. Perhaps he is thirsty as well. 佢肚餓囉; 或者又係頸渴添.
22. Give him something to eat, and to drink. 俾野佢食, 俾野佢飲囉.
23. Call the nurse to carry him. Take him out for a walk. 叫奶媽嚟把佢. 去同佢行街.
24. He is unwilling to come. Never mind whether he is willing or not. 佢唔肯嚟. 唔打理佢肯唔肯.
25. She has no husband; she is a widow. 佢冇老公 (or 男人) 嘅. 佢係寡母婆
26. A grandson and granddaughter live with her. 一個孫,一個孫女同佢住.
27. This is my nephew. 呢個係我姪吖.
28. Is he a native of the place? 佢係本地人唔係呢.
29. Why does he come here? 佢做乜嚟呢處呢.
30. He has come to buy things for his grandfather. 佢嚟同亞公買野.
31. When is he going back? Do you know? 佢幾時翻去呢. 你知唔知呀.
32. In two or three days with his cousin. 三兩日同表兄翻去囉.

LESSON VI.—Relationships.

1. ᶜNéi hai² ₛmi ʽyau* ₍ni? — You are what man eh?⁵³
2. ᶜK'ui hai² ᶜngo ᶜlò-tau² lok₀. — He is my father.³⁹
3. ᶜNéi ᶜyau ᶜlò-ᶜmò ᶜmò ₍ni? — You have mother not eh?⁵³
4. ᶜNéi ʽkéi-ₛshí ʽts'ui*-₍ts'an ₍ni? — You what time marry eh?⁵³
5. Shap₂ ʽkéi ₍nín, or shap₂ ₍nín ᶜyau ₍to lo'. — Ten odd years, or ten years have more.³¹
6. ᶜYau ʽtsai ᶜnui ᶜmò á'? — Have sons daughters not eh?²
7. ₍Yau ʽkéi-ko' ᶜuni, ᶜmò ʽtsai. [ʽtái* ₍ni?] — Have several [C.] daughters, no sons.
8. Chí'-tái² (or chŭ' tái² ko', or ke') ᶜyau ʽkéi — Greatest (or greatest one) [or C.] have how big eh?⁵³
9. ₍Kam ₍nín ᶜyau shap₂ ʽkéi sui'. — This year have ten odd years.
10. Ká' ʽcho (or ʽká*) ₍m ₍ts'ang ₍á? Ch'ut₂ ₍mín — Married not yet eh?¹ Gone-out of doors not-yet
11. ᶜNéi ᶜyau ʽkéi ₍to ₍hing-tai² ₍ni?. [méí' ₍ni?] — You have how many brothers?⁵³ [eh?⁵³]
12. Yat₂ kò' tái²-ʽlò, yat₂ ko' sai'-ʽlò. — One [C.] elder brother, one [C.] younger brother.
13. ᶜYau ʽtsz-múí² ᶜmò ₍ni? — Have sisters not eh?⁵³
14. Yat₂ ko' Á'-ʽtso, yat₂ ko' Á'-ʽmúi*. — One [C.] elder-sister, one [C.] younger-sister.
15. ᶜNéi ʽts'ui* ᶜlò-₍p'o méí²-₍ts'nng ₍ni? [lok₀.] — You married wife not yet eh?⁵³
16. Méí²-₍ts'nng. (or ₍in-₍ts'ang, or ₍meng) ʽts'ui* — Not yet, (or not yet, or not-yet) married.³⁹
17. ᶜNgo ₍m wá² tak₂ ting² ʽkéi-ₛshí ʽts'ui*-₍ts'an.¹ — I not say can certain what time marry.
18. ᶜNgo ʽnui-ʽyan* ʽhai nk₂-ʽk'éi. [ʽlò-₍p'o kwá'.] — My wife (lit. woman) in house.
19. ᶜNéi ch'ut₂ ₍nín ʽts'ui* (often pronounced ʽts'ò) — You coming year marry wife probably?¹⁸
20. Tsò²-mat₂ ᶜnéi ko' sai'-₍mau-ʽtsai hám' ₍ni? — Why your [C.] child cries eh?⁵³
21. ᶜK'ui ᶜt'ò-ugo² lo'. Wák₂-ʽche yan² hai² — He hungry.³¹ Perhaps also is thirsty besides.
    ʽkengt-hot₀ ₍t'ím.
22. ʽPéi ᶜye ᶜk'ui shik₂. ʽPúi ᶜye ᶜk'ui ᶜyam ₍lo. — Give things him eat. Give thing him drink.³⁰
23. Kıú' ᶜnái-má ₍lai 'p'ò* ʽk'ni. Hui' ₍t'ung — Call nurse come carry him. Go with him walk
    ᶜk'ui ₍háugt ₍kái. [₍m ʽbang. — streets.
24. ᶜK'ui ₍m ʽhang ₍lai. ₍M 'tá-ʽlei ʽk'ui ʽhang — He not willing come. Not mind he willing not
25. ᶜK'ui ᶜmò ᶜlò-₍kung (or ₍nám 'yan*) ke', — She no husband (or man); she is widow. [willing.
    ᶜk'ui hai² ʽkwá-ᶜmò-₍p'o.
26. Yat₂ ko' ᶜsün, yat₂ ko' ᶜsün-ᶜnui ₍t'ung ʽk'ui — One [C.] grandson, one [C.] granddaughter with
27. ₍Ni-ko' hai² ᶜngo chat₂ á. [chü² ke'. — This is my nephew.¹ [her live.
28. ᶜK'ui hai² ʽpún-téi²-ᶜyan ₍m hai² ₍ni? — He is native not is ch?⁵³
29. ᶜK'ui tsò²-mat₂ ₍lai ᶜui-shü' ₍ni? — He why comes this place eh?⁵³
30. ᶜK'ni ₍lai ₍t'ung Á'-₍kung ᶜmái ᶜye. — He comes for grandfather buy things.
31. ᶜK'ui ʽkéi-ₛshí ʽfán hui' ₍ni? ᶜNéi chí' ₍m — He what time back go eh?⁵³ You know not
    ₍chí á'? — know eh?² [back go.³¹
32. ₍Sám ᶜlöng yat₂ ₍t'ung ʽpúi-₍hing ₍fán hní' lo'. — Three two days with consin (of different surname)

1. This is a more polite form than the above.

LESSON VII.—Opposites.

1.	This man is very tall and large.	呢個人好高大蟠.
2.	I am shorter than he.	我矮過佢咯.
3.	That cow is fat.	啣隻牛肥.
4.	This sheep is thin.	呢隻綿羊瘦.
5.	This string is too long.	呢條繩長過頭.
6.	The thread is too short; it is not enough.	呢條線短得齋唔够使咯.
7.	This is a very large house.	呢間屋好大間個.
8.	The road is so narrow you cannot walk on it.	呢條路咁窄唔行得咯.
9.	This chair is strong.	呢張椅堅固.
10.	This table is very shaky.	呢張檯好浮.
11.	He is very strong.	佢身子好壯健.
12.	I am weaker than he.	我軟弱過佢.
13.	This table-cloth is wet.	呢張檯布濕.
14.	Dry it in the sun, and bring it back.	晒乾掉翻嚟喇.
15.	This rock is very hard.	呢磧石好硬.
16.	You must boil this meat till it is soft.	你要烚到呢的肉腍 *or* 呢啲肉你要烚到腍.
17.	Your hands are dirty.	你對手汚糟囉蟠.
18.	It would be best for you to wash them clean.	你去洗乾淨至好咯.
19.	I want hot water.	我要熟水.
20.	I do not want cold water.	唔要凍水.
21.	The sea is very deep.	大海好深呀.
22.	Rivers are more shallow than seas.	河淺過海.
23.	It is very far by water.	水路好遠咯.
24.	By land it is not as far by half.	打路去冇一半咁遠.
25.	Those plantains are not ripe yet.	個啲蕉未熟咯.
26.	These coolie oranges are too unripe.	呢啲橙生過頭.
27.	I don't want those eggs boiled so hard.	個啲蛋唔好烚(得)[1]咁老.
28.	I want to eat the oysters raw.	蠔我愛生食.
29.	There are a great many water-buffaloes.	有好多水牛.
30.	There are very few goats.	有好少草羊.
31.	He is a very clever man.	佢係好聰明嘅人.
32.	You are very stupid.	你十分愚蠢咯.

1. This word may be omitted or not.

LESSON VII.—Opposites.

1. ₍Nī-ko⁾ ₅yan ʿhò ₍kò tái² po⁾. This man very tall large.⁶⁰
2. ⁵Ngo ʿai kwo⁾ ⁵k'ui lok₀. I shorter than he.⁵³
3. 'Ko* chek₀ ₅ngau ₅féi. That [C.] cow fat.
4. ₍Ni chek₀ ₅míu-₅yöng shau⁾. This [C.] sheep thin.
5. ₍Ni ₅t'íú ₅shing ₍ch'òng-'kwo*-₅t'au. This piece string too-long.
6. ₍Ni ₅t'íú sín⁾ 'tŭn-tak₅-tsai²; ₅m kau⁾ ʿshai lok₀. This piece thread too-short; not enough use.⁵³
7. ₍Ni ₅kán uk₂ ʿhò tái² ₍kán ko⁾. This [C.] house very large one [or C.]¹⁶
8. ₍Ni ₅t'íú lo² kòm⁾ chák₀ ₅m ₅hángṭ tak₂ lok₀. This length road so narrow not walk can.⁵³
9. ₍Ni ₅chöng 'yí ₍kín-kú⁾. This [C.] chair strong.
10. ₍Ni ₅chöng 't'oi* ʿhò ₅fau. This [C.] table very weak.
11. ⁵K'ui ₅shan-'tsz ʿhò chong⁾-kín². His body very strong.
12. ⁵Ngo ⁵yūn-yòk₂ kwo⁾ ⁵k'ui. I weaker than he.
13. ₍Ni ₅chöng 't'oi*-po⁾ shap₂. This [C.] table-cloth wet.
14. Shái⁾ ₍kon ₍ning ₅fán ₍lai ₍lá. Sun dry bring back come.²¹
15. ₍Ni kau² shek₂ ʿhò ngáng². This piece rock very hard.
16. ⁵Néi yíú⁾ sháp₂ tò⁾ ₍ni-₅ti yuk₂ ₅nam, or ₍Ni ₅ti yuk₂ ⁵néi yíú⁾ sháp₂ tò⁾ ₅nam. You must boil until this meat tender, or This meat you must boil till tender.
17. ⁵Néi tni⁾ ʿshau ₀¹-₅tsò lo⁾ po⁾. Your pair-of hands dirty.³¹ ²¹
18. ⁵Néi hui⁾ ʿsai ₍kou-tseng²ṭ chí⁾-'hò lok₀. You go wash clean best.⁵³
19. ⁵Ngo yíú⁾ yít₂ ʿshui. I want hot water.
20. ₍M̆yíú⁾ tung⁾ ʿshui. Not want cold water.
21. Tái²-'boi ʿhò ₅sham á⁾. Great ocean very deep.²
22. ₍Ho 'ts'ín kwo⁾ 'hoi. Rivers shallower than seas.
23. ʿShui lo² ʿhò ⁵yūn lok₀. Water road very far.⁵³
24. ʿTá lo² hni⁾ ⁵mò yat₂ pún⁾ kòm⁾ ⁵yūn. By road going not one half so far.
25. Ko⁾-₅ti ₅tsíú méi² shuk₂ lok₀. Those plantains not-yet ripe.⁵³
26. ₍Ni-₅ti 'ch'áng* ₅shápṭ kwo⁾-₅t'au. These coolie-oranges unripe too over much (lit. head).
27. Ko⁾-₅ti 'tán* ₅m 'hò sháp₂ (tak₂) kòm⁾ ⁵ỉò. Those eggs not good boil (can) so old.
28. Hò, ₅ngo oi⁾ ₅shángṭ shik₂. Oysters, I want raw eat.
29. ⁵Yau ʿhò ₅to ʿshui-₅ngau. Have great many water cows (or oxen).
30. ⁵Yau ʿhò shíú ʿts'ò-₅yöng. Have very few goats.
31. ⁵K'ui hai² ʿhò ₅ts'ung-₅ming ke⁾ ₅yan. He is very clever man.
32. ⁵Néi shap₂ ₅fan ₅yū-ʿch'un lok₀. You ten parts stupid.⁵³

1. Sometimes pronounced ú.

LESSON VIII.—Monetary.

1. One dollar. 一個銀錢,一文.
2. A dollar and a half. 個半銀錢
3. Half a dollar. Over a dollar. [nounce. 半個銀錢, (or) 半文, 個幾銀錢.
4. This word 'ngau' is very difficult to pro- 呢個銀字好難講呀.
5. Do you say so? Do you pronounce it so? 你係咁話咩 你係咁講咩
6. That is easier to pronounce. 咟個易啲講羅
7. A dollar is divided into ten 'ho,' (ten-cent 一個銀錢分十毫.
8. One 'ho' is divided into ten cents. [picces). 一毫子分十仙 [毫六.
9. Ten dollars and sixty-six cents. 十個銀錢零六毫六, or 十個六
10. Can you change accounts in taels into dollars? 兩數你喩伸元數唔喩呀
11. One tael is equal to a dollar and forty cents. 一兩銀值得個四銀錢.
12. Nine mace. Nine cash. [dollars to me. 九錢銀, 九個錢
13. You agreed to hand over eighteen hundred 你應承交千八銀過我[1]
14. One tael, seven mace, six candareens, six léi. 一兩七錢六分六.
15. What is a dollar worth in cash? 一個銀錢找得幾多錢.
16. It is worth one thousand and forty cash. 找得一千零四十錢.
17. How much wages do you want a month? 你一個月要幾多人工呢.
18. I want eight dollars a month. This is too much. 要八個銀錢個月, 多過頭吖
19. Your expenses are few; you do not need so 你使費少唔使要咁多.
20. If I find my own food, it is not much. [much. 係食自己唔係多吖.
21. The master does not provide you with food, of course you find yourself. 唔係食事頭, 係食自己嘅定喇
22. I can't reduce my terms. 唔減得咯.
23. Do you know how to do the work? I have 你曉做唔曉呀 我做過咯.
24. You must not spend this money. [done it. 你唔好使呢啲錢.
25. You ought to send it home. 你應該寄翻去屋.
26. Does he gamble? I think he does. 佢賭錢咩 我估係吖.
27. Does he play at cards, or dominoes? [dice. 佢打乜野牌, 紙牌嗎骨牌呢.
28. Both; he also plays-at fán tán, pò tsz and with 兩樣都有, 又揸灘, 打寶字
29. If he gambles, I shall not employ him. 佢係賭錢, 我唔請佢. [嘢色.
30. You tell him what I say. I have. 你話佢聽. 話咯.
31. He says he won't dare do so. 佢話唔敢做咯.
32. I take it he is acquainted with his work. Probably he is. 我睇得佢係熟手咯, 大概係呀.

---

1. The 銀 in such a phrase is ambiguous: it may mean dollars, or taels.

LESSON VIII.—Monetary.

1. Yat, ko' ₅ngan 'ts'ín,* or yat, ₅man*. — One [C.] silver cash, or one dollar.
2. Ko' pún' ₅ngan-'ts'ín.* [₅ngan-'ts'ín.* — One (and a) half dollar.
3. Pún' ko' ₅ngan-'ts'ín*, or pún' ₅man. Ko' 'kéi — Half a dollar, or half dollar. One (and) odd dollar.
4. ₅Ni-ko' ₅ngau tsz² 'hò ₅nán 'kong á'. — This ngan character very difficult to-speak.
5. ⁵Néi hai² 'kòm wá² ₅me? ⁵Néi hai² 'kòm 'koung — You do so say do-you?³⁹ You do so pronounce eh.³⁹
6. 'Ko-ko' yí²- ₅ti 'kong lo'. [₅me? — That easier to pronounce.³¹
7. Yat, ko' ₅ngan-'ts'ín* ₅fan shap, ₅hò. — One [C.] dollar divided ten dimes.
8. Yat, ₅hò-'tsz ₅fan shap, ₅sín*. — One dime divided ten cents.
9. Shap,-ko' ₅ngan-'ts'ín* ₅lengt luk, ₅hò luk,, or shap, ko' luk, ₅hò luk,. [á'? — Ten dollars and six dimes six (cents) or ten [C.] six dimes six. [counts not can eh?²
10. 'Löng shò' ⁵néi 'wúi ₅shau ₅yün sho' ₅m ⁵wúi — Tael accounts you can carry-out-into dollar ac-
11. Yat, 'löng 'ngau* chik, ts-tak, ko' sz' ₅ngan — One tael silver worth one four dollar.
12. 'Kau ₅ts'ín-'ngan.* 'Kau ko' 'ts'ín*.['ts'ín*. — Nine mace silver. Nine [C.] cash.
13. ⁵Néi ₅ying-₅shing ₅káu ₅ts'ín pát, ₅ngan* 'kwo* — You agreed hand-over thousand eight money to me.
14. Yat, 'löng₅ts'at₅ ₅ts'ín)luk, ₅fan)luk,. [⁵ngo. — One tael seven mace six cundareens six (léi).
15. Yat, ko' ₅ngan-₅ts'ín 'cháu tak, 'kéi ₅to 'ts'ín*? — One [C.] dollar change can how many cash?
16. 'Cháu tak, yat, ₅ts'ín ₅lengt sz' shap, 'ts'ín*. — Change can one thousand and forty cash.
17. ⁵Néi yat, ko' yüt, yíú' 'kéi ₅to ₅yan-₅kung ₅ni? — You one [C.] month want how much wages eh?⁵³
18. Yíú' pát₀ ko' ₅ngan-'ts'ín* ko' yüt,. ₅To — Want eight [C.] dollars a month. Much too.¹
    'kwo*-₅t'au á.
19. ⁵Néi 'shai fai' 'shíú, ₅m 'shai yíú' kòm' ₅to. — Your expenses little not need want so much.
20. Hai² shik, tsz²-'kéi ₅m hai² ₅to ₅á. — Do eat self not is much.¹
21. ₅M hai² shik, ₅sz²-'t'au,* hai² shik, taz²-'kéi — Not do eat master's, do eat self — certainly.²¹
22. ₅M 'kám tak, lok₀. [ke' 'ting* ₅lá. — Not reduce can.³²
23. ⁵Néi 'híú tsò² ₅m 'híú á'? ⁵Ngo tsò² kwo' lok₀. — You know do not know eh?² I done already.³²
24. ⁵Néi ₅m 'hò 'shai ni-₅ti 'ts'ín.* — You not good use this money.
25. ⁵Néi ₅ying-₅koi kéi' ₅fán hui' ₅kwai. — You ought send back go home.
26. ⁵K'ui 'tò-'ts'ín* ₅me? ⁵Ngo 'kú hai² ₅á. — He gamble eh?³⁹ I think does.¹
27. ⁵K'ui 'tá mat, ⁵ye 'p'ái*, 'chí ₅p'ái péi² kwat, — He play-at what, dominoes-or-cards, paper cards, ₅p'ái ₅ni? or bone tablets eh?⁵³
28. ⁵Löng yöng² ₅tò ⁵yau; yau² ₅chá ₅t'án, 'ta 'pò — Two kinds also have; further play-at fán-tan, play-'tsz*, chák, shik,. at pò-tsz, throw dice.
29. ⁵K'ui hai² 'tò-'ts'ín* ⁵ngo ₅m 'ts'engt ⁵k'ui. — He does gamble, I not engage him.
30. ⁵Néi wá² ⁵k'ui ₅t'eng.*† 'Wá* lok₀. — You tell him to-hear. Told.³²
31. ⁵K'ui wá¹ ₅m 'kòm tsò² lok₀. [k'oi — He says not dare do.³²
32. ⁵Ngo 't'ai-tak, ⁵k'ui hai² shuk, 'shau lo'. — I see-can he is acquainted 'hand.³¹ Probably is.²

LESSON IX.—Commercial.

1.	How much is this?	呢啲幾多銀 (or 錢) 呢.
2.	What is the price of that?	個啲幾多價錢呢.
3.	It is too dear.	貴過頭, or 貴得嚌咯.
4.	I shall not buy it. I don't want it.	我唔買呀. 唔要咯.
5.	Have you any cheaper ones?	有平啲嘅冇呀
6.	This is cheaper.	呢個平啲啊
7.	How do you sell this rice?	呢的米點賣呢
8.	Oh! I don't stand out so. Reduce your price.	唉吔. 唔麻唔咄減價唎.
9.	Increase your offer. You are dear.	你添啲唎. 你貴吖.
10.	No. They are first quality of goods.	唔係貴吖, 係第一好貨咯.
11.	Is it good? Mine are the best.	好唔好吖. 我嘅至好咯.
12.	I have seen better ones before.	我舊時見過好啲嘅.
13.	Have you any better ones?	重有好啲嘅冇呢.
14.	Bring them for me to see.	搾嚟俾我睇.
15.	If suitable I shall certainly buy.	合使我是必買吖.
16.	It does not matter if they are dearer.	貴的都唔計帶吖.
17.	There are none as good as these throughout Hongkong.	通香港都冇呢啲咁好嘅.
18.	It is imitation. No; it is genuine.	係假嘅. 唔係; 係真嘅.
19.	You don't know good from bad.	你都唔識好醜嘅咯.
20.	I do. I have been in that business.	識吖, 我都做過個啲生意咯.
21.	I am afraid it is old, is it not? No it is new.	係舊嘅罅咧. 唔係, 係新嘅.
22.	This is no use. It is useless.	呢個冇用咯, 唔中用咯.
23.	He wants too high a price.	佢要得價錢多咯.
24.	You offer too little. Don't be so stingy.	你俾得少吖, 唔好咁慳吖.
25.	It will not pay cost price.	唔够本 (or 本錢) 吖.
26.	How long will it last?	使得幾耐呢.
27.	I guarantee it will last four years.	我包用四年咯.
28.	That is a promissory note is it?	個張係揭單咩.
29.	How much is the capital and interest?	本銀利息 (or simply 本利, or 本息) 幾多呀.
30.	The interest is only three dollars per mensem.	每月三個銀錢利息咯.
31.	That's very heavy interest. No, it is rather little interest.	好重利呀. 唔係吖, 幾平利呀.
32.	The capital is one hundred dollars payable on demand.	本銀一百元隨時取回.

LESSON IX.—Commercial.

1. ₍Ní-₍ti ʿkéi ₍to ʾngan* (or ʾts'ín*)¹ ₍ni? | This how much money (or cash) eh?⁵⁶
2. Kó'-₍ti ʿkéi ₍to ká'-₍ts'ín ₍ni? | That how much price eh?⁵³
3. Kwai' ʾkwo* ₍t'au, or kwaí' tak₍-tsai² lo'. | Dear over much, or dear much too.
4. ˢNgo ₍m ˢmái á'. ₍M yíú' lok₀. | I not buy.² Not want.³²
5. ˢYan ₍p'eugt-₍ti ke' ˢmò á'? | Have cheaper ones not eh?²
6. ₍Ni-ko' ₍p'eng-₍ti o'? | This cheaper.⁵⁶
7. ₍Ni-₍ti ˢmai ʿtím mái² ₍ni? | This rice how sell eh?⁵³
8. ₍Ai ₍rá, ₍mś-ʾmá*-ʾtéi*, ʿkam ká' ₍lá. | Oh! Let-it-pass. Reduce price.²¹
9. ˢNéi ₍t'ím ₍ti ₍lá. ˢNéi kwai' ₍á. | You increase little.²¹ You dear.¹
10. ₍M hai² kwai' ₍á, hai² tai' ynt, ʿbò fo' lok₀. | Not is dear,¹ are No. 1 good articles.³²
11. ʿHò ₍m ʾbò ₍á? ˢNgo-ke' chi'-ʿbò lok₀. | Good not good eh?¹ Mine best.³²
12. ˢNgo kau² ₍shí kín' kwo' ʿbò ₍ti ke'. | I old time (formerly) seen have better ones.
13. Chung² ˢyau ʿbò-₍ti ke' ˢmò ₍ui? | Besides have better ones not eh?⁵³
14. ₍Ning ₍lai ʿpéi ˢngo ʿt'ai. | Bring come give me see.
15. Hòp₍ ʿshai ˢngo shí'-pít, ˢmái ₍á. | Suitable for-use I certainly buy.¹
16. Kwai'-₍ti ₍tò ₍m kai' tái' ₍á. [ke'. | Dearer even not reckon (it) great (cost).¹
17. ₍T'ung* ₍Höng-ʿkoug ₍tò ˢmò ₍ni-₍ti kòm' ʿbò | Throughout Hongkong even not these so good.¹⁵
18. Hai² ʿká ke'. ₍M hai²; hai² ₍chán ke'. | Is false.¹⁵ Not is; is true.¹⁵
19. ˢNéi ₍tò ₍m shik₍ ʿbò ʿch'au ke' lok₀. | You even not know good bad ones.³¹
20. Shik₍ ₍á. ˢNgo ₍tò tsò² kwo' ₍ko ₍tí ₍sháugt yí' lok₀. | Know — I also done over that business.—
21. Hai² kau² ke' lá' kwá'. ₍M hai², hai² ₍san ke'. | Is old one²¹ probably-'tis-isn't-it?¹³ Not is, is
22. ₍Ni-ko' ˢmò yung² lok₀. ₍M ₍chung yung² | This no use.³² Useless.³² [new.¹⁵
23. ˢK'ui yíú'-tak, ká'-₍ts'ín ₍to lok₀. [lok₀. | He wants price much.³²
24. ˢNéi ʿpéi-tak, ʿshíú ₍á. ₍M ʿbò kòm' ʿhán ₍á. | You offer little.¹ Not good so stingy.¹
25. ₍M kau' ʿpún (or ʿpún ₍ts'ín) ₍á. | Not enough (to equal) cost-price¹, (or original cost
26. ʿShai tak₍ ʿkéi noi² ₍ni? | Use can how long eh?⁵³ [money).
27. ˢNgo ₍pán yung² sz' ₍nín lok₀. | I guarantee use four years.³²
28. ʿKo ₍chöng hai² k'ít₀ ₍tán ₍me? | That [C.] is promissary note is-it?³⁹
29. ʾTùn ʾngan* léi²-sik, (or simply ʿpún léi², or ʿpún sik,) ʿkéi ₍to á'? | Capital money interest, (or principal interest) how much eh?¹
30. ˢMúi yüt₍ ₍sám-ko' ₍ngan-ʾts'ín* léi' sik₍ che'. | Each month three dollars interest only.⁸
31. ʿHo ʿch'ung* léi² á'. ₍M hai² ₍á; ʿkéi ₍p'eugt léi² á'. [ʿwúi. | Very heavy interest.² Not is;¹ rather cheap interest.² [back.
32. ʾPún ʾngan* yat₍ pák₀ ₍yün, ₍ts'ni ₍shí ʿts'úi | Capital money one hundred dollars, any time take

---

1 Use the former if the price is likely to be given in silver, and the latter if in cash.

LESSON X.—Commercial.

1.	What business is he in?	佢做乜野生意呢.
2.	I am a general merchant.	我做南北行嘅.
3.	Where is your hong?	你間行喺邊處呀.
4.	What is it called (*its style*)?	乜野字號呢.
5.	How long have you been in business?	你做生意有幾耐呀.
6.	Call the compradore.	叫買辦嚟嗻.
7.	Have you made up your accounts?	你計數唔曾呀.
8.	I have not made them up completely yet.	唔曾計清楚咯.
9.	Compare accounts with me.	同我對數喇.
10.	Wait a bit, this item is wrong.	等吓咋, 呢條錯咯.
11.	It must be gone over again. That will do.	要計過咯. 做得囉.
12.	Has that money been shroffed?	睇過個啲銀唔曾呀.
13.	Call the shroff to shroff it.	叫睇銀嘅嚟睇喇.
14.	If there are any bad ones, go and change them.	有唔好嘅要換嗻.
15.	Weigh these dollars.	兌呢啲銀喇.
16.	Ten of them are not full weight; they are	十個唔够重呀, 輕吋.
17.	Who is the accountant here? [light.	呢處邊個做掌櫃呢.
18.	My friend. This is the manager.	我朋友. 呢個係做司事人咯.
19.	Has he a share in the business?	生意佢有份冇呀.
20.	What goods are these?	呢啲係乜野貨呢.
21.	All miscellaneous goods.	喊嗻哈都係雜貨咯.
22.	Have they passed the Customs?	過稅唔曾呢.
23.	They have passed. Where is the Bill of	過嘅咯. 攬載紙呢.
24.	He wants to open a shop. [Lading?	佢想開間舖.
25.	I am afraid he will lose his money (*lit.* capital).	我慌佢蝕本呀.
26.	Where is his shop? [dull.	佢個間舖喺邊處呢.
27.	There is not much business here. It is very	呢處冇乜生意呀, 好淡吋.
28.	What were the good-will, stock-in-trade and fittings sold for? [him, was it?	招牌舖底傢生頂得幾多銀呢.
29.	Then it was you that sold that business to	噉個啲生意係你頂過佢咩.
30.	Call men to carry the goods, into the go-down. I will not come to-morrow, as it is Sunday.	叫人抬貨落貨倉喇. 聽日禮拜我唔嚟咯.
31.	When does the steamer leave? There are a great many passengers.	火船幾時開身呢. 有大多搭客咯.
32.	I want to send some letters (*or* a letter) home to the country.	我要寄信翻屋鄉下.

LESSON X.—Commercial.

1. ⁵K'ui tsò² ₅mi-⁵ye ₅sháng†-yî² ₒui? He does what thing business eh?⁵³
2. ⁵Ngo tsò² ₅nám-pak₅ 'hong*-ke². I do south-north hong's.
3. ⁵Néi ₅kán 'hong* 'hai ₒpín-shū² á²? Your [C.] hong at what place eh?²
4. ₒMi-(⁵ye) tsz²-hò² ₒni? What (thing) style eh?⁵³
5. ⁵Néi tsò² ₅sháng†-yî² ⁵yau 'kéi 'noi* á²? You do business have how long eh?²
6. Kíú² ⁵mái-'pán* ₅lai 'chá. Call compradore come first.⁵
7. ⁵Néi 'kui* shò² ₅m-₅ts'ang á²? You reckon accounts not yet eh?²
8. ₅M-₅ts'ang kai² ₅ts'ing-'ch'o lok₀. Not yet reckoned clearly.³²
9. ₅T'ung ⁵ngo tui² shò² ₅lá. With me compare accounts.²¹
10. ⁵Tang ⁵há chá², ₒni ₅t'úi ts'o² lok₀. Wait bit first,⁶ this item wroug.³²
11. Yíú² kai² kwo² lok₀. Tsó² tak₅ lo². Must reckon again.³² Do can.³¹
12. 'T'ai kwo² ko²-₀ti 'ugau* ₅m-₅ts'aug á²? Looked over that money not yet eh?²
13. Kíú² 't'ai-'ngan*-ke² ₅lai 't'ai ₅lá. Call shroffing one come look.²
14. ⁵Yau ₒm 'hò ke² yíú² wún² po². Have not good ones must chauge.⁶⁰
15. Tui² ₒni-₀ti ₅ngan-₅lá. Weigh these dollars.²¹
16. Shap₂-ko² ₒm kau² 'ch'ung*† á². ₅Heng†₅ á. Ten not euough heavy.² Light.¹
17. ⁵Ni-shū² ₒpín-ko² tsò² 'chöng-'kwai* ₒni? This place who [C.] is accountant eh?⁵³
18. ⁵Ngo ₒp'ang-⁵yau. ₅Ni-ko² hai² tsò² ₅sz-sz²-₅yan lok₀. My friend. This [C.] is being manager.³²
19. ⁵Sháng†-yî² ⁵k'ui ⁵yau 'fan* ⁵mò á²? Business he has share not eh?²
20. ₅Ni-₀ti hai² ₅mi-⁵ye fo² ₒni? These are what goods eh?⁵³
21. Hám²-pá²-láng² ₅tò hai² tsáp₂-fo² lok₀. All even are miscellaneous goods.³²
22. 'Kwo* shui² ₅m-₅ts'ang ₒni? Passed customs not yet eh?⁵³
23. Kwo² 'cho lok₀. ⁵Lám tsoi² 'chí ₒni? Passed [s. of p. t.].³² Bill-of-Lading eh?⁵³
24. ⁵K'ni ⁵söng ₅hoi ₅káu p'ò². He wishes open [C.] shop.
25. ⁵Ngo ₒfong ⁵k'ui shit₅ ₒpún á². I fear he lose capital.² [eh?⁵³
26. ⁵K'ui 'ko ₅kán p'ò² 'hai ₒpín-shū² ₒni? His that [C.] shop (that shop of his) at what place
27. ⁵Ni shū² ⁵mò mat₅ ₅sháng†-yî² á²; 'hò tám² ₅á. This place not much business;² very dull.¹
28. ₅Chíú ₒp'ái, p'ò² ₒtai, ká²-₅sháng† 'ting tak₅ ⁵kéi ₒto 'ngan* ₒni? [⁵k'ni ₒme? Sign board, shop residue, furniture, sold able how much money eh?¹³ [it?³⁹
29. 'Kóm, 'ko-₀ti ₅sháng†-yî² hai² ⁵néi 'ting kwo² Then that business 'twas you sold (it) to him was-
30. Kíú² ⁵yau ₅t'oi fo² lok₀ fo²-₀ts'ong ₅lá. ₅T'ing yat₅ ⁵Lái-pái² ⁵ngo ₒm ₅lai lok₀. Call men carry goods down go-down.²¹ To-morrow Sunday I not come.³²
31. 'Fo-₅shün ⁵kéi-₅shí ₅hoi-₅shan ₒni? ⁵Yan tái² ₒto táp₂-hák₀ lok₀. Steamer what time start eh?⁵³ Have great many passengers.³²
32. ⁵Ngo yíú² 'kéi² sun² ₅fán ₅kwai ₅böng-'há*. I want send letter back home country.

LESSON XI.—Medical.

1. This gentleman is a doctor. 呢位係醫生咯.
2. Is he a surgeon, or physician? 佢係外科醫生嘑內科呢.
3. Call a Chinese doctor to feel my pulse. 請唐人醫生嚟睇脈呀.
4. I am not very well to-day. 我今日唔多自然咯.
5. What is the matter with you? 你有乜野病呢.
6. My head aches. 頭痢呀.
7. Have you been sick? 有嘔冇呢.
8. I have not, but I feel inclined to be so. 冇嘔想嘔咡.
9. Is there anything else the matter? 重有乜野病冇呢.
10. I have also the stomach-ache. 我肚都痛吓.
11. That is not serious. 個啲冇乜相干嚛.
12. Take a little medicine. 食啲藥喇.
13. What medicine ought I to take? 我應食乜野藥呢.
14. Wait till I come back. I am going to the hospital now. 等我翻嚟咋. 我而家去醫生館.
15. I will send a man with medicine for you. 我打發人捽藥嚟俾你.
16. You have fever. I will give you a draught. 你發熱囉. 我俾藥水你食.
17. I have ague. Take this powder. 我發冷囉. 食呢啲藥散.
18. Do you feel your throat dry? 你見喉嚨乾咩.
19. I do, and it is very painful. 見乾囉. 又見好痛添咯.
20. Don't drink so much water. 咪飲咁多水吁.
21. Take a little chicken broth. Take a little conges. 食的雞湯. 食的粥吁.
22. Are you able to sleep at night? 晚頭瞓得唔瞓得呢.
23. Has he got cold? Does he cough? 佢冷親咩. 佢咳嗎.
24. At times he does, at times he doesn't. 有時有, 有時冇.
25. Put on a plaster. Does he drink? 貼膏藥. 佢飲酒唔飲呀.
26. I am afraid he smokes opium. 我慌佢食鴉片煙嘅.
27. Perhaps he does. I am afraid he does. 怕係呀. 或者係都唔定呀.
28. How long has he been ill? 佢病有幾耐呢.
29. He has been feeling weak for a long time? 佢好耐見軟弱囉.
30. Tell him to take some cooling medicine. 叫佢食啲涼藥喇.
31. Did he feel better after taking the pills? 佢食咄藥丸見好的嗎.
32. No, he was much worse. 唔係, 越發傻咯.

1 攸 'Yam could be used; but the above form is better.

LESSON XI.—Medical.

1. ₋Ni ʽwai* hai² ₋yí-₋sháng† lok₀. This gentleman is doctor.³²
2. ˢKʽui hai² ngoi²-₋fo ₋yí-₋sháng†, péi² noi²-₋fo ₋ni? He is external practice doctor, or internal practice eh?⁵³
3. ʽTsʽeng¹ ₋Tʽong-₋yan ₋yí-₋sháng† ₋lai ʽtʽai mak₂ á'. Invite Chinese doctor come feel pulse.²
4. ˢNgo ₋kam-yat₂ ₋m ₀to tsz²-₋yín lok₀. I to-day not very well.³²
5. ˢNéi ˢyau mat₂-ˢye peng²† ₋ni? You have what thing sickness eh?⁵³
6. ₋Tʽau tsʽek₀† a'. Headache.²
7. ˢYau ʽau ˢmò ₋ni? Have sick not₂eh?⁵³
8. ˢMò ʽau, ʽsöng ʽau ₋che. Not sick. Wish to be sick only.⁷
9. Chung¹ ˢyau ₋mi-ˢye pong²† ˢmò ₋ui? Besides have what sickness not eh?⁵³
10. ˢNgo ˢtʽò ₋tò tʽung² á. My stomach also pains.¹
11. Ko'-₋ti ˢmò mat₂ ₋söng-₋kon ká². That not much matter.¹⁴
12. Shik₂ ₋ti yök₂ ₋lá. Eat some medicine.²¹
13. ˢNgo ₋ying shik₂ ₋mi-ˢye yök₂ ₋ni? I ought to-eat what medicine eh?⁵³
14. ʽTang ˢngo ₋fán ₋lai chá', ˢNgo ₋yí-₋ká hui³ ₋yí-₋sháng-ˢkún. Wait I back come until.⁶ I at-present go hospital.
15. ˢNgo ˢtá-fát₀ ₋yan ₋ning yök₂ ₋lai ʽpéi ˢnéi? I send man bring medicine come give you.
16. ˢNéi fát₀-yít₂ lo'. ˢNgo ʽpéi yök₂ ˢshui ˢnéi shik₂. You have-fever.³¹ I give medicine water (i.e. liquid medicine) you eat.
17. ˢNgo fát₀-ˢláng lo'. Shik₂ ₋ni ₋ti yök₂ ʽsán. I have-ague.³¹ Eat this medicine powder.
18. ˢNéi kín³ ₋hau-ˢlung ₋kon ₋me? You feel throat dry eh?³⁹
19. Kín³ ₋kon lo'. Yau² kíu³ ʽhò tʽung² tʽím lok₀. Feel dry.³¹ Also feel very painful besides.³²
20. ˢMai ʽyam kòm³ ₋to ʽshui á. Don't drink so much water.¹
21. Shik₂ ₋ti ₋kai ₋tʽong, shik₂ ₋ti chuk₂ á. Eat some chicken soup. Eat some congee.¹
22. ˢMán-₋tʽau fan³-tak₂ ₋m fan³-tak₂ ₋ui? Night sleep can, not sleep can eh?⁵³
23. ˢKʽui ˢláng-ˢtsʽau ₋me? ˢKʽui kʽat₂ má²? He cold caught eh?³⁹ He cough eh?³⁵
24. ˢYau ₋shí ˢyau; ˢyau ₋shí ˢmò. Have times have; have times not.
25. Tʽíp₀ ₋kò yök₂. ˢKʽui ʽyam ʽtsau ₋m ˢyam á'? Stick-on plaster. He drink wine not drink eh?²
26. ˢNgo ₋fong ˢkʽui shik₂ ₋á-pʽín³ ₋yín ke'. I fear he smokes opium.¹⁵
27. Pʽá³ hai² á'. Wák₂ ʽche hai² ₋tò ₋m ting² á'. Fear does.² Perhaps does also not certain.³
28. ˢKʽui peng²† ˢyau ʽkéi-ʽnoi* ₋ni? He ill have how long eh?⁵³
29. ˢKʽui ʽhò noi² kín³ ˢyūn-yök₂ lo'. He very long feel weak.³¹
30. Kíu³ ˢkʽui shik₂ ₋ti ₋löng yök₂ ₋lá. Tell him eat some cooling medicine.²¹
31. ˢKʽui shik₂-ʽcho yök₂-'yūn* (or ₋yūn) kín³ He eat [s. of p. t.] pills feel better eh?³³
32. ₋M hai², yüt₂-fát₀ pai² lok₀. [ʽhò-₋ti ₋má?] Not is, the-rather the-worse.³²

LESSON XII.—Ecclesiastical.

1.	Is this a convent or not?	呢間係庵唔係呢.
2.	Are there any priests?	有和尚冇呀.
3.	There are no priests; there are nuns.	冇和尚,有尼姑啫.
4.	How many are there? Are there many or few?	有幾多個呢,多嘞少呢.
5.	Over twenty. Twenty and more.	二十零個. 二十個有多咯.
6.	What do they, the priests, do?	佢哋呢, 和尚呢, 做乜野呢.
7.	Read the Sutras the whole day long, so they say.	成日念經咖.
8.	Do you believe it? No one does.	你信唔信吖. 冇人信嘅.
9.	That is a temple. I do not know whether it is a Buddhist, or Taouist one. Which is it?	個間係廟. 唔知係佛教嘅, 嘞道教嘅呢.
10.	It is a Buddhist temple.	係佛教嘅.
11.	What is the difference?	有乜分別呢.
12.	There is a great difference.	有大分別咯, or 大有分別咯.
13.	What idols are those?	個的係乜野菩薩呢.
14.	The three Precious Buddhas.	係三寶佛咯.
15.	He is a Protestant missionary.	佢係講耶穌嘅.
16.	Have you become a convert? I have not.	你入教唔曾呀. 未曾呀.
17.	Why have you not?	做乜你唔曾入教嘅咩.
18.	Is there a chapel here?	呢處有禮拜堂冇呢.
19.	There are two; and there is someone preaching every day.	有兩間咯, 日日有人講書.
20.	Are they Protestant or Catholic?	係天主教嘅, 嘞耶穌教嘅呢.
21.	One is Protestant.	一間係耶穌教嘅.
22.	The other is Catholic.	一間係天主教嘅.
23.	Who are the Catholic Missionaries?	神父係乜人呀.
24.	They are all Frenchmen.	個個都係法蘭西人呀.
25.	Have they families?	佢哋有家眷冇呢.
26.	They are not allowed to marry.	唔准佢取老婆嘅.
27.	They wear Chinese clothes.	佢扮唐裝嘅咯.
28.	What is the intention in this?	有乜意思呢.
29.	They want to be like Chinese.	佢想學翻唐人一樣.
30.	Is there any other reason?	重有乜緣故冇呢.
31.	You must ask them to know.	要問佢就知嚹.
32.	I am a Chinese, and do not know.	我係唐人,唔知到吖.

LESSON XII.—Ecclesiastical.

1. ͵Ní ͵kán hnì² ͵om ͵m hnì² ͵ní? This [C.] is convent not is eh?[53]
2. ⁵Yau ͵wo-ˈshöng* ⁵mò á'? Have (Buddhist) priests not eh?[2]
3. ⁵Mò ͵wo-ˈshöng*; ⁵yau ͵néi-͵kwú ͵che. No (Buddhist) priests, have nuus.[7]
4. ⁵Yau ˈkéi ͵to ko' ͵ni? ͵To péi² ˈshú ͵ni? Have how many ones eh.[53] Many or few eh?[53]
5. Yí²-shap͵ ͵lengt ko', or yí² shap͵ ko' ⁵yau ͵to lok₀. Twenty odd ones, or twenty ones have more.[32]
6. ⁵K'ui-téi² ͵ni, ͵wo-ˈshöng* ͵ni, tsò² ͵mi-⁵ye They,[53] priests,[53] do what thing eh?[53]
7. ͵Sheugt yat͵ ním²-͵king wo'. [͵ni? Whole day recite sutras, (so they) say.[65]
8. ⁵Néi sun' ͵m sun' ͵á? ⁵Mò ͵yan sun' ke'. You believe not believe eh?[1] No man believes.[15]
9. Ko' ͵kán hnì² mìú². ͵M ͵chí hnì² Fnt͵-káu' ke', péi² Tò²-káu'-ke' ͵ni? That [C.] is temple. Not know is Buddhist sect's, or Taouist sect's, which-is it?[53]
10. Hai² Fnt͵-káu' ke'. Is Buddhist sect's.
11. ⁵Yau mat͵ ͵fan-pít͵ ͵ni? Have what difference eh?[53]
12. ⁵Yau tái² ͵fau-pít͵ lok₀, or tái² ⁵yau ͵fan-pít͵ Have great difference,[32] or great have difference.[32]
13. Ko'-͵ti hnì² mat͵-⁵ye ͵p'ò-sát₀ ͵ni? [lok₀. Those are what idols eh?[53]
14. Hai² ͵Sám ˈPò Fnt͵ lok₀. Are Three Precious Buddhas.[32]
15. ⁵k'ui hai² ͵kong ͵Ye-͵sò ke'. He is speak Jesus one?[15]
16. ⁵Néi yap͵ káu' ͵m-͵ts'ang á'? Méi² ͵ts'ang á'? You entered the-faith not yet eh?[2] Not yet.[2]
17. Tsò² mat͵ ⁵néi ͵m ͵ts'aug yap͵ káu' ke' ͵me? What thing you not yet entered the-faith eh?[39]
18. ͵Ni-shù' ⁵yau ⁵Lói-pái' ͵t'ong ⁵mò ͵ni? This place have Sabbath Hall not eh?[53]
19. ⁵Yau ˈlöng ͵kán lok₀. Yat͵ yat͵ ⁵yau ͵yau ˈkong ͵shú. Have two [C.][32] Day by day have man preach.
20. Hai² ͵T'ín-ˈChü-káu' ke', péi² ͵Ye-͵sò-káu' Are Heaven's Lord's faith's one, or Jesus' faith's
21. Yat͵ ͵kán hai² ͵Ye-͵sò káu' ke'. [ke' ͵ni? One [C.] is Jesus' faith's one.[15] [one eh?[53]
22. Yat͵ ͵kán hai² ͵T'ín ˈChü káu' ke̜'. One [C.] is Heaven's Lord's faith's one.[15]
23. ͵Shau-fú² hai² ͵mi-⁵yan* á'? Priests (Romish) are what men eh?[2]
24. Ko'-ko' ͵tò hai² Fát₀ ͵lán-͵sai ͵yau á'. Everyone even is French-man.[2]
25. ⁵K'ui-téi² ⁵yau ͵ká-kün' ⁵mò ͵ni? They have families not eh?[53]
26. ͵M ͵chun ⁵k'ui ˈts'ui ⁵lò-͵p'o ke'. Not allowed to-them marry wives.[15]
27. ⁵K'ui páu² ͵T'ong-͵chong ke' lok₀. They dress Chinese style.[15][34]
28. ⁵Yau mat͵ yí²-sz' ͵ni? Have what meaning eh?[53]
29. ⁵K'ú ˈsöng hok͵ ͵fán ͵T'ong-͵yan yat͵ ⁵yöng². They wish copy again Chinese (lit. T'ong men, i.e. men of the T'ong Dynasty.)
30. Chung² ⁵yau mat͵ ͵yiu-kwú ⁵mò ͵ni? Besides have what reason have not eh?[53]
31. Yíú' mau² ⁵k'ui tsau² ͵chí lo'. Must ask them then know.[81]
32. ⁵Ngo hai² ͵T'ong-͵yan, ͵m ͵chí-tò' ͵á. I am Chinese, not know.[1]

LESSON XIII.—Nautical.

1. This is a steamer. 呢隻係火船.
2. That is a sailing vessel. [steam-launch. 個隻係桅棒船.
3. There is no wind to-day. We must go in a 今日冇風要搭火船仔去咯.
4. How many passengers are there on board? 船上有幾多搭客呢.
5. Are there fully a thousand, or thereabout? 有成千個咁噃冇呀.
6. There are mostly Chinese, who are going to Singapore. 唐人多咯,去星架波嘅.
7. Where is the Chief Officer? 大伙呢, or 大伙喺邊處吖.
8. This is the Captain; that is the Second Mate. 呢個係船主,嗰個係二伙.
9. When shall we reach port? 幾時到埠呀.
10. This vessel can go very fast. 呢隻船行得好快.
11. How many li will it go in an hour? 一點鐘行得幾多里路度呢.
12. It will probably go over fifty li. 約嗼車得五十多里路.
13. Is it the Chief, or Second Engineer who has 係大車,嗎二車埋砦呢.
14. Do you ever sail? [gone on shore? 有時喺哩冇呀.
15. How much coal do you use a day? 一日喺幾多炭呢.
16. It depends upon the speed of the ship. 睇個隻船行快,嗎行慢嚟.
17. If she goes fast more is used; 車快就燒多.
18. If she goes slow then a smaller quantity. 車慢就燒少.
19. Come up on deck. Do not go near the funnel. 上船面喇 咪行埋烟通個處呀.
20. Is this a passage boat, or a ferry-boat? 呢隻渡船,嗎橫水渡呢.
21. It is a passage boat: this is a Kau-lung passage boat. 係渡呀; 呢隻係九龍渡呀.
22. When do you start; and when do you arrive? 你幾時開身,幾時到 (or 埋頭) 呢.
23. Where is the ladies' cabin; and the pantry? 女艙呢,管事房呢.
24. Call the carpenter, to mend that door. 叫鬪木佬嚟, 整翻好個度門.
25. The hinges are off, and the lock is broken. 個啲鉸用咗,個鎖又爛.
26. It has no lock. The key has been lost. 冇鎖囉. 唔見個條鎖匙咯.
27. Make another. 整過第二條喇.
28. First take a padlock, and lock the door securely. 先使把荷包鎖,鎖緊個度門至得.
29. How many sailors and firemen are there on board? 船上有幾多水手,幾多燒火呀.
30. What is the capacity of the vessel? 個船裝得幾多貨呢.
31. What is her draft? Seven feet eight. 食幾深水呀. 七尺八.
32. They are just going to hoist sail. 就扯哩囉.

LESSON XIII.—Nautical.

1. ₂Ni chek₀ hai² ʽfo-ₛhūn. This [C.] is steamer.
2. ʽKo chek₀ hai² ₛwai-ʼpʻáng* ₛshūn.[huí² lok₀. That [C.] is sailing ship.
3. ₂Kam yat₂ ʽmò ₂fung. Yíu² táp₀ ʽfo ₂shūn ʽtsai To-day no wind. Must by fire ship diminutive go.³²
4. ₂Shün shōng² ʽyau ʽkéi ₂to táp₀-ʽhák₀ ₂ni? Ship on have how many passengers eh?⁵³
5. ʽYau ₂shengt ₂tsʻín koʼ kòm¹ tsai² ʽmò á²? Have fully thousand ones so thereabouts not eh?²
6. ₂Tʻong-ₛyan ₂to loʼ. Hui¹ ₂Sing-káʼ-ₛpo keʼ. Chinese most.³¹ Going Singapore.¹⁵
7. Tái² ʽfo ₂ui? or Tái² ʽfo ʽhui ₂pín-shü¹ ₂á? Chief mate eh?⁵³ or Chief mate at what place eh?¹
8. ₂Ni-koʼ hai² ₂shün-ʽchü; ʽko-koʼ hai² yí² ʽfo. This one is Captain; that one is second mate.
9. ʽKéi ₂shí tòʼ fau² á²? What time arrive port eh?²
10. ₂Ni chek₀ ₂shūn ₂háng tak₂ ʽlò fái¹. [₂ni? This [C.] vessel go can very fast. [about eh?⁵³
11. Yat₂ ʽtím-₂chung ₂háng tak₂ ʽkéi ₂to ʽléi lò² ʽtò* One hour of-the-clock go can how many miles road
12. Yök₀ mok₀ chʻe tak₂ ʽug-shap₂ ₂to ʽléi lò². Probably steam can fifty more li road.
13. Hai² Tai² ₂chʻe, péi² yí² chʻe ₂mái chái¹ ₂ni? Is it the Chief engineer, or second engineer gone a-
14. ʽYau ₂shí ʽshai ʽléi ʽmò á²? Have times use sails have not eh?² [shore eh?⁵³
15. Yat₂ yat₂ ʽshai ʽkéi ₂to tʻán² ₂ni? One day use how much coal eh?⁵³
16. ʽTʻai ʽko chek₀ ₂shün ₂hang fái¹, péi² ₂háng See that [C.] vessel go fast, or go slow.
17. ₂Chʻe fái¹ tsan² ₂shíú ₂to. [mán² che. Steam fast then burn more.
18. ₂Chʻe mán² tsan² ₂shíú ʽshíú. Steam slow then burn little.
19. ʽSbōng ₂shün ʽmin* ₂lá. ʽMai ₂háng ₂mái Ascend shipʼs surface.²¹ Donʼt walk near funnel
   ₂yín ₂tʻung koʼ shü¹ á². that place.²
20. ₂Ni chek₀ ʽtò*, péi² ₂wáng-ʽshui ʽtò* ₂ni? This [C.] passage-boat, or ferry-boat eh?⁵³ [boat.²
21. Hai² ʽtò* á²; ₂ni chek₀ hai² ʽKan-₂lung ʽtò* á². Is passage-boat,² this [C.] is Kau-lung passage-
22. ʽNéi ʽkéi-₂shí ʽhoi-₂shan; ʽkéi-₂shí tòʼ (or You what time start; what time arrive (or touch
   ₂mái ₂tʻau) ₂ni? bows) eh?⁵³
23. ʽNui ₂chʻong ₂ni? ʽKwún-sz² ʽfong* ₂ni? Womenʼs cabin eh?⁵³ Pantry eh?⁵³
24. Kíú¹ tau²-múk₂-ʽlò ₂lai, ʽching-₂fán-ʽhò ʽko Call carpenter come, make again good that [C.]
   tò² ₂mün. door. [broken.
25. Koʼ-₂ti káu¹ lat₂ ʽcho, koʼ ʽso yau² lán². Those hinges come-off [s. of p. t.] the lock moreover
26. ʽMò ʽso loʼ. ₂M kín² ʽko ₂tʻiú ʽso-₂shí lok₀. No lock.³¹ Not see that [C.] lock key.³²
27. ʽChing kwoʼ tai²-yí² ₂tʻiú lá¹. [₂mün chí² tak₂. Make again another [C.]²² [before it-will-do.
28. ₂Sín ʽshai ʽpá ₂ho-₂pán ʽso, ʽso ʽkan koʼ tò² First use [C.] purse-lock lock firmly that [C.] door
29. ₂Shün shōng² ʽyau ʽkéi ₂to ʽshui-ʽshau, ʽkéi Ship on have how many sailors (lit. water hands);
   ₂to ₂shíú-ʽfo á²? how many firemen (lit. burn fire) eh?²
30. Koʼ ₂shün ₂chong tak₂ ʽkéi ₂to foʼ ₂ni? That vessel hold can how much goods eh?⁵³
31. Shik₂ ʽkéi ₂sham ʽshui á²? Tsʻat₂ chʻek₀ pat₀. Eat how deep water eh?² Seven feet eight.
32. Tsau² chʻe ʽléi loʼ. Just-about hauling-up sails.³¹

LESSON XIV.—Judicial.

1. I want to summons this man. 我想告呢個人.
2. He is a thief, and has stolen things of mine. 佢做賊偷我野咯.
3. Have you any witnesses? 你有證人冇吖.
4. I have witnesses; they have not come yet. 有證人；唔曾嚟咯.
5. Issue subpœnas for them to come. 出證人票, 叫佢嚟喇.
6. Has the constable arrived? 差人 (差役 or 綠衣) 到嗎.
7. He is at the Gaol. 佢喺監房.
8. This is the Yamen. 呢間衙門囉.
9. What Yamen? 邊間衙門呢.
10. The Consul's Yamen (Consulate). 領事官衙門囉.
11. Who is the present Consul? 而家邊個做領事官呢.
12. Mr. Fut (lit. Mr. Buddha). 係佛大人呀.
13. I will trouble you to present this petition to His Lordship, the Chief Justice. 多煩你同我遞呢張禀過按察司大人.
14. Kindly tell me what to say. 唔該你教我點講呀.
15. Are you Plaintiff, or Defendant? 你係原告, 嘅被告呢.
16. You must tell the truth, and only say what you have seen and heard yourself. 要照直講, 親眼見, 親耳聽, 至好講出嚟.
17. Then I must just say what I know myself. 噉我硬要講本身所知嘅事咯.
18. That is right; that is quite right; no mistake. 啱咯, 啱嘅咯, 冇錯咯.
19. Your evidence is not believed. 你口供唔入信呀.
20. The evidence given on both sides does not agree. 兩頭口供唔合吖.
21. One of you must be telling lies. 是但有個講大話咯.
22. No, I am not. All Hongkong knows about it. 唔係, 冇講大話. 通香港都知呢件事咯.
23. If you had said, "the whole neighbourhood knows," I might have believed you. 你話通街坊都知, 我或者可以信你吖.
24. Will His Lordship allow us to go to the temple and swear on a cock's head? 大人准我地去廟斬鷄頭唔准呢.
25. How many prisoners are there to-day? 今日有幾多犯呢.
26. There is a murderer, five thieves, two burglars, and three kidnappers. 有個兇手, 五個賊, 兩個打明火嘅, 三個拐帶嘅.

1. 差人 $_c$ch'ai $_,$yan, and 差役 $_c$ch'ai yik$_,$ are better than 綠衣 luk$_,$ yi, which is vulgar.

LESSON XIV.—Judicial.

1. ⁵Ngo ⁶söng kò³ ͼni-ko³ ͵yau. I wish prosecute this man.
2. ⁵K'ui tsò² ¹ts'ák*,¹ ͼt'au ⁵ngo ⁵ye lok₀. He is thief, steal my things.³²
3. Néi ⁵yau ching³-͵yan ⁶mò ͵á? You have witness not eh?¹
4. ⁵Yau ching³-͵yan, ͵m-͵ts'ang ͵lai lok₀. Have witness, not yet come.³²
5. Ch'ut͵ ching³-͵yau-p'iú¹ kíu³ ⁵k'ui ͵lai ͵lá*. Issue subpœnas call them come.²¹
6. ͼCh'áí͵yan (or ͼch'áí yik͵, or luk͵ ͵yí) tò³ má²? Police man (or police man, or green coat) arrived
7. ⁵K'ui ¹hai ͼkám-ͼfong. He at Gaol.   [eh?³⁵
8. ͵Ni ͼkán ͵ngá-ͼmún lo³. This [C.] Yamen.³¹
9. Pín-ͼkán ͵ngá-'mún* ͵ni? Which [C.] Yamen eh?⁵⁸
10. ⁵Ling-sz²-ͼkwún ͵ngá-'mún* lo³. Consul's Yamen.³¹
11. ͵Yí-ͼká ͼpin-ko³ tsò² ⁵Ling-sz²-ͼkwún ͵ni? At-present who is consul eh?⁵³
12. Hai² Fat͵ Tái²-͵Yan á³. It is Fat Mr. (lit. Mr. Buddha).²
13. ͼTo ͵tán ⁵néi ͵t'ung ⁵ngo tai² ͵ni ͼchöng ͼpan kwo³ On³-Ch'át₀-ͼSz Tái²-͵Yan. Much trouble you for me present this [C.] petition to Chief-Justice His-Lordship.
14. ͵M ͼkoi ⁵néi ͼkáu⁵ ⁵ngo ⁶tím ͼkong á³. Not deserve you teach me how speak.²
15. ⁵Néi hai² ͼYüu-kò³, péi² Péí²-kò³ ͵ui? You are Plaintiff, or Defendant eh?⁵³
16. Yíú³ chíú³ chik͵ ͼkong, ͼts'an ⁵ngáu kín³, ͼts'au ⁵yí ͼt'eng, chí³ ⁶hò ⁶kong ch'ut͵ ͵lai. Must according-to straight-forwardness speak; own eyes seen, own ears heard only good speak out come.
17. ⁶Kom ⁵ngo ngáng² yíú³ ⁶kong ⁶pún ͼshan ⁶sho ͼchí ke² sz² lok₀. Then I just must speak own person that know—matters.³²
18. Ngám lok₀; ͵ugám sái² lok₀; ⁵mò t'so³ lok₀. Right;³² right entirely;³² no mistake.³¹
19. ⁵Nei ⁶hau-ͼkung ͵m yap͵ sun³ á³. Your evidence not enter belief.²
20. ⁵Löng ͵t'au ⁶hnu-ͼkung ͵m hòp͵ á. Both sides evidence not agree.¹
21. Shí²-tán² ⁵yau* ko³ ⁶kong tái²-wá¹ lok₀. Certainly (of the two) there-is one speaking lies.³¹
22. ͵M hai²; ⁵mò ⁶kong tái²-wá¹; ͵t'ung ͵Hōng ⁵Kong ͼtò ͼchí ͵ui kíu² sz² lok₀. Not is, not speaking lies. All Hongkong even knows this [C.] matter.³²
23. ⁵Néi wá², "ͼt'ung ͼkái-ͼfong ͼtò ͼchí," ⁵ngo wák͵ ͼche ⁶ho ⁵yí sun³ ⁶néi á. You say, "all neighbourhood even knows," I perhaps might believe you.¹
24. Tái²-͵Yan ͼchun ⁵ngo-téi² hui³ ¹míú* ͼchám ͼkai ͵t'au ͵m ͼchun ͵ni? His-Lordship allow us go temple chop-off fowl's head not allow eh?⁵³
25. ͼKam-mat͵ ⁵yau ⁵kéi ͼto ¹fán* ͵ni? This day have how many prisoners eh?⁵³
26. ⁵Yau ko³ ͼhung-⁶shau, ⁵ng-ko³ ⁶ts'ák,¹ ⁵löng ko³ ⁶tá-ͼming-⁶fo ke³, ͼsám ko³ ⁶kwái-tái³ ke³. Have a murderer, five [C.] thieves, two [C.] burglars,¹⁵ three [C.] kidnappers,¹⁵ .

1. This is a rising yap͵ tone.

LESSON XIV.—Judicial.—(*Continued*).

27. Then there are a great number of cases. 噉有好多案件咯.
28. Those are the lawyers at the table. 坐埋檯嘅係狀師咯.
29. The case has been up for hearing several times; when will judgment be given? 審幾堂嚹, 幾時定案呢.
30. How do I know? Ask the Interpreter to enquire for you. 我點知呀. 拜託傳話同你問吓喇.
31. The case was tried at the Magistracy, and the Magistrate allowed the defendant to be bailed out. 係巡理廳審過, 大老爺准擔保被告出嚟咯.
32. Do you wish to arrest the man, or put execution in force against his goods? 你想拉個人, 或 (or 噉) 封佢貨呢.

LESSON XV.—Educational.

1. Ah! here we are. This is a Government Free School. [classes. 啊, 到咯, 呢間係皇家義學.
2. There are sixty scholars, divided into four 有六十個學生, 分四班嘅.
3. The master is a friend of mine, and a Chinese B.A. 個先生係我朋友, 佢係秀才.
4. Has he got any assistant? 有人幫教冇呢.
5. Not at present, but he wishes to engage one after the New Year. [I suppose. 現時冇, 但係過年想請個.
6. There will be holidays at the end of the year 年尾放假嚹吡.
7. Certainly, we Chinese think it of the utmost importance to keep the New Year. 定嘅喇, 我地唐人過年算至緊要嘅咯.
8. What book is this boy reading? 呢個呢, 讀也野書呢.
9. That is the Trimetrical Classic, the book that a Chinese boy first reads. 個部係三字經咯, 唐人細佬仔先讀個部嘅咯.
10. Then it is a simple book; for probably you proceed from the simple to the difficult. 噉就係淺書咯, 大概自淺而深嚟學嘅.
11. It is neither very simple, nor very difficult: the words are most of them simple, but the meaning is sometimes very abstruse. 又唔係幾淺, 又唔係幾深, 字大多淺嘅, 但意思有時好深嘅.
12. How many years have you been at school? 你讀幾多年書呢.

LESSON XIV.—Judicial.—(Continued).

27. ꜝKòm ˢyau ꜝhò ₜto on³-ꜝkín* lok₀.   Then have great many cases.⁸²
28. ¹T'so* ₘmái ꜝt'oi* ko³ hai² chong²-ₛsz lok₀.   Sit at table those are lawyers.³²
29. ꜝSham ꜝkéi ₛt'ong lo³; ꜝkéi-ₛshí ting¹ ou³ ₙni?   Try several sittings;³¹ what time fix case eh?⁵³
30. ˢNgo ꜝtím ₜchí á³? Pái¹-t'ok₀ ꜝch'ûn-ꜝwá* ₛt'ung ˢnéi ¹man* ˢhá ₜlá.   I how know eh?² Beg on-your-behalf Interpreter for you ask a-bit.³¹
31. ꜝHai ₜTs'un-ˢlei-ₜt'eng ꜝsham kwo³, Tái²-ˢlò-ₛye ꜝchun ₜtám-ꜝpò Péi²-kò³ ch'ut₂ ₜlai lok₀.   At Magistracy tried over, His-Worship allowed bail Defendant out come.³²
32. ˢNéi ꜝsöng ₜlái ko³ ₜyau, wák₀ (or péi²) ₜfung ˢk'ui fo³ ₙni?   You wish arrest the man, or seize his goods eh?⁵³

LESSON XV.—Educational.

1. O²! th³ lo³. ₙNi ₜkán hai² ₛWong-ₜKá yi²   Ah! Arrived.³¹ This [C.] is Government Free
   hok₂.   Study.
2. ˢYau luk₂-shap₂ ko³ hok₂-ₜshángt, ₜfan sz³   Have sixty [C.] scholars divided-into four
   ₜpán ke³.   classes.¹⁵
3. Ko³ ₜSín-ₜShángt hai² ˢngo ₛp'ang-ˢyau;   The teacher is my friend; he is B.A.
   ˢk'ui hai² Sau³-ₛts'oi.
4. ˢYau ₜyan ₜpong-káu³ ˢmò ₙni?   Have man assist teach not eh?⁵³
5. Yín²-ₛshí ˢmò, tán²-hai² ꜝkwo* ₙnín ꜝsöng   At-present no, but over (New) Year wishes engage
   ꜝts'eng ko³.   one.
6. ₙNín ˢméi fong³-ká³ lo³-kwá³.   Year end holidays³¹ probably.¹⁷
7. ꜝTing*-ke³ ₜlá, ˢngo téi² ₜT'ong-ₜyan kwo³   Certainly,⁵¹ ²¹ we Chinese passing (New)-year
   ₜnín sin³ chí² ꜝkau-yíú³ ke³ lok₀.   consider most important.¹⁵ ³²
8. ₙNi-ko³ ₜpi, tuk₂ mat₂-ˢye ₛshü ₙni?   This [C.] now, reads what book eh?⁵³
9. Ko³ pò² hai² ₛSám-Tsz²-ₜking lo³. ₜT'ong-   That [C.] is Three Character Classic.³¹ Chinese
   ₜyan sai³-ₜman-ꜝtsai ₛsín tuk₂ ko³ pò²   children first read that [C.]¹⁵ ³²
   ke³ lok₀.
10. ꜝKom tsau² hai² ꜝts'ín ₛshü lok₀. Tái²-ꜝk'oi   Then just is easy book.³² Probably from simple
    tsz² ꜝts'ín·yí ₜsham ₜlai hok₂ ke³.   to difficult come study.¹⁵
11. Yau² ₘm hai² ꜝkéi ꜝts'ín, yau² ₘm hai² ꜝkéi   Also not is very shallow, also not is very deep.
    ₜsham. Tsz² tái² ₜto ꜝts'ín ke³, tán² yí-   Characters greater-many shallow,¹⁵ but sense
    sz³ ˢyau-ₛshí ꜝhò ₜsham ke³.   have times very deep.¹⁵
12. ˢNéi tuk₂ ꜝkei ₜto ₜnín ₛshü ₙni?   You read how many years books eh?⁵³

LESSON XV.—Educational.—(*Continued*).

13.	I have studied between ten and twenty years.	我讀十幾年書咯.
14.	Then you must be very learned. [learned.	噉你就係好聰明嘅咯.
15.	Oh no! I cannot consider myself as very	唔係,我唔敢話自己好聰明嘅
16.	Where is your desk; where is your seat?	你個書位 (*or* 書憻, *or* 檯) 呢, 你嘅椅呢.
17.	I do not belong to this school, I have only come to visit—to see the teacher.	我唔係做學生吖,我不過嚟坐吓咡,嚟見吓個教館先生啫.
18.	Oh! probably you are a student. Have you passed any examinations yet?	啊你係讀書人咔,考過試唔曾呢.
19.	I have gone up several times, but have not graduated; my brother has taken his M.A.	考過兩三勻,未曾入,我大佬已經中舉咯.
20.	When does this class say its lessons?	呢班幾時念書呢.
21.	We Chinese don't do that way; when a boy knows his lesson he comes up and repeats it, the whole class does not come up at once.	我地唐人唔係噉嘅,一個讀熟,就一個嚟背,唔係成班一齊上嚟念嘅.
22.	If he does not know it, what then?	或唔識呢,點呢.
23.	He has to go back to his place and learn it well, if he is lazy he is beaten.	要翻去位讀熟咯,若係懶惰就打佢咯.
24.	These are reading the Four Books, and those the Five Classics.	呢啲讀四書,個啲讀五經.
25.	It would be well to hang up two more maps in this school of yours.	你呢間書館,掛多兩幅地理圖都好吖.
26.	How many have commenced to write essays?	有幾多個開筆作文章嘅呢.
27.	A number of the scholars can construct antithetical sentences I suppose.	有好多學生噲對'對咔.
28.	Bring ink, penholder, and pen nibs. I have brought them.	摖墨水,筆竿,筆嘴嚟喇. 拈嚟咯.
29.	Has the Government Inspector of Schools been to see this school?	皇家書館嘅監督,有嚟睇過呢間館冇呢.
30.	He has; he has been several times. He comes every now and then.	有,嚟過好幾勻咯,耐不耐都嚟嘅.
31.	How many names are there on the roll?	日記紙有幾多人名呢.
32.	There are sixty odd; two or three are absent on sick leave.	有六十幾個,有兩三個因有病告假.

LESSON XV.—Educational.—(*Continued*).

13. ʽNgo tnk₂ shap₂ ʽkéi ͵nín ͵shū lok₀. [lok₀. | I read ten odd years books.³²
14. ʽKòm ʽnéi tsan³ hai² ʽhò ͵tsʽung-͵ming ke⁾ | Then you even are very learned.¹⁵ ³²
15. ͵M hai², ʽngo ͵m ʽkòm wá² tsz²-ʽkéi ʽhò | Not am, I not dare say myself very learned.¹⁵
    ͵tsʽung-͵ming ke⁾.
16. ʽNéi ko⁾ ͵shū-ʽwai* (*or* ͵shū-ʽtʽoi*, *or* ʽtʽoi*) | Your [*C.*] desk (*or* table) eh ;⁵³ your seat eh ?⁵³
    ͵ni ; ʽnéi-ke⁾ ʽyí ͵ni ?
17. ʽNgo ͵m hai²-tsò² hok₂-͵sháng† ͵ǎ, ʽngo pat₂- | I not am school-boy,¹ I only come sit a-little-
    kwo⁾ ͵lai ʽtsʽo* ʽhá ͵che, ͵lai kíu⁾ ʽhá ko⁾ | while only,⁷ come see a-bit that teach school
    káu⁾-ʽkwún ͵Sín-͵Sháng (*or* ͵Seng†) che⁾. | gentleman (*or* contracted form) only.⁸
18. O² ! ʽnéi hai² tuk₂-͵shū-͵yan kwá⁾. ʽHán | Oh ! you are read-book-man probably.¹⁸ Ex-
    kwo⁾ shī² ͵m-͵tsʽaug ͵ni ? | amined passed not yet eh ?⁵³
19. ʽHáu kwo⁾ ʽlòng ͵sám ͵wan, méi²-͵tsʽang yap₂; | Examinations over two three times, not yet entered;
    ʽngo tái²-ʽlò ʽyí-͵king ʽchung* ʽkui lok₀. | my elder brother already passed M.A.³²
20. ͵Ni ͵pán ʽkéi-͵shi ním²-͵shū ͵ni ? | This class what time say lesson eh ?⁵³
21. ʽNgo-tei² ͵Tʽong-͵yan ͵m hai² ʽkòm ke⁾, yat₂ | We Chinese not are so,¹⁵ one [*C.*] learned thorough-
    ko⁾ tuk₂-shnk₁, tsau⁾ yat₂ ko⁾ ͵lai púi⁾, | ly then one [*C.*] comes back-It, (*i.e. says his*
    ͵m hai² ͵sheng† ͵pán yat₂ ʽtsʽai* ʽshöng | *lesson with his back to the teacher : so that he*
    ͵lai ním² ke⁾. | *cannot see the book the teacher holds*) not is
    | whole class one together up come say.⁵³
22. Wák₂ ͵m shik₂ ͵ni, ʽtím ͵ni ? | If not know eh, how then ?⁵³
23. Yiú⁾ ͵fán hui² ʽwai* tnk₂ shnk₂ lok₀, yök₂· | Must back go seat read thoroughly,³² if is lazy
    hai² ʽlán-to² tsau⁾ ʽtá ʽkʽui lok₀. | then beat him.³² [Classics.
24. ͵Ni-͵ti tuk₂ Sz⁾-͵Shū, ʽko-͵ti tuk₂ ʽNg-͵King. | These learning Four Books ; those learning Five
25. ʽNéi ͵ni ͵kán ͵shū-ʽkwún kwá⁾ ͵to ʽlöng fnk₂ | You this [*C.*] school hang more two [*C.*] maps
    téi² ʽléi-͵tʽò ͵tò ʽhò ͵á. | also good.¹
26. ʽYau kéi⁾ ͵to ko⁾ ͵hoi pat₂ tsok₀ ͵man-͵chöng | Have how many [*C.*] start (with) pens compose
    ke⁾ ͵ni ? | essays.¹⁵ ⁵³ [I-suppose.¹⁸
27. ʽYau ʽhò ͵to hok₂-͵sháng† ʽwúi tui⁾ ʽtui kwá⁾. | Have great many scholars can make antitheses
28. ͵Níng mak₂ ʽshni, pat₂ ͵kon, pat₂ ʽtsui ͵lai | Bring ink, pen holder, pen-nib come.²¹ Brought
    ͵lá. ͵Ním ͵lai lok₀. | come.³²
29. ͵Wong-͵Ká ͵shū-ʽkwún-ke⁾ ͵Kám-tuk₁, ʽyau | Government Schools' Inspector have come look
    ͵lai ʽtʽai kwo⁾ ͵ni ͵kán ʽkwún ʽmò ͵ni ? | over this [*C.*] school not eh ?⁵³
30. ʽYau ͵lai kwo⁾ ʽhò ʽkéi ͵wan lok₀, noi²- | Have come over good few times,³¹ now-and-then
    pat₂-ʽnoi* ͵tò ͵lai ke⁾. | also come.¹⁵
31. Yat₂-ʽkéi⁾-ʽchí ʽyau ʽkéi ͵to ͵yan ʽmeng* ͵ni ? | Roll have how many persons' names eh ?⁵³
32. ʽYau luk₂-shap₂ ʽkéi ko⁾; ʽyau ʽlöng ͵sám | Have sixty odd ones. Have two three [*C.*] be-
    ko⁾ ͵yan ʽyau peng²† kò⁾ ʽká⁾. | cause have sickness got leave.

Directions for the Rendering of English Grammatical Forms and Idioms in Chinese and vice versâ.

CAUTION.—The following directions and notes refer only to the Cantonese colloquial, though in many instances it will be found that the forms of expression and construction are equally applicable to both the vernacular and book-language.

I. Chinese being to a great extent a monosyllabic language, there is no change in the word itself such as takes place in English and many other languages by declension and conjugation. The following pages will shew how such forms are to be expressed in Chinese.

II. It is scarcely too much to say that position is everything in a Chinese sentence: it takes the place in a great measure that declensions and conjugations do in Western languages, and often shows to what part of speech the word belongs.

NOUNS.

NUMBER.

III. There is no difference, as a general rule, between the Singular and Plural of Nouns, as:—

人 ˏyan, *man.* 人 ˏyan, *men.*

IV. The Plural is understood from the sense, as:—

人嗌講說話 ˏyan 'wúi 'kong shüt₀ wá², *men can speak.*
雀嗌飛 tsök₀ 'wúi ˏféi, *birds can fly.*

Note.—This is not a very trustworthy test, as the above sentences might be rendered in the Singular in English.

Caution.—When speaking in Chinese do not attempt to render English Plurals in such a manner in Chinese as to show that they refer to more than one, unless particular attention is to be drawn towards the fact that more than one is spoken of, or unless No. V. is applicable.

V. The Plural is shewn to be meant in Chinese (and must be expressed in English) by the qualifying words, where such words occur, or by the general context, as:—

個啲人 ko' ˏti ˏyan, *those men.*
日日有幾個人嚟 yat₂ yat₂ 'yau 'kéi ko' ˏyan ˏlai, *several men come every day.*

NUMBER.

VI. The sign of the Plural, 哋 téi², is often added to the word man, 人 ͵yan; but such a combination is not always best rendered by "men;" but may be put into English in various ways, as:—

唔係我做嘅 人哋做嘅 ͵m hai² ˈngo tsò² ke', ͵yan téi² tsò² ke', *it was not I that did it; it was some one else.*

人哋係噉講 ͵yan téi² hai² ˈkòm ˈkong, *people say so.*

人哋講 ͵yan téi² ˈkong, *it is said*—on dit.

人哋話我人子係乜誰呢 Yan téi² wá² ˈngo ͵yan ˈtaz hai² mat, ˈshui⁰ ͵ni? *Whom do men say that I the son of man am?*

Note.— 人 ͵yan alone is also used in this sense, as:—

人話係噉 ͵yau wá² hai² ˈkòm, *it is said to be so* (i.e. men say it is so.)

VII. The Plural is sometimes formed by the reduplication of the Noun, as:—

人人知咯 ͵yan ͵yan ͵chí lok₀, *all men know.*

Note 1.—This repetition of the noun shows, as above, that the whole of the class for which the noun is a name—in its entirety, or the whole of the portion which is then the subject of thought or conversation is referred to.

Note 2.—Such a form may often be equally well, or better rendered into English as follows:—

人人都知 ͵yan ͵yan ͵tò ͵chí, *every one knows it.*

人人都做嘅 唔使怕吖 ͵yan ͵yan ͵tò tso² ke', ͵m ˈshai p'á² ͵á, *every body does it, you need not be afraid.*

VIII. Sometimes a collective and exhaustive phrase is used to express what in English would oftener be expressed by a simple Plural and Adjective, as:—

所有咁多人嚟齊嗮 ˈsho ˈyau kòm' ͵to ͵yan ͵lai ͵ts'ai sái', *all the men came.* (As many men as there were all came without an exception).

人呢 有咁多去咁多 ͵yan ͵ni, ˈyau kòm' ͵to hui' kòm' ͵to, *all the men went.* (Of the men, as many as there were went.)

IX. Very often a Numeral is added to the Noun (or Pronoun), owing to the necessary ambiguity when no Plural is otherwise expressed, when in English the simple Plural would be sufficient without any such device, as:—

佢六個嚟 ˈk'ui luk₂ ko' ͵lai, *they six came.*

Remark.—Without 六, 佢 might equally well mean *he, she* or *it.*

Note.— 等 ˈtang is given in some books as a sign of the Plural. It is booky and is not often used as an affix to the noun (or pronoun) in every day conversation.

NOUNS.

CASE.

X. Strictly speaking there is no case in Chinese; See No. I.

XI. There is then no means of distinguishing whether a noun (or pronoun) in Chinese is to be rendered in English by the Nominative, or Objective Cases or other Cases (for Possessive Case see No. XV, XVI, XVII, and XVIII) except by its position, or the obvious meaning, sometimes shewn by Prepositions, &c., as:—

我俾 ^{s}ngo ^{c}péi, *I give.*
俾我 ^{c}péi ^{s}ngo, *give me.*
俾過我 ^{c}péi kwo^3 ^{s}ngo, *give (it) to me.*

Remark.—The position of 我 ^{s}ngo shows whether it is *I*, or *me*, the same word being used in Chinese for both.

佢話我 ^{s}k'ui wá^2 ^{s}ngo, *he scolded me.*

Note.—佢話我 ^{s}k'ui wá^2 ^{s}ngo, may mean, *he scolded me*, or *he said to me*; but in the latter case there is another word added to amplify the meaning, as:—佢話我知 ^{s}k'ui wá^2 ^{s}ngo $_c$chí, or 佢話我聽 ^{s}k'ui wá^2 ^{s}ngo $_c$t'eng†, *he told me.*

XII. The position of the Subject or Object with regard to the verb may be stated generally to be the same as in an English sentence. See No. XIV though.

XIII. When two Verbs are used in Chinese to express what in English is shewn by one Verb, the Objective or Dative is placed between the two Verbs, as:—

佢話我聽 ^{s}k'ui wá^2 ^{s}ngo $_c$t'eng†, *he told me.*
佢打發我去 ^{s}k'ui ^{c}tá fát$_o$ ^{s}ngo hui^3, *he sent me.*

Remark.—The meaning of the above and similar phrases will be better got at by paraphrasing them, as:—

佢話我知 ^{s}k'ui wá^2 ^{s}ngo $_c$chí, *he told me*, i.e. he spoke to me about it in such a way that I acquired a knowledge of it, or more simply, he told me so that I knew about it, or, he informed me about it.

XIV. When particular attention is to be drawn to the object in the sentence, then it and its qualifying words take precedence of all other words in the sentence, as:—

個啲生意你做有幾耐呢 Ko^3 $_c$ti $_c$sháng yi^3 ^{s}néi tsò^2 ^{s}yau ^{c}kéi ^{t}noi* $_c$ui? *How long have you been in that business?*
嗰啲屋我賣咗咯 ^{c}ko $_c$ti uk$_o$ ^{s}ngo mái^2 ^{c}cho lok$_o$, *I have sold those houses.*

XV. The Possessive Case may be, and is often, expressed by the addition of 嘅 ke^3 to the Noun (or Pronoun), as:—

人嘅 $_c$yan ke^3, *man's.*

CASE.

人哋嘅 ,yan téi² ke', *men's.*
我嘅 ʻngo ke', *mine.*

XVI. 嘅 ke' is often understood and not expressed at all, as:—

我屋 ʻngo uk, *my house.*

XVII. A Personal Pronoun preceding a Noun may be in the Possessive case, or in apposition to the Noun which follows it, as:—

我事頭 ʻngo sz² 't'au*, *my master, or I, the master.*

Note.—In the latter case the tone may be more strongly marked, or a slight pause, represented in English by the comma, may be made after the Pronoun.

XVIII. The word 之 ʻchi is even used with certain words to mark the Possessive though essentially a book word; this occurs but seldom in the purest colloquial.

GENDER.

XIX. Many nouns in Chinese may be used with equal appropriateness as names for males or females, or for both combined. They are used with equal correctness for either, or for both males and females when there is no necessity to draw a distinction, or when the sex is known to the hearer. The context or sense will generally show whether a Masculine, or Feminine word, or one common to both Genders is to be used to convey the meaning of the Chinese word into English.

Such Chinese nouns are rendered Masculine or Feminine when it is desirable from a Chinese point of view to point out the difference.

有幾多人呢 ʻyan ʻkei ₍to ₍yan ₍ni?, *How many men are there?*, or *How many persons are there?*

佢老婆係西洋人 ʻk'ui ʻlò ₍p'o hai² ₍Sai ₍yōng ₍yan, *his wife is a Portuguese* (i.e. western ocean person.)

男女有幾多人呢 ₍Nám ʻnui ʻyau ʻkei ₍to ₍yan ₍ni? *How many persons are there, male and female?*

XX. The Genders are distinguished by prefixing the words 男 ₍nám, *male*, and 女 ʻnui, *female*, respectively to the noun when it refers to the human species, as:—

男人 ₍nám ʻyan*, *man.*
女人 ʻnui ʻyan*, *woman.*
男仔 ₍nám ʻtsai, *boy.*
女仔 ʻnui ʻtsai, *girl.*

XXI. The Genders are also distinguished by affixing 公 ₍kung and 婆 ₍p'o* respectively for males and females, as:—

GENDER.

伯爺公 pák₀ ‚ye* ‚kung, *an old man, a greybeard.*
伯爺婆 pák₀ ‚ye* ‚p'o, *an old woman, an old wife.*
媒人公 ‚múi ‚yan ‚kung, *a male go-between.*
媒人婆 ‚múi ‚yan ‚p'o, *a female go-between.*
主人公 ʻchü ‚yan ‚kung, *a master.*
主人婆 ʻchü ‚yan ‚p'o, *a mistress.*
事頭公 sz² ‚t'au ‚kung, *a master.*
事頭婆 sz² ‚t'au ‚p'o, *a mistress.*
屋主 uk, ʻchü, *a landlord.*
屋主婆 uk, ʻchü ‚p'o, *a landlady.*

Note.—伯爺 pák₀ ‚ye,* alone is Masculine and not common to both Genders.

事頭 sz² ‚t'au* alone is more generally Masculine, though applicable to both males and females.

屋主公 uk, ʻchü ‚kung is allowable, but seldom used. 屋主 uk, ʻchü alone is Masculine and Feminine.

XXII. 佬 ʻlò and 婆 ‚p'ò are used in the same way as 公 ‚kung and 婆 ‚p'o, as:—

蛋家佬 tán² ‚ká ʻlò, *a boatman.*
蛋家婆 tán² ‚ká ‚p'o, *a boatwoman.*

XXIII. The Genders are distinguished by the use of 公 ‚kung, or 牯 ʻkú for the Masculine and 嫲 ʻná for the Feminine for animals and birds, as:—

雞 ‚kai, *a fowl*; 雞公 ‚kai ‚kung, *a cock*; 雞嫲 ‚kai ʻná, *a hen.*
狗 ʻkau, *a dog*; 狗公 ʻkau ‚kung or 狗牯 ʻkau ʻkú, *a male dog*; 狗嫲 ʻkau ʻná, *a bitch.*
馬 ʻmá, *a horse*; 馬牯 ʻmá ʻkú, *a stallion* (馬公 ʻmá ‚kung is not used); 馬嫲 ʻmá ʻná, *a mare.*
牛 ‚ngau, *an ox, or cow*; 牛牯 ‚ngau ʻkú, *or* 牛公 ‚ngau ‚kung, *a bull*; 牛嫲 ‚ngau ʻná, *a cow.*

None.—嫲 ʻná is even applied to women when spoken of together with their children, as:—

兩仔嫲 ʻlöng ʻtsai ʻná, *mother and child.*
三仔嫲 ‚sám ʻtsai ʻná, *mother and children.*

The word 仔 ʻtsai is common to both genders here.

The Masculine for 嫲 ʻná used in such a manner is 爺 ‚ye, as:—

兩仔爺 ʻlöng ʻtsai ‚ye, *father and son.*

NOUNS.

GENDER.

三仔爺 ,sám 'tsai ,ye, *father and two sons;*
伯爺 ,pák。 ,ye*, and 老姆 ˚ló 'ná are used for father and mother; the latter is rather vulgar.

Remark.—It is remarkable, that with all the Chinese reverence for age and the superiority of those who are older over those who are younger, that in two or three Colloquial idiomatic phrases in common use the younger and inferior is named first before the elder and superior. Those given above for father and son, &c, and mother and child, &c, are two of them. Besides those there is 兩嬸母 ˚löng 'shani ˚mò, *two sisters-in-law,* (two brother's wives are thus styled), 兩弟兄 ˚löng tai² ,hing, *two brothers.*

Other words are sometimes given as expressing Gender ; but the beginner will find that they are but seldom used in *Colloquial,* and that the above are quite sufficient for all practical purposes, as far as the vernacular is concerned.

XXIV. 仔 'tsai used by itself is Masculine, as:—

係我仔 hai² ˚ngo 'tsai, *it is my son.*

女 ˚nui is the Feminine, as:—

我冇女 ˚ngo ˚mò ˚nui, *I have no daughters.*

In combination the compound word of which 仔 'tsai is a part is common to both Genders, if it refers to living objects (See Note), as :—

細伇仔 sai' ,man 'tsai, *a child.*
猪仔 ,chü 'tsai, *a little pig.*
狗仔 'kau 'tsai, *a puppy.*

Exceptions:— 男仔 ,mán 'tsai, *a boy,* Masculine.
女仔 ˚nui 'tsai, *a girl,* Feminine.
事仔 sz² 'tsai, *a "boy"* (servant) Masculine.

Note.— 仔 'tsai when used as a diminutive with Nouns, whether they apply to objects without sex, or living beings, has no effect on the Gender of the Noun, as :—

檯仔 't'oi* 'tsai, *a small table.*
部仔 'pò* 'tsai, *a pass book, or small manuscript book.*
艇仔 ˚t'eng 'tsai, *a small boat.*
亞臊仔 á' ,ò 'tsai, *a baby.*

XXV. It will be seen from the above that Gender is not generally either inherent to, or a necessary condition of a Chinese word. It is made use of to prevent confusion, and is often not used even where to our ears it seems as if confusion were already worse confounded without its use.

NOUNS.

GENDER.

Remark.—As a rule abstain from the use of sex-denoting words, when others will do equally well.

XXVI. Notice that in Chinese the names of the eight principal points of the compass are reversed in their order to what they are in English:—

1st. As to the order of naming the four cardinal points, instead of saying North, South, East, West, they say 東西南北 ‚Tung ‚Sai ‚Nám Pak‚, *East, West, South, North.*

2nd. The order of the component parts of the names of the other principal points of the compass, the names of which are compounded of the names of the four cardinal points, is reversed in Chinese, as:—

Chinese.	English.
東北 ‚Tung-Pak‚	*North-East.*
西北 ‚Sai-Pak‚	*North-West.*
東南 ‚Tung-‚Nám	*South-East.*
西南 ‚Sai-‚Nám	*South-West.*

XXVII. The word denoting relation is placed after the name of the individual. When names of relationship are used in connection with the name of the individual to whom this relationship belongs, or on whom it is bestowed, the name of the individual comes first and is followed by the name of the relationship, contrary to the practice in English, as:—

亞三叔 A' ‚Sám shuk‚, *uncle A Sam.*

Note.—It is politeness amongst the Chinese; 1st, to give a title of relationship to every one with whom they are acquainted; 2nd, to everybody to whom they wish to be polite, though perfect strangers to them even to the extent of never having set eyes on them before. The title of relationship thus bestowed on an individual, to whom the speaker is not in any way related, depends upon the age of the person addressed and of course the sex. The large terminology, which the Chinese possess for indicating the different shades of relationship, lends itself readily to all the gradations of respect considered necessary in thus addressing strangers and adopting them for the moment as relations. If the stranger looks older than was at first sight supposed and a favour is being asked, to which it may be thought a ready response is not likely from appearances to be given, a more respectful degree of relationship can readily be substituted for the one originally bestowed on the spur of the moment without sufficient thought. Do not therefore suppose that when a Chinese speaks of uncle and sister-in-law So and So that these people are his relations.

GENDER.

Remark.—To those who have been in the United States the analogy of this custom to that prevalent in the Southern States of addressing elderly negroes and negresses as Uncles and Aunts will be apparent.

XXVIII. 先生 ₛsín ₛsháng†, literally, *elder born*, but which is applied to teachers, is also used in the same way that *Monsieur* and *Herr* are in French and German respectively, as:—

陳先生 ₛCh'an ₛSín ₛsháng†, *Mr. Ch'an.*
係呀,先生 hai²-á', ₛSín ₛsháng†, *Yes, it is so, Sir.*
有個先生嚟 ʿyau kó' ₛsín ₛsháng† ₛlai, *a gentleman (or teacher) came.*
個先生係噉吩咐嚟做 ko' ₛsín ₛsháng† hai² ʿkom ₛfan fú' ₛlai tsò², *the gentleman directed it to be so done.*

Note.—The feminine of 先生 ₛsín ₛsháng† is 師奶 ₛsz ₛnái.

XXIX. Notice that titles in Chinese come after the name of the person, as:—

陳大人 ₛCh'an Tái² ₛyan, *His Excellency Ch'an.*

XXX. Notice that in Chinese the surname, as in our directories, precedes the other names which an individual bears, as:—

林亞有 ₛLam Á' ʿYau.

Note.—The 亞 Á' is not really a part of the name. The surname and name in the example if given alone would be 林有 ₛLam ʿYau, but this particle 亞 Á' is often prefixed to a Chinese individual name (They can scarcely be called Christian names) when it consists of only one syllable.

XXXI. Amongst phrases expressive of quantity occur such as 大半, tái² pún', 小半, ʿsíù pún', which mean two divisions of any thing, one being rather more than the half, and the other rather less.

ARTICLES.

XXXII. There are no Articles in Chinese.

XXXIII. 一 yat, is often used before a Noun where in English the Indefinite Article is used, and 個 ko', *that*, where the Definite Article would be employed in English, as:—

一個人 yat, ko' ₛyan, *a man.*
個人 ko' ₛyan, *the man.*

Note.—When the Numeral Adjective is thus used it must always be accompanied by the appropriate Classifier for the Noun, as above.

ARTICLES.

XXXIV. But the words which may take the place of the Article in English are often omitted, as:—

成日 ʻsheung† yat᷄, *the whole day.*

As in French no Article is used in Chinese before the word *half*, as:—

(一) 斤半 (yat᷄,) ʻkan púi¹, *a catty and a half.*

> Remark.—The 一 yat᷄ which might be thought to take the place of the Article is not often used in this connection unless particular attention is to be called to the *one*.

XXXV. The use of the English Definite Article *the* before an Adjective to express a class of persons, as *the virtuous*, is expressed in Chinese by 類 lui following the Adjective.

CLASSIFIERS.

XXXVI. A Chinese does not say as we do in English a board, a ship, a man, &c., but he generally uses some word, such for instance as, piece, just as we generally speak of a pair of trousers, a brace of snipe, a set of instruments, &c.

XXXVII. These words have been termed Classifiers, as certain ones are used for certain classes of objects and they cannot be used for others and *vice versa*. They have been described as constituting a secondary class of Nouns.

XXXVIII. They are largely used in the Chinese language, more especially is this the case in the colloquial. The Cantonese colloquial has its full share of them. Every Noun has its appropriate one or more. No confusion must take place in their use. Mistakes in the use of these Classifiers may insult a Chinese, as for instance to speak of a man as 一隻人 yat, chek₀ ʻyan instead of 一個人 yat, ko' ʻyan, 隻 chek₀ being only applied in pure *Cantonese* to animals, birds, and certain inanimate objects, &c., though in the Hakka Dialect the former mode of expression is quite correct. The learner must therefore pay the greatest attention to these important words, of which an alphabetical list of those in colloquial use with examples of the way in which they are used are given below.

XXXIX. Genuine Classifiers are those which are merely distinctive, or descriptive to a more or less degree of quality, but which have no numerical, or quantitative meaning attached to them. These distinctions are in many cases to the English ear so apparently arbitrary and subtle as to defy translation.

> Remark.—The pidgin English word '*piecee*' used before a Noun, as:—*one piecee man* is the rough attempt at what is untranslateable.

CLASSIFIERS.

Remark.—Many words which are constantly used in Combination with Nouns have had the conventional term of Classifiers applied to them by foreigners, though being merely either simple Nouns, or Nouns of Multitude. They have thus been grouped together with the Genuine Classifiers, the latter being "words which have no analogous terms in our own language" to represent them. The designation, thus given to a number of Nouns simply used in a partitive sense has been a misnomer, and at the same time misleading, as the distinctive character and beauties of the use of Genuine Classifiers has thus been lost sight of.

XL. The Classifier comes immediately before the Noun, the Numeral preceding it, as:—

一個人 yat, ko' ₅yan, a—man.

Note.—This rule applies to the cases where a Noun is only accompanied by a Numeral and consequently of necessity a Classifier as well.

XLI. The Classifier is used occasionally after the Noun. It is used after the Noun in enumerating articles as in a list, or catalogue, or when particular attention is to be drawn towards the number, but this is more the case in the book language. It is not every Classifier that can thus come after its Noun, when used alone with its Noun. 個 ko' for instance cannot be used after 人 ₅yan alone without a Numeral, but 隻 chek₀ can be used after 船 ₅shün, as:—

睇吓船隻有幾多個 ᶜt'ai ʰhá ₅shün chek₀, ᶜyau ᶜkéi ₅to ko', see how many boats (or vessels) there are. This sentence would, however, be generally used as a subordinate one in a compound sentence and not used alone as a simple question. The more natural form would be, 睇吓有幾多隻船喺處 ᶜt'ai ʰhá ᶜyau ᶜkéi ₅to chek₀ ₅shün ʰhai shü', see how many boats (or vessels) there are here.

Note.— 個 ko' can be used after 人 ₅yan when a Numeral comes between them, as :— 人(有)三個 ₅yan (ᶜyau) ₅sám ko', of men there were three.

XLII. A more common use of the Classifier after the Noun is when it is accompanied by a Numeral in which case any Classifier may follow its Noun, when particular emphasis is to be given to the Noun. It is then brought out with more distinctness than when rapidly said with the words in their common order. When so said it is well to make a momentary pause after the Noun, which would be represented in English by a comma, as:— '

人, 三個 ₅yan, ₅sám ko', three men, or of men there were three, or as to men there were three of them.

Note 1.—When the Classifier is used after the Noun it does not appear before the Noun as well.

CLASSIFIERS.

Note 2.—When a Classifier is used after a Noun whether it forms in this connection a Compound Noun, or is still simply a Noun and its Classifier, it sometimes happens in order to enumerate the number a Numeral and a Classifier again require to be employed; in such a case the same Classifier is never employed again, as:—

案件一宗 on' kín² yat, ,tsung, *a case at law*.
船位一個 ,shün 'wai* yat, ko', *a seat on board a boat*, (your place on board a boat, or ship that your passage entitles you to.)

It is also to be noted that if the order were to be reversed different Classifiers would require to be employed, as:—

一宗案件 yat, ,tsung on' kín², *and* 一個船位 yat, ko' ,shün 'wai*.

XLIII. If an Adjective is used with a Noun accompanied by a Classifier and Numeral, the Adjective is placed between the Classifier and the Noun, as:—

一隻大船 yat, chek₀ taí² ,shün, *a—large ship*.

XLIV. Adjectives and the Adverbs which qualify them, when unaccompanied by Numerals, precede the Classifier, as:—

大個人 taí² ko' ,yan, *a large man, or an adult*.
好長條街 'hó ,ch'öng ,t'íu ,kaí, *a very long street*.

XLV. When a Demonstrative Adjective Pronoun is used, as well as an Adjective, the former precedes the Classifier and the Adjective or Adjectives immediately precede the Noun (See Note to XLVI.), as:—

個張長椅 ko' ,chöng ,ch'öng 'yí, *that—long chair*.
呢部大紅書 ,ni pò' taí² ,hung ,shü, *this—large red book*.

XLVI. When two Adjectives are used without any Numeral to qualify the Noun, the Classifier may come between the two, as:—

大張長椅 taí² ,chöng ,ch'öng 'yí, *a—large long chair*.
咀細件青色衫 'ko saí' kín² ,ts'engt shik, ,shám, *that small—blue coloured jacket*.

Note.—It will be seen from the last example that XLV. has exceptions.

XLVII. But it is often better to put the Adjectives together, especially when a Demonstrative Adjective Pronoun is used, as:—

咀件細青色衫 'ko kín² saí' ,ts'engt shik, ,shám, *that—small dark blue jacket*.

CLASSIFIERS.

XLVIII. When a Numeral is used the Classifier either takes the first position after the Numeral, the Adjective then following it and preceding the Noun, or the Classifier comes after Numeral and Adjective —(See XLIX.), as:—

一間大屋 yat, ‚kán táí² uk,, *a large house.*
一大間屋 yat, táí² ‚kán uk,, *a large house.*

XLIX. When, however, the Adjective expresses Nationality it invariably immediately precedes the Noun and follows the Classifier, whether a Numeral Adjective appears in the sentence or not, as:—

一個英國人 yat, ko' ‚Ying kwok₀ ‚yan, *an—Englishman.*
咽個唐人 ‘ko ko' ‚T'ong ‚yan, *that—Chinese.*

L. The Demonstrative Adjective Pronoun and Classifier are often used together before a noun, the commonest combinations of the two being 呢個 ‚ni ko' and 咽個 ‘ko ko'.

Note 1.—Some Dictionaries give these two forms as *this* and *that.* This, however, is incorrect. The 呢 ‚ni represents the English "this," 個 ko' is untranslateable; unfortunately, according to our ideas, 呢 ‚ni cannot always be used alone, but must often be accompanied by a Classifier. 個 ko' is a Classifier and, being one of the commonest in use, has been supposed by Europeans to be a part of the word *this,* or *that,* as the case may be. That this opinion is erroneous and the view here enunciated is correct the change of classifier before the different classes of Nouns will show, for it is still adhered to when used with 呢 ‚ni and 個 ko', and the use of 呢 ‚ni and 個 ko' alone before a certain class of Nouns also proves it as:—呢回 ‚ni ‚wúi *this time,* 咽時 ‘ko ‚shí *that time.*

Note 2.—呢 ‚ni and 個 ko' are used alone before Nouns of time and place, as above, without the need of any Classifier. 個 ko' can be used alone oftener than 呢 ‚ni, as:—個人 ko' ‚yan, *that man.* It is often best rendered by *the* in English.

Note 3.—When more emphasis or rather more distinctness in pointing out the particular object meant is required the 個 ko' is repeated, as, however, the reduplication of 個 ko' i.e. 個個 ko' ko' is used to mean *every, each one,* or *all,* to prevent mistakes the former of the two, when one is to be a Demonstrative Adjective Pronoun and the other a Classifier, is put into an upper rising tone as 咽個 ‘ko ko' and consequently written in a slightly different form to indicate that it is a colloquial word. Note the difference between the two, as:—

個個條處咯 ko' ko' ‘hai shü' lok₀, *all (every one, or each one, is) are here.*
咽個人條處咯 ‘ko ko' ‚yan ‘hai shü' lok₀, *that—man is here.*

CLASSIFIERS.

Remark.—It will be well for the learner to bear the above remarks in mind, or else he will commit many egregious errors. For example it will be quite correct when asked, " Who did this?" to reply 呢個人 ,ni ko' ,yan or 呢個 ,ni ko' simply ; for 個 ko' is a Classifier that can be used with 人 ,yan; but it would be incorrect to say in answer to, "Which piece of thread did you drop?" to say 呢個 ,ni ko'; for 個 ko' is not the proper Classifier for thread, 條 ,t'íu must be used in this case.

LI. The Classifier must be used with 呢 ,ni, but 個 ko' can be used alone, as:—

呢間屋 ,ni ,kán uk,, *this—house*.
個屋 ko' uk,, *that house*.

Exception.—呢 ,ni (as well as 個 ko') is used alone before common Nouns of Place and Time.

LII. When the Demonstrative and Classifier are thus combined it often happens that the Classifier is dropped in the Plural, 啲 ,ti, the Plural addition to 呢 ,ni taking its place, as:—

呢隻船 ,ni chek₀ ,shün, *this—ship*.
呢啲船 ,ni-,ti ,shün, *these ships*.
啹棵樹 'ko ,p'o shü², *that—tree*.
啹啲樹 'ko-,ti shü², *those trees*.

LIII. If, however, the Classifier is retained in the Plural, it is then necessary that it should either be preceded by a Numeral, or that the word 幾 'kéi, *several*, should be used between the Demonstrative and the Noun, as:—

呢幾隻狗 ,ni 'kéi chek₀ 'kau, *these several—dogs*.
三十部書 ,sám-shap₂ pó² ,shü, *thirty—books*.

LIV. A Classifier may be used alone without its Noun. This is the case when the Noun has been already used in the sentence or in a preceding sentence. Or even if the context shows plainly then the Classifier may be used instead of the Noun, in which case it is best rendered in English by *one*. The Noun may then be dropped and its place taken by its appropriate Classifier, the classifier being used in this way as in English we might use an Adjective substantively, or a Numeral Adjective without its Noun, or a Personal Pronoun, or the indefinite Pronoun *one*, as:—

個隻船好大個 ko' chek₀ ,shün 'hò tái² ko', *the vessel was a very large one*.
有幾多人嚟 有三個嚟 'Yau 'kéi ,to ,yan ,lni? 'Yau ,sám ko' ,lni.
How many men came? There were three came.

CLASSIFIERS.

有一個叫做陳亞日 ₅yau yat₋ ko' kíú' tsò² ₅Ch'an Á' Yat₂, *there is one called Ch'an Á Yat.*

LV. The Classifier is often used where in English the Indefinite Article would appear, as:—

三個銀錢個月 ₅sám ko' ₅ngan 'ts'ín° ko' yüt₂, *three dollars a month.*

Remark.—The Rules given above are equally applicable to the Genuine Classifiers as well as to other words such as 'pair,' &c. commonly miscalled Classifiers when used in Chinese.

LVI. List of Classifiers and other words used before nouns.

1. 'Chán 盞 is applied to lamps, &c., as:—

一盞燈 yat₂, 'chán ₅tang, *a lamp.*
一盞火 yat₂, 'chán 'fo, *a lighted lamp.*
一盞油 yat₂, 'chán ₅yau, *a lamp-saucer full of oil.*

Note.—The Classifier 盞 'chán after 燈 ₅tang *lamp*, i.e. used in combination with it, as:—燈盞 ₅tang 'chán, forms a Compound Noun. It is the name given to the saucer-like portion of a Chinese lamp which holds the oil and wick.

2. Chek₀ 隻 is used for boats, ships, birds, animals, the hands, the feet, plates, balls of opium, &c., &c., as:—

三隻手 ₅sám chek₀ 'shau, *a pilferer.*
大隻船 tái² chek₀ ₅shün, *a large ship.*
八隻烟坭 pát₂ chek₀ ₅yín ₅nai, *eight balls of opium.*
一隻唐人狗 yat₂ chek₀ ₅T'ong ₅yan 'kau, *a Chinese dog.*

Exception.—The Classifier 個 ko' is more appropriate with 熊人 ₅hung ₅yan, *a bear.*

3. ₅Chí 枝 is applied to sticks, walking sticks, muskets, &c., pencils, pens, flowers, branches of trees, pieces of ginseng, cinnamon, &c., &c., forks, lamps, flags, masts, flagstaffs, candles, incense-sticks, a band or body of soldiers from two upwards, oars, &c., as:—

一枝筆 yat₂, ₅chí pat₂, *a pen, or pencil.*
一枝花 yat₂, ₅chí fá, *a flower.*
一枝樹枝 yat₂, ₅chí shü² ₅chí, *a branch of a tree.*

4. ₅Chong 椿 is used with 事情 sz² ts'ing, *an affair, a concern,* 'where the object of the speaker is to speak specially of one matter amongst a number. It is

CLASSIFIERS.

a means of particularising.' '件 kín² is much more common with 事情 sz² ₅tsʻing.'

5. ₅Chʻong 牀, *a bed*, is used with coverlet, mattress, and very rarely with carpet, as:—

一牀褥 yat, ₅chʻoug yuk₂, *a mattress.*

6. ₅Chöng 張 though it means to spread out is not applied only to articles that may be spread out, such as sheets, table-covers, mats, documents, letters, newspapers, (where the latter are unsealed or opened out, not closed in envelopes, or wrappers, &c.) curtains, carpets, beds, tables; but also to chairs, stools, &c., as:—

一張八仙檯 yat, ₅chöng pát₀ ₅ aín ʽtʻoi,* *an octagonal table.*
一張睡椅 yat, ₅chöng shui² ʽyí, *an easy chair.*
一張信 yat, ₅chöng sun³, *a letter* (not enclosed in an envelope).
打開咖張新聞紙 ʽtá ₅hoí ʽko ₅chöng ₅san ₅man ʽchí, *open out that newspaper.*

7. ₅Chʻöng 塲 is used for matters, or business, &c., as:—

一塲好心 yat, ₅chʻöng ʽhò ₅sam, *a good action.*
打一塲交 ʽtá yat, ₅chʻöng ₅káu, *to have a fight.*
打一塲官府 ʽtá yat, ₅chʻöng ₅kwún ʽfú, *to take a case to Court.*

8. 炷 Chü³ is applied to cash, or incense sticks, games of fán-tán, &c., as:—

一炷錢 yat, chü³ ₅tsʻín, *a pile,* or *heap,* or *lot of cash.*
一炷香 yat, chü³ ₅höng, *a cluster of incense sticks.*
一炷攤 yat, chü³ ₅tán, *a game of fán-tán.*

9. Fái³ 塊 is used with cloth, leaves of trees, or plants, mirrors, stones, wood, iron, copper, paper, &c., as:—

一塊樹葉 yat, fái³ shü² yíp₂, *a leaf.*
一塊木 yat, fái³ muk₂, *a piece of wood.*
一塊石 yat, fái³ shek₂, *a piece of stone.*

10. Fuk, 幅 is applied to walls, pictures, maps, pieces of ground, cloth, &c., as:—

一幅田 yat, fuk, ₅tʻín, *a field.*
一幅字 yat, fuk, tsz², *a scroll.*
一幅畫 yat, fuk, ʽwá*, *a picture.*

CLASSIFIERS.

11. ꜀Fún 欵 is applied to sections, or articles of laws, treaties, petitions, business, news, cash, cases in Court, &c., as:—

一欵事 yat, ꜀fún sz², *a matter of business.*
一欵生意 yat, ꜀fún ₌shäng† yi², *a business.*
一欵錢 yat, ꜀fún ₌ts'ín, *one kind of cash.*
一欵案件 yat, ꜀fún on² kín², *a case (in Court).*

12. ₌Fung 封 is used for letters and despatches, &c., as:—

一封信 yat, ₌fung sun², *a letter.*
一封文書 yat, ₌fung ₌man ₌shü, *a despatch.*

13. ꜀Há 吓 is used for sighs, and in a number of phrases where short periods of time are expressed, as:—

唞一吓氣 ꜀t'au yat, ꜀há héi², *to give a gasp, or sigh.*

14. ꜀Hau 口 is applied to small arms, to knives, swords, &c., and individuals, as:—

一口對面笑 yat, ꜀hau tui².mín² síu², *a revolver, or pistol, &c., &c.*
一口六口連 yat, ꜀hau lúk, ꜀hau ꜀lín* (or ꜀lím), *a six-barrelled revolver.*
拐帶人口 ꜀kwái tái² ₌yan ꜀han, *to kidnap.*
一口人 yat, ꜀hau ₌yau, *an individual.*
一口鐵鑊 yat, ꜀hau t'ít₀ wok₌, *an iron cooking pan.*
一口劍 yat, ꜀hau kím², *a sword.*
三口刀 sám ꜀hau ₌tò, *three knives.*

15. ꜀Hòm 砍 is applied to cannon, muskets, &c., as:—

一砍大炮 yat, ꜀hòm tái¹ p'áu², *a cannon.*
一砍鎗 yat, ꜀hòm ₌ts'öng, *a musket,* (&c.)
一砍米 yat, ꜀hòm ꜂mai, *a mortar full of rice.*

16. Ká² 駕 is used with fire-engines, carriages, jinrickshas, &c., as:—

一駕(馬)車 yat, ká² (꜂má) ₌ch'e, *a carriage.*
一駕水車 yat, ká² ꜂shui ₌ch'e, *a fire-engine.*

17. Ká² 架 is the Classifier of screens, pictures, pier-glasses, and whatever is framed, as:—

一架鏡 yat, ká² keng²†, *a mirror.*

CLASSIFIERS.

18. ˌKán 間 is applied to houses, or shops, and most buildings, rooms, monasteries, convents, temples, &c., &c., as :—

一間屋 yat, ˌkán uk, *a house.*
一間舖 yat, ˌkán p'ò, *a shop.*
七間房 ts'at, ˌkán 'fong*, *seven rooms.*
喺呢間廳 ʰhai 'ko ˌkán ˌt'engt, *in the sitting room.*

Exception.—Do not use 間 ˌkán before the word *pagoda.*

19. Kín² 件 is used for articles of clothing, matters of business, goods, such as balls of opium, cases in Court, cushions, &c., &c., mirrors, glass, &c., as :—

一件事 yat, kín² sz², *a matter of business.*
一件衫 yat, kín² ˌshám, *a jacket.*
一件案 yat, kín² on', *a case in Court.*
一件木板 yat, kín² muk, ˈpán, *a board.*

20. Ko' 個, 箇, 个 is used before the names of the human species and many inanimate objects; no definite rule can be laid down as to its use. On the other hand it is absurd to say that it can be used with 'other substantives when the correct classifier is unknown.'

一個人 yat, ko' ˌyan, *a man.*
一個鐘 yat, ko' ˌchung, *a bell.*

21. 'Kün 卷 is applied to pictures, maps, plans, books, as :—

書卷 ˌshü 'kün, *books.*
一卷地理圖 yat, 'kün tei² ˈléi ˌt'ò, *a map.*

22. 'Kwún 管 is applied to needles, nails, pencils, fifes, flutes, flageolets, pipes, water-pipes, quills, and tubular objects, &c., as :—

一管針 yat, 'kwún ˌcham, *a needle.*
一管簫 yat, 'kwún ˌsiú, *a flute.*

23. ˌMan 文 is used for cash and coins, &c., as :—

一文錢 yat, ˌman* 'ts'ín*, *a cash.*
一文銀錢 yat, ˌman* ˌngau 'ts'ín*, *a dollar.*

24. Mín² 面 is applied to gongs, looking-glasses, shields, &c., as :—

一面鑼 yat, mín² ˌlo, *a gong.*
一面鏡 yat, mín² keng't, *a looking-glass.*
一面藤牌碟 yat, mín² ˌt'ang ˌp'ái típ, *a rattan shield.*

CLASSIFIERS.

25. ₂Mún 門 is applied to pieces of artillery, anchors, rudders, matters of business, &c., as:—

一門炮 yat, ₂mún p'áu³, *a piece of artillery.*
一門生意 yat, ₂mún ₂shángt yí², *a business.*
一門事業 yat, ₂mún sz² yíp₂, *a matter of business.*

26. Nap, 粒 is applied to seeds, grains, buttons, grains of sand, shot, peanuts, fleas and other vermin, mites (of humanity), spots on the person, &c., as:—

一粒鈕 yat, nap, ʻnau, *a button.*
一粒星 yat, nap, ₂sing, *a star.*

27. ʻNgán 眼 is used with, or for, needles, lamps, nails, wells, &c., as:—

一眼針 yat, ʻugan ₂cham, *a needle.*

28. ʻPá 把 is used for articles that can be grasped though not confined to such things alone, as, knives, umbrellas, a head of hair, torches, a bunch of chopsticks, sheaves of grain, or large bundles of grass, firebrands (both literal and figurative,) as:—

一把刀 yat, ʻpá ₂tò, *a knife.*
一把遮 yat, ʻpá ₂che, *an umbrella.*

29. ʻPán 板 is applied to *tableau vivant*, as:—

一板色 yat, ʻpán shik₂, *a tableau vivant.*

30. P'at, 匹 is used for horses, &c., as:—

一匹馬 yat, p'at, ʻmá, *a horse.*

31. ₂P'ín 篇 is used with essays of all kinds, as:—

一篇文章 yat, ₂p'ín ₂man ₂chöng, *an essay.*

Note.—篇 ₂p ín is here used in a different manner to what it is when it is used with the word book, as:— 一篇書 yat, ₂p'ín ₂shü. In this connection it is not a Classifier but means a *page* of a book.

32. ₂P'ò 舖 is used for trees, vegetables, &c., as:—

一舖樹 yat, ₂p'o shü², *a tree.*
一舖菜 yat, ₂p'o ts'oi³, *a vegetable.*

33. ₂P'ò 鋪 is used with bed, as:—

一鋪牀 yat, ₂p'ò ₂ch'ong, *a bed.*

34. Pò² 部 is used for books, as:—

幾部書 ʻkéi pò² ₂shü, *several books.*

CLASSIFIERS.

35. 'Pún 本 is used for volumes of books, acts of plays, &c., as:—
　一本書 yat, 'pún ,shü, *a book*.
　一本戲 yat, 'pún héi', *an act (of a play)*.

36. P'ung² 甏 is applied to bad odours, and walls, &c., as:—
　一甏隨 yat, p'ung² ,ts'ui, *a stench*.
　一甏墻 yat, p'ung² ,ts'öng, *a wall*.

37. ,Shing 乘 is applied to carriages, sedan chairs, &c., as:—
　一乘轎 yat, ,shing 'kiú*, *a sedan chair*.
　一乘車 yat, ,shing ,ch'e, *a carriage*.

38. 'Sho 所 is used with buildings, places, &c., as:—
　一所花園 yat, 'sho ,fá ,yün, *a garden*.

39. Shü'† 處 is used with places, &c., as:—
　一處地坊 yat, shü'† téi² ,fong, *a place*.

40. Tái' 帶 is used with walls, trees, &c., as:—
　一帶圍墻 yat, tái' ,wai ,ts'öng, *a surrounding wall*.
　一帶樹木 yat, tái' shü² muk,, *a row of trees*.
　一帶水 yat, tái' 'shui, *a neighbourhood*, or *locality*.

41. Tát₀ 笪 is used for spots, or marks, &c., &c., as:—
　一笪地坊 yat, tát₀ téi² ,fong, *a spot, a place*.
　一笪印跡 yat, tát₀ yan' tsik,, *a mark*.

42. ,Tau 篼 is used as a Classifier of trees, as:—
　一篼樹 yat, ,tau shü², *a tree*.

43. 'Tím 點 is applied to dots, spots, hours, drops of fluid, souls, inspirations, actions of the mind, &c., as:—
　一點靈魂 yat, 'tím ,ling ,wan, *a soul*.
　一點靈機 yat, 'tím ,ling ,ke, *a sudden inspiration, a happy thought*.
　一點好心 yat, 'tím 'hó ,sam, *a kind heart*.

44. 'Ting 頂 is applied to hats, caps, sedan chairs, &c., as:—
　一頂轎 yat, 'ting 'kiú*, *a sedan chair*.
　一頂帽 yat, 'teng† 'mò*, *a hat*.

Note.—This word is often pronounced 'teng. It is pronounced 'ting or 'teng when speaking of a sedan chair; and 'teng when referring to a hat or cap. It is however very generally in colloquial pronounced 'neng when used with the word *hat*, as:—yat, 'neng 'mò*, *a hat*.

CLASSIFIERS.

45. T'íp₀ 貼 is applied to charms, plasters, &c., as:—

一貼符 yat, t'íp₀ fú², a charm.
一貼膏藥 yat, t'íp₀ ₍kò yök₂, a plaster.

46. ₍T'íú 條 is used for a handkerchief, a single stocking, a pair of trousers, a road, a street, snakes, whips, girdles, fish, worms, rivers, pieces of thread, sticks, pieces of wood, rattan, bamboo, reins, a single body or person, a passage or hall in a house, villages, seas, &c., as:—

一條路 yat, ₍t'íú lò², a road.
一條河 yat, ₍t'íú ₍ho, a river.
一條蛇 yat, ₍t'íú ₍she, a snake.
一條魚 yat, ₍t'íú 'yü*, a fish.
一條褲 yat, ₍t'íú fú', a pair of trousers.
一條柴 yat, ₍t'íú ₍sháí†, a piece of wood.

Note.—With regard to the last two examples, the first might be translated, a *length of trousers*, that being the Chinese equivalent of *pair* when that word is applied to trousers. In the same way the second might be rendered a *length of wood*, or *stick of wood*, i.e. a piece of wood that is not simply square, or round, or flat; but whose predominating quality is length.

47. 'Tö, or 'To 朶 is applied to flowers, flames of fire, or the flame of a lamp, &c., as:—

一朶花 yat, 'tö ₍fá, a flower.
一朶火 yat, 'tö 'fo, a light.

48. Tò³ 道 is applied to charms, Imperial commands, &c., &c., as:—

一道符 yat, tò³ ₍fú, a charm.
一道聖旨 yat, tò² shing³ 'chí, an Imperial command.
一道文書 yat, tò² ₍man ₍shü, a despatch.

49. Tò² 度 is not always applied to places over, or through which one can pass. It is used for bridges, doors, an official residence, or office, a despatch, seas, rivers, embankments, staircases, &c., as:—

一度橋 yat, tò² ₍k'íú, a bridge.
一度門 yat, tò² ₍mún, a door.
一度海 yat, tò² 'hoi, a sea.
一度樓梯 yat, tò² ₍lau ₍t'ai, a staircase.

50. ₍T'oi 檯 is applied to theatrical plays, &c., as:—

一檯戲 yat, ₍t'oi héi³, a play.

CLASSIFIERS.

51. ₅T'ong 堂 is applied to curtains, suits, ladders, &c., as :—

一 堂 蚊 帳 yat₃ ₅t'ong ₅man chòng², *a mosquito net.*

一 堂 梯 橫 yat₃ ₅t'ong ₅t'ai ₅wáng, *a ladder.*

52. Tso² 座 is applied to houses, pagodas, temples, hills and mountains, cities, idols (images), lighthouses, forts, &c., as :—

一 座 廟 yat₃ tso² 'miú*, *a temple.*

一 座 塔 yat₃ tso² t'áp₀, *a pagoda.*

一 座 樓 yat₃ tso² 'lau*, *a house.*

一 座 祠 堂 yat₃ tso² ts'z ₅t'ong, *a monastery.*

53. ₅Tsün 尊 is used with idols, Buddhas, and sometimes with cannon, as :—

一 尊 佛 yat₃ ₅tsüu fat₃, *a Buddha.*

Note.—This Classifier is only used with the word cannon by literary men. No. 25 is the one oftener and more commonly used.

54. ₅Tsung 宗 is applied to cases in court, affairs, business matters, &c., as :—

一 宗 事 幹 yat₃ ₅tsung sz² kon', *a matter.*

一 宗 案 件 yat₃ ₅tsung òn' kin², *a case.*

55. Tün² 段, or 端 ₅Tün is applied to pieces of news, or pieces of ground, essays, &c., as :—

一 段 文 字 yat₃ tün² ₅man tsz², *an essay.*

一 段 古 yat₃ tün² 'kwú, *a story of olden times.*

56. ₅T'ün 團 is applied to earth, cotton, snow, whatever can be held in the hand, and harmonious feelings, good intentions, &c., &c., as :—

一 團 線 yat₃ ₅t'ün sín', *a roll of thread.*

一 團 坭 yat₃ ₅t'ün ₅nai, *a lump of earth.*

一 團 和 氣 yat₃ ₅t'ün wo² hei', *a peaceful time.*

57. Wai² 位 is applied to respectable persons, &c., as :—

三 位 先 生 sám 'wai* Sín ₅Shángt, *three gentlemen.*

一 位 女 客 yat₃ 'wai* ₅núi hák₀, *a lady visitor.*

一 位 神 yat₃ 'wai* ₅shan, *a god.*

一 位 菩 薩 yat₃ 'wai* ₅p'ò sát₀, *an idol.*

一 位 官 府 yat₃ 'wai* ₅kwún 'fú, *an official.*

58. ₅Yün 員 is applied to officers of government, as :—

一 員 案 察 yat₃ ₅yün òn' ts'át₀, *a judge.*

一 員 欽 差 yat₃ ₅yün ₅yam ₅ch'ái, *an ambassador.*

59. ₅Yün 圓 is applied to coins, as :—

一 圓 銀 yat₃ ₅yün 'ngan*, *a dollar.*

CLASSIFIERS.

Note.—It may be noted that some of the above words had better not, in some connections, be considered as Classifiers; but are sometimes better rendered in English partitively.

LVII. Besides the above the following may sometimes be heard.

1. ͵Chü 株 as a Classifier of trees.

Note.—This is a book language Classifier; but it is occasionally used in conversation by literati.

2. ͵Kan 根 as a Classifier of trees.

Note —This is used by natives of other parts of China, and is not a pure Cantonese use of the word.

LVIII. Avoid the following in Colloquial.

1. ʽMéi 尾, a tail, which is used in the book language as a Classifier of fish, as:—鮀魚十尾 ʽwán ʽyü* shap͵ ʽméi, ten tench. In the Colloquial 條 ͵tʽíu should be used.

2. Foʼ 顆 a clod, used in the book language as a Classifier of pearls, beads and similar articles. 粒 nap͵ is the word which should be used in the Colloquial.

3. ͵Fong 方 a square, is used in the book language as a Classifier of squares of ink, inkstones, junkets of beef, mutton, pork, &c.

Note.—This latter however might be rendered in English by the words *square*, or *piece*, and might be looked upon as a partitive construction.

LIX. The following is a list of words generally included in Lists of Classifiers, but omitted in this book from the List of Genuine Classifiers given above, and for the most part consisting of Nouns used partitively.

1. Chʽan² 陣 is used with showers, times, noises, fits of temper, gusts, puffs, and flashes of light, as:—

一陣風 yat͵ chan² ͵fung, *a gust of wind*.
一陣光 yat͵ chan² ͵kwong, *a flash of light*.
一陣雨 yat͵ chan² ʽyü, *a shower*.
一陣火氣 yat͵ chan² ʽfo héiʼ, *a fit of anger*.

2. Chát₀ 札 is used for rolls, or packages, bunches of flowers, bundles of papers and letters, as:—

一札紙 yat͵ chát₀ ʽchí, *a bundle of paper, or papers*.
一札花 yat͵ chát₀ ͵fá, *a bouquet*.
啯札野 ʽko chát₀ ʽye, *that bundle of things*.

3. Chü² 炷 is used with regard to incense, as—

一炷香 yat͵ chü² ͵hŏng *a bunch of incense sticks*.

CLASSIFIERS.

4. Chün' 串 is applied to anything strung together, as a string of cash, or beads, as:—

一串珠 yat, chün' ,chü, *a string of beads.*

5. Fü' 副 is used for sets of beads, tools, buttons, bedding, writing materials, bed-boards, coffins, &c., as:—

一副檯椅 yat, fü' ,to'i 'yí, *a set of chairs and tables.*
一副架撑 yat, fü' ká' ,ch'áng, *a set of implements.*
一副長生 ynt, fü' ,ch'öng ,shángt, *a coffin, or set of coffin boards*, (generally applied to one when bought before death.)

6. ,Hong 行 a column of words, or row of objects, or men, &c., as:—

一行字 ynt, ,hong tsz², *a column of character.*

7. 'Kwú 股 is applied to shares in business and heads of essays, &c., as:—

一股份 yat, 'kwú fan², *a share* (in business).
一股生意 yat, 'kwú ,shángt yí', *a business of one share.*
一股文章 yat, 'kwú ,man ,chöng, *a head of an essay.*

8. Kui' 句 is applied to sentences, phrases, &c., as:—

一句說話 yat, kui' shüt, wá², *a sentence.*

9. Kuk, 局 is applied to games of chess, to gentry and people of a neighbourhood, or company for public business, &c., as:—

一局棋 ynt, kuk, ,k'éi, *a game of chess.*
一局紳衿 ynt, kuk, ,shan ,k'am, *the body of gentry.*
一局百姓 yat, kuk, pák, sing', *the body of the people.*

10. ,Kw'an 羣 is used for droves, flocks, herds, crowds, schools of fish, flights of flies, &c., as:—

一羣綿羊 yat, ,kw'an ,mín ,yöng, *a flock of sheep.*
一羣烏蠅 yat, ,kw'an ,wú ,ying*, *a lot of flies.*
一羣人 ynt, ,kw'an ,yan, *a crowd of men.*

11. ,P'at, 疋 is applied to pieces of cloth, silk, game, &c., as:—

一疋布 yat, p'nt, pó', *a piece of cloth.*

12. ,Páu 包 is used for bales, bundles, or packages, &c., as:—

一包書 vat, ,páu ,shü, *a bundle of books.*
一包衣物 ynt, ,páu ,yí mat, *a bundle of clothing.*
一包貨 vat, ,páu fo', *a bale of goods.*

13. Tám' 担 is applied to burdens, weights, &c., as:—

一担水桶 yat, tám' 'shui 't'ung, *a pair of water pails.*
一担籮 yat, tám' ,lo, *a couple of carrying baskets.*

CLASSIFIERS AND ADJECTIVES.

CLASSIFIERS.

一担貨物 yat, tám' fo' mat, *a picul of goods,* (i.e. a hundred catties, or 133 lbs.)
一担山水 yat, tám' ‚shán ‘shui, *a load of hill water.*
八担炭 pát₀ tám' t'án', *eight piculs of coal,* (nearly half a ton.)

14. Tui² 隊 is used for a crowd of people, a flock of birds, or animals, a school of fish, a fleet of ships, &c., &c., as:—

一隊人 yat, tui² ‚yan, *a crowd of people.*
一隊雀鳥 yat, tui² tsok₀ ‘niú, *a flight of birds.*
一隊魚 yat, tui² ‘yü", *a school of fish.*

ADJECTIVES.

LX. The Adjective, when used attributively, or predicatively, occupies the same position in the sentence that it does in an English one.

Exception.—It is the first word in the phrase, or sentence when the principal, or only idea used is in regard to the quality expressed by the Adjective. The Chinese habit of leaving out even the verb in a sentence accounts often for the Adjective taking the foremost place, as:—

熱過頭 yit, kwo' ‚t'au, *it is too hot.*
長得滯 ‚ch'öng tak, tsai², *it is too long.*
短咯,唔夠使 ‘tün lok₀, ‚m kau' ‘shai, *it is short, there is not enough for use.*

Note.—The verb is not always necessary in Chinese when it is used predicately in English, therefore the position of the Adjective with regard to the Noun shows whether it (the Adjective) is used in the predicate or otherwise. When the latter is the case it follows the Noun, and it precedes it when it is used attributively.

Exceptions.—The Adjective follows as well as precedes the Nouns in a few cases in Chinese. In these cases the meaning differs according to the position of the Adjective before or after the Noun.

荔枝乾 ‘lai ‚chi ‚kon, *dried li-chis* (the dried fruit).
乾荔枝 ‚kon ‘lai ‚chi, *a dry (without juice) li-chi.*
龍眼乾 ‚lung ‘ngán ‚kon, *dried lung-ngans* (as above).
乾龍眼 ‚kon ‚lung ‘ngán, *dry lung-ngans* (as above).
魚生 ‚yü ‚shángt, *a dish composed of uncooked fish dished up with condiments is so termed.*
生魚 ‚shángt 'yü", *fresh fish.*

LXI. The Comparative Degree of Adjectives is formed by the word 啲 ‚ti being added to the Adjective, as:—

好 ‘hò, *good,* 好啲 ‘hò ‚ti, *a little better,* or *better.*

ADJECTIVES.

Note.—This might be called a qualified Comparative; for it is limited in its meaning and does not have the fulness of meaning of the English Comparative. It also differs from the Comparatives given below. In common conversation, however, its limited meaning is often lost sight of.

LXII. The words 更 kang' or 重 chung² are prefixed to the Adjective in its Positive Degree and often in its Qualified Comparative Degree and form a Comparative, being identical with the English Comparative, as:—

大 tái², *large*; 更大 kang' tái², *or* 更大啲 kang' tái² ti, *larger*.

Note.—啲 ti is also used after the Adjective sometimes when 更 kang' and 重 chung² have already been employed before the Adjective, as:— 更好啲 kang' ʻhò ti, 重好啲 chung² ʻhò ti, *better*. These forms are both quite admissible and in common use.

LXIII. What French Grammarians call the Comparative of Equality is expressed in Chinese as follows:—

個隻咁大 ko' chek̬ kom² tái², *as large as that one*.
好似呢條咁長 ʻhò ˢtsz ˬní ˌtʻíú kom² ˬchʻöng, *as long as this one*, (lit. *like this one so long*).

LXIV. The Repeated Comparative is often rendered by 越 yüt̬ as:—越大越好 yüt̬ tái² yüt̬ ʻhò, *the larger the better*.

Note.—That it is to be rendered in English by the Definite Article *the* and the Comparative.

LXV. The Repeated Comparative is sometimes rendered without the 越 yüt̬ the juxtaposition of the two Comparatives showing well enough what is meant, as:—

大啲好啲 tái² ti ʻhò ti, *the larger the better*.

Note.—It is perhaps as well or better to render the above, as, *it would be better to be larger*.

LXVI. The Superlative Degree is formed by prefixing 至 chí², 頂 ʻting, 極 kik̬, or 上 shöng² to the Adjective, as:—

長 ˬchʻöng, *long*; 至長 chí² ˬchʻöng, *longest*.
好 ʻhò, *good*; 頂好 ʻting ʻhò, *the best*.
吤 ˈyai, *bad*; 極吤 kik̬ ˈyai,* *the worst*.
好 ʻhò, *good*; 上好 shöng² ʻhò, *the best*.

Remark. The last form is also used as a Comparative, as:— 上貨 shöng² fo' *superior goods*.

Note 1.— 第一好 tái² yat̬ ʻhò, literally, "No. 1 good," is sometimes used when in English we would say, *the best*.

ADJECTIVES.

Note 2.—十分 shap₂ ₍fan used before an Adjective should be rendered by *very* and the Superlative Degree, or the latter alone as the sense may direct, as :—

十分遠 shap₂ ₍fan ʻyün, *very far*, or *very far indeed*.
十分好 shap₂ ₍fau ʻhò, *very good*, or *the best*.

Note 3.—In a sentence with a Verb *best* is better relegated to the end of the sentence though it is permissible to put it at the beginning, as :—至好嘅做 chi² ʻhò ʻkom tsò², or 嘅做至好咯 ʻkom tsò² chi² ʻhò lok₀, or 極好係嘅做 kik₂ ʻhò hai² ʻkom tsò², or 嘅做係極好 ʻkom tsò² hai² kik₂ ʻhò, *it is best to do it so*, or *to do it so is best*. But with 十分好 shap₂ ₍fan ʻhò and 第一好 tai² yat₃ ʻhò and 頂好 ʻting ʻhò it must be placed at the end.

The reason of 十分 shap₂ ₍fan being thus employed is that, the decimal system being in use amongst the Chinese, ten parts, or divisions of any thing form in a Chinese mind the idea of completeness: so 十分好 shap₂ ₍fan ʻhò gives a Chinese the idea that whatever is spoken of in that way is completely, entirely—in all its tenths, which go to make up the whole, good; or rather that the quality of goodness is, as it were, divided into ten parts, certain things to which the quality of goodness appertains only possessing certain tenths of this goodness, whereas the one to which 十分 shap₂ ₍fan is applied possesses the goodness in its fulness of ten parts. It is curious to notice, however, that exaggeration has rendered it necessary to introduce a still stronger form than 十分 shap₂ ₍fan, when the latter form expresses, as above stated, completeness: completeness or entirety having been used in an exaggerated sense when it was not strictly applicable, a still stronger expression has been felt to be necessary to express the idea of completeness, or entirety in a higher or the highest degree, hence the phrase 十二分(好) shap₂ yi² ₍fan (ʻhò), which might be rendered by *the very very (best)*.

Remark.—The Adjective itself undergoes no change, it will be noticed: this will best be seen by literally translating the forms which represent the Comparative and Superlative Degrees in English, as:

好 ʻhò, *good*, 好啲 ʻhò ₍ti, *good a-little-more*; 更好 kang' ʻhò, *more good*.
十二分好 shap₂ yi² ₍fau ʻhò, *twelve parts good, &c. &c.*

LXVII. When the word *than* is used in English with a Comparative, the Adjective in Chinese need not be accompanied by any sign of the Comparative Degree—the *than* showing conclusively that it cannot be put into the Positive Degree in English, as:—

乾過咱個 ₍kòn kwo' ʻko ko', *dryer than that* — (one).

Note.—According to the genius of the Chinese language there is no necessity, when the sense is shewn plainly enough by the context, to add words. One reason of this may be

ADJECTIVES.

that a multiplicity of little words has a tendency to obscure the meaning in a monosyllabic language devoid of inflexion and conjugation.

At the same time both 啲 ˏti and 更 kang' may be used as well when 過 kwo' appears in a sentence, as:—

更大過呢啲 kang' tái² kwo' ˏni ˏti, *larger than these.*
長啲過嗰個 chōng ˏti kwo' ˈko ko', *longer (or a little longer) than that — (one).*
更大啲過佢嘅 kang' tái² ˏti kwo' ˈk'ui ke', *larger than his (or rather larger than his.)*

The use of 啲 ˏti and 更 kang' often give more force to the Comparative when used with 過 kwo' forming to some extent a Comparative of Intensity, as opposed to a simple Comparative.

LXVIII. Many Adjectives are formed from Nouns by the addition of 嘅 ke', as:—

英國 ˏYing Kwok₀, *England.* 英國嘅 ˏYing Kwok₀ ke', *English.*

Note 1.—The 嘅 ke' is, however, often dropped, and it is often better to drop it when the Adjective is used attributively, as:—

英國人 ˏYing Kwok₀ ˏyan, *an Englishman.*
英國野 ˏYing Kwok₀ ˢye, *English things.*

Note 2.—When used predicatively, however, it is better to retain the 嘅 ke', as:—

佢係英國嘅人 ˈk'ui hai² ˏYing Kwok₀ ko' ˏyan, *he is an Englishman.*

Remark.—The 嘅 ke' is sometimes useful in differentiating the meaning of words or terms which might otherwise be confused together, as for example:—

大人 Tái² ˏyan, *His Excellency, His Lordship, &c.,* or it may be translated by its primary meaning that of *a large or great man;* but if 嘅 ke' be inserted any ambiguity is gone at once, it cannot then be a title, as:—大人嘅 tái² ˏyan ke', *a great, or large, or tall man.*

LXIX. The Chinese always say "new and old" and not "old and new," as:—

新舊約書 ˏSan Kau² Yōk₀ (ˏShū), *the Old and New Testaments,* lit. New Old Covenants (or Convenant Books.)

NUMERAL ADJECTIVES.

LXX. The Cardinal Numerals, given on page 3, are strictly speaking the only Numeral Adjectives in Chinese, the other forms of Numeral Adjectives being

NUMERAL ADJECTIVES.

expressed by their combination with other words, or with themselves. Those given at the beginning of the book will be sufficient to guide the student in the use of these words.

Note.— 十 shap$_2$, ten if meant in Chinese is generally understood, or so represented as to be understood It may be omitted or not when used with other numbers, the position of the figure which represents the number of tens plainly showing that it must be tens and nothing else. When there is no ten shown in English, say as in 101, the one is shewn to belong to the units by the insertion of 零 ,lengt between the two ones, as:— 一百 零一 yat,·pák$_o$,lengt yat, ; without it the figures would stand for 110, as:— 一百一 yat, pák$_o$ yat,. The one, it will be noticed, is also omitted before figures, as:— hundred and one instead of a or one hundred and one. 零 ,lengt may be introduced between any of the figures expressing numbers as: 二十零一 — yi^2 shap$_2$,lengt yat,, twenty and one, or between all of them, as 一百零二十零一 — yat, pák$_o$,lengt yi^2 shap$_2$,lengt yat,, one hundred and twenty and one, but it is better for the beginner to use it sparingly, except when its use points out what in English is shown by the insertion of a cypher between the figures.

LXXI. In speaking of time an ambiguity may arise as to whether for instance the speaker means "half past one," or "an hour and a half," unless something else is said as well which will show clearly what is meant, as:—

一點鐘 yat, 'tím ,chung, which may mean, *one o'clock*, or *one hour*.

Note. 1.—To make sure as to which is meant it is often as well to ask questions similar to the following:— 個陣時打咀一點鐘未呀 Ko' chan^2 ,shí 'tá 'cho yat, 'tím ,chung méi^2 á'? *Had it struck one o'clock then?* To be followed by the questions 噉係一點咯 'kom hai^2 yat, 'tím lok$_o$? *Then it was one o'clock?* 係要成點鐘嚟做咩 Hai^2 yíu^3 ,shengt 'tím ,chung lai tso^2 ,mé? *Did it take a whole hour to do?* If in the latter case this is not what was meant, the answer will be something like the following 唔係個陣時係一點鐘咯 ,m hai^2, ko' chan^2 ,shí hai^2 yat, 'tím ,chung lok$_o$, *no, it was one o'clock then.*

Remark.—It is by such methods that one has to resolve the precise facts out of what seem ambiguous statements in Chinese.

Note 2.—At the same time it must be remembered that where there seems no want of clearness in the English context, the contrary may be the case in Chinese, owing to the want of tense and other matters incident to the language; so it is better that the foreign student should use some word or phrase, when a certain length of time is meant, to show without doubt to the Chinese hearer that such is the meaning and that an hour of the day is not intended.

NUMERAL ADJECTIVES.

Note 3.—A reference to the old English style of stating the hour and its meaning will show the Chinese idiom, which is the same:—e.g. *seven of the clock*, i.e. *seven hours of the clock* or *seven strokes of the clock* as it is in Chinese.

LXXII. The same order is observed in the construction of a phrase representing time on the clock, &c. as in phrases denoting weights, &c., as:—

六點半 luk, ʻtím pún', *half past six.*
八點(過)一(個)骨 pát₀ ʻtím (kwoʼ) yat, (koʼ) kwat,, *a quarter past eight.*
五點四個字 ʻng ʻtím sz' koʼ tsz², or 五點搭四 ʻng ʻtím táp₀ sz', *twenty minutes past five.*
三點(過, or 零)十個呫呢 ,sám ʻtím (kwoʼ, or ,leng†) shap, koʼ ,mín ,ní, *ten minutes past three.*

LXXIII. 多少 ,to ʻshíú is often used in Chinese when speaking approximately of a number and has the sense of *more or less*; or it may be often rendered by *some*, or *a few*, with a nearer approach to the idea in the Chinese mind when using it. When used with a definite number it may also be rendered by *thereabouts*, as well as by *more or less*, as:—

有多少係處 ʻyau ,to ʻshíú ʻhai shü', *there are more or less*, or *there are a few*, or *there are some.*
有十個多少係處 ʻyau shap, koʼ ,to ʻshíú ʻhai shü', *there are ten or thereabouts*, or *there are ten more or less.*

LXXIV. The Ordinal Numerals are represented in Chinese by the use of 第 tai² with the Cardinal Numerals, as:—

第一 tai² yat, *first* (or *No.* 1).

Note 1.—個 koʼ is generally used after them in the higher numbers; it may be used, however, or not with all of them.

Note 2.—第二 tai² yi² is also used to mean *next*, or *another* as 第二個月 tai² yi² koʼ yüt,, *next month*, or *another month.*

DATES.

As the Ordinal Numerals are largely used in dates it may prove useful to the beginner to have their combination with other words noted.

Note.—That in Colloquial there are no distinctive names for the days of the week, or month; but that like quakers the Chinese largely use the Ordinal Numerals for this purpose. In speaking of years they are commonly called the *first, second,* and so on years of such and such a reign, though the cycle of sixty years is also used.

NUMERAL ADJECTIVES.

LXXV. In giving the date the Chinese invert, according to our ideas, the order of the words. The year comes first, then the month, and finally the day, as:—

同治十年八月十三 T'ung Chí² shap₂ nín pát₀ yüt₂ shap₂ sám, *the thirteenth of the eighth moon of the tenth year of T'ung Chí.*

四月初七 sz' yüt₂ ch'o ts'at₂, *the seventh of the fourth moon.*

Note.—That as in English it is not necessary, when it is quite plain from the context that the day of the month is meant, to say day; the word day is left out, as in the sentences above. The Chinese carry this further than the English, for the last denomination of anything mentioned, when others are mentioned before it, is not expressed, the number of such a denomination only being given, as:—.

一個九銀錢 yat₂ ko' kau ngan 'tsín*, *one dollar and ninety (cents understood),* (lit. one [C.] nine silver cash.)

八錢 — pát₀ ts'ín yat₂, *eight mace and one (candarin understood.)*

LXXVI. The word 初 ch'o is used before the days of the moon (or Chinese month) from the 1st to the 10th inclusive, and even if the word month does not occur in the conversation the use of this prefix shows when the first ten days of the month are spoken of that the number which follows it refers to a day of a month and not to anything else. Nothing is prefixed to the numbers representing the remaining two thirds of the days of the month, as:—

初一 ch'o yat₂, *the first of the moon.*

十三 shap₂ sám, *the thirteenth.*

LXXVII. It is a very common division to make of the month into three, and when one is uncertain as to the exact day when anything occured, &c., instead of saying in the beginning, middle, or end of the month, though all these terms are used, it is more common to say, 初幾 ch'o 'kéi, 十幾 shap₂ 'kéi and 廿幾 ye², or yá² 'kéi, or 二十幾 yí² shap₂ 'kéi, as:—

初幾打風颶 ch'o 'kéi tá fung kau², *there was a storm in the 1st decade of the moon.*

我十幾翻去歸鄉吓 ngo shap₂ 'kéi fán hoi' kwai höng 'há, *I returned home in the 2nd decade of the moon.*

廿幾有回音唎 ye² 'kéi yau wúi yam kwá², *I think there will be an answer in the 3rd decade of the moon.*

Note.—The beginning of the month is rendered as 月頭 yüt₂ t'au.
The middle „ „ 月中 yüt₂ chung.
The end „ „ 月尾 yüt₂ méi.

Remark.—月中 yüt₂ chung also means in the course of the month.

NUMERAL ADJECTIVES.

LXXVIII. The word 號 hò² is used after any and every day of the English month, and this when the word month occurs in the sentence shows (sometimes the context will show it otherwise) that the number of which 號 hò² forms a suffix refers to a day of the English month, as:—

一號 yat, hò², *the first of the month* (*English*), supposing that what has been already said shows that it is a day of the month that is being spoken of.

英人二號 ₍Ying ₍yan yī² hò², *the second of the English month* (lit. *English man 2nd day* [*of month understood*]).

英月(份)二十號 ₍Ying yüt₂ (fan²) yī² shap₂ hò², *the twentieth of the English month*.

LXXIX. New Year's eve is called 年卅呀晚 ₍nin ₍sā* ú² ˢmán j.e. the night of the thirtieth of the year, notwithstanding whether it really is the 29th, or 30th of the month; for, owing to the Chinese month being variable in its length, (some months having twenty-nine days and others thirty) it sometimes happens that the day that is so called is only the 29th of the month.

LXXX. New Year's day is 年初一 ₍nín ₍ch'o yat₂, i.e. the first day of the year.

LXXXI. A month of thirty days is known as 月大 yüt₂ tái², *a large month*, and one of twenty-nine as 月少 yüt₂ ˢshíú, *a small month*. These are the respective number of days in a Chinese month.

Note.—It has already been said (See *Dates* under Ordinal Numbers No. LXXIV), that the Ordinal numbers are employed in dates. It will however be found that:—

(*a.*) With regard to years it is sufficient and more correct to say, for example, 同治三年 ₍T'ung Chí² ₍sām ₍níu, *the third year of T'ung Chi*, without using the 第 tai² before the 三 ₍sām, &c.

(*b.*) With regard to the months of the year the same holds good, as:—今年八月 ₍kam ₍nín pāt₀ yüt₂, *the eighth month of this year*.

Exception.—This only holds good when Numerals are employed; for example, it is impossible to put 第 tai² before 正 ₍ching, as:—正月 ₍ching yüt₂, the first month of the year. In fact this month may be said to be the only one which has a name, as above, applied to it in colloquial, for though 正 ₍ching may mean the *first* when applied to months it is not a Numeral. It is worth nothing that 正 ₍ching thus used is in a different tone to what it is in when it is used otherwise, then it is pronounced 正 ching³. It may further be noted that if the word 第 tai² is used before 月 yüt₂ it should then be rendered into English by the first month that say such and such a thing happened, irrespective of whether

NUMERAL ADJECTIVES.

it be the first month of the year or not. It is not then to be considered as the first month of the regular year.

(c.) There is likewise no need to use the 第 tai² before the days of the English, or Chinese month. Before the first ten days of the Chinese month it is impossible to use it as there is no place for it to come in.

(d.) 第 tai² can only be used in connection with the days of the week in the following manner, as for instance, *the third day of that week*, 咱個禮拜第三日 'ko ko' ˢlai pái' tai² ˌsám yat.

LXXXII. The names of the days of the week are in Cantonese, as follows:—

Sunday 禮拜(日) ˢlai pái' (yat).
Monday 禮拜一 ˢlai pái' yat.
Tuesday 禮拜二 ˢlai pái' yi².
Wednesday 禮拜三 ˢlai pái' ˌsám.
Thursday 禮拜四 ˢlai pái' sz².
Friday 禮拜五 ˢlai pái' ˢug.
Saturday 禮拜六 ˢlai pái' luk.

LXXXIII. The 日 yat, in 禮拜日 ˢlai pái' yat, can be dropped whenever the context shows plainly that the 禮拜 ˢlai pái' used alone refers to the day and does not mean "week," for 禮拜 ˢlai pái' alone also means "week."

第二個禮拜嚟 tai² yi² ko' ˢlai pái' ˌlai, means, *come next week*.

Note.—The difference between Sunday and Monday when the 日 yat, is used is very subtle to the English ear: it consists only in a different tone to the last word, as:—

Sunday 禮拜日 ˢlai pái' yat.
Monday 禮拜一 ˢlai pái' yat.

LXXXIV. The Distributive Numerals are represented in Chinese by the reduplication of the Cardinal Numerals, accompanied by 個 ko', as:—

一個一個嚟 yat, ko' yat, ko' ˌlai, *come one by one*.

Note.—逐個, or 逐個逐個 chuk, ko', or chuk, ko' chuk, ko', is also used for *one by one*, or *each by each*.

LXXXV. The Numeral Adverbs, *once, twice, thrice, &c.*, to be turned into Chinese must be translated from their literal meaning in English into Chinese, as:—

I did it once, i.e., I did it on one occasion 我做過一限 ˢngo tsò² kwo' yat, chòng'.
Strike him once, i.e., Strike him one time 打佢一吓 'tá ˢk'ui yat, ˢhá.
I have been twice, i.e., I have been two times 我去過兩勻 ˢngo hui' kwo' ˢlóng ˌwan.
I have heard him twice, i.e., I have heard him two times 我聽佢兩回咯 ˢngo ˌt'eng1 ˢk'ui ˢlóng wúi² lo'.

NUMERAL ADJECTIVES.

LXXXVI. Amongst expressions denoting time such as the following are of frequent occurrence:—

The time it would take to drink a cup of tea, 飲一盃茶咁耐 ‛yam yat, ‛pui ₌ch‛á kom³ noi², or ‛noi*.

The time it would take to drink a cup of hot tea, 飲一盃熱茶咁耐 ‛yam yat, ‛pui yĭt, ‛ch‛á kom³ noi².

The time it would take to eat a meal of rice, 食一餐飯咁耐 shik₂ yat, ‛ts‛an fán² kom³ noi².

The time it would take to eat a bowl of rice, 食一碗飯咁耐 shik₂ yat, ‛wún fán² kom³ noi².

The time it would take to smoke a cigar, 食一口烟咁耐 shik₂ yat, ‛hau ‛yín kom³ noi².

The time it would take for an incense stick to burn, 燒一枝香咁耐 shíú yat, ‛chí ‛höng kom³ noi².

PRONOUNS.

PERSONAL PRONOUNS.

LXXXVII. Personal Pronouns are often left out in a Chinese sentence.

Note 1.—Personal Pronouns of the 1st and 2nd Persons are often understood, the sense showing what person is meant, as in the 2nd person of the English Imperative, as :—

今朝做嚟 ‛kam ‛chíú tsò² ₌lai, *I did it this morning.*

做咯 tsò² lok₀, *it is done.*

Note 2.—The Personal Pronouns of the 3rd Person are often left out in a Chinese sentence when it is well enough understood to what the sentence refers, as :—

個啲係鷄蛋，係唔好嘅咯 ko³ ₌ti hai² ₌kai ‛tán* ; hai² ₌m ‛hó ke³ lok₀, *those are hen's eggs; they are bad.*

Note 3.—All the Personal Pronouns are in the 下上 há² ‛shöng, or lower rising tone, as :— 我 ‛ngo, 你 ‛néi, 佢 ‛k‛ui.

LXXXVIII. When the Plural is shewn 哋 téi² is the sign of it, as :—

佢 ‛k‛ui, *he, she,* or *it*; 佢哋 ‛k‛ui téi², *they.*

Remark.—Though Plural forms exist for the Personal Pronouns, the Singular form is often used where in English we would use the Plural, especially when the context shows that more than one is meant, as when more than one has been already mentioned, as :—

佢三個話我知 ‛k‛ui ₌sám ko³ wá² ‛ngo chí, *they three told me.*

PRONOUNS.

LXXXIX. When the Possessive is expressed 嘅 ke᾿ is the sign of it, as:— 我嘅 ⸢ngo ke᾿, *mine*.

XC. The Declension of the English Personal Pronouns are therefore represented in Chinese as follows:—

First Personal Pronoun.

Singular.

I, 我 ⸢ngo.
My, 我, *or* 我嘅 ⸢ngo, *or* ⸢ngo ke᾿.
Mine, 我嘅 ⸢ngo ke᾿.
Me, 我 ⸢ngo.

Plural.

We, 我哋 ⸢ngo téi².
Our, 我哋, *or* 我地嘅 ⸢ngo téi², *or* ⸢ngo téi² ke᾿.
Ours, 我哋嘅 ⸢ngo téi² ke᾿.
Us, 我哋 ⸢ngo téi².

Second Personal Pronoun.

Singular.

You, 你 ⸢néi.
Your, 你, *or* 你嘅 ⸢néi, *or* ⸢néi ke᾿.
Yours, 你嘅 ⸢néi ke᾿.
You, 你 ⸢néi.

Plural.

You, 你哋 ⸢néi téi².
Your, 你哋, *or* 你地嘅 ⸢néi téi², *or* ⸢néi téi² ke᾿.
Yours, 你地嘅 ⸢néi téi² ke᾿.
You, 你哋 ⸢néi téi².

Third Personal Pronoun.

Singular.

He, she, *or* it, 佢 ⸢k'ui.
His, her, *or* its, 佢, *or* 佢嘅 ⸢k'ui, *or* ⸢k'ui ke᾿.
His, Hers, *or* its, 佢嘅 ⸢k'ui ke᾿, (when used predicatively).
Him, her, *or* it, 佢 ⸢k'ui.

Plural.

They, 佢, *or* 佢地 ⸢k'ui *or* ⸢k'ui téi².
Their, 佢哋, *or* 佢地嘅 ⸢k'ui téi², *or* ⸢k'ui téi² ke᾿.
Theirs, 佢地嘅 ⸢k'ui téi² ke᾿.
Them, 佢 ⸢k'ui.

PRONOUNS.

Caution.—The learner must not forget that the signs of the Plural and Possessive may often be omitted.

Note.—The want of Gender in the Third Person occasions some degree of ambiguity, as well as the often optional use, or rather disuse of the signs of the Plural and Possessive.

XCI. The Nominative of the Personal Pronoun with the Reflective Pronoun is sometimes placed before or after the Verb and sometimes the Verb is placed between the two as in English, as:—

我打自記 ʰngo ʻta tsz² ʻkei, *I strike myself.*
我自記去 ʰngo tsz² ʻkei hui', *I went myself,* lit. *(I myself went.)*

Note 1.—Note the difference between 我打自記 ʰngo ta tsz² ʻkei, *I strike myself,* and 我自記打（佢） ʰngo tsz² ʻkei ʻta (ʻkʻui), *I myself strike (him),* as in English.

Note 2.—To those who find a difficulty in the tones it may be of assistance to remember that all the Personal Pronouns are in the Lower Rising Tone or hả² ₚhýg, as:—我 ʰngo, *I*; 你 ʰnei, *you;* 佢 ʰkʻui, *he.*

INTERROGATIVE PRONOUNS.

XCII. There are several words which may be used in connection with appropriate Classifiers to express the ideas conveyed in English by *who, what,* or *which.* The Classifier appropriate to the object spoken of is always used with them whether the Noun be employed or not. If the Noun is not employed the Classifier may be considered as being used substantively. The first word which may thus be used is 邊 ₚpin which alone in itself may be taken to mean *which,* the words that are used with it showing whether it means when used with these words *which, what,* or *who,* as for instance:—邊個 ₚpin koʼ. . Here in the first place we must find out to what the Classifier 個 koʼ refers. Is it a man or men who have been spoken of, or who are referred to? Then 邊 ₚpin must be translated either as, *who,* or *which.* If an animal, or some inanimate object then it must be translated by *which.* Likewise remember when doing the converse, i.e. putting one of these English words into Chinese to get hold of the appropriate Classifier for what is spoken about, as for instance if you want to say *which table,* or the word *which* alone, referring at the time to a table, do not on any account say 邊個 ₚpin koʼ, for 個 koʼ is not the Classifier to use with table, but say 邊張 ₚpin ₚchöng.

Note.—That 邊 ₚpin is used with all the Classifiers just in the same way as 一, 二, 三, yat, yiʼ, ₂sám, *one, two, three,* and all the other Numerals would be used with all the Classifiers. This seems simple and plain enough and yet some of our dictionaries

PRONOUNS.

for the use of English-speaking people learning Chinese have fallen into the error of saying that 邊個 ₍pin ko' is *who*, or *which* ! ! ! Why not say at once that 一個 yat₎ ko' is *one*, and then add on each of the Classifiers in turn to 一 yat₎ and state, that 'curious to say the Chinese have many ways of expressing one, in fact no less than sixty'? (For there are nearly sixty different Classifiers in Cantonese.) This would be as much the fact as saying that 邊個 ₍pin ko' meant *who*, or *which*. The importance of the matter is great and it is not one to be thought of no consequence, and yet this class of mistakes is in daily use by foreigners speaking Chinese, most egregious error though it be, thanks in part to our dictionaries, which, if not in error themselves, are not explicit enough on this and kindred points. The absurdity of the thing may be further shown by adding 人 ₍yan, *man* on to 邊個 ₍pin ko', for it is often used with the Noun 人 ₍yan, *man* when referring to men (as it is with other Nouns when referring to other objects), as: 邊個人 ₍pin ko² ₍yan *who*, or *which man*, and then say that these three words together mean *what*.

XCIII. To form the Possessive Case the sign of the Possessive 嘅 ke' is used, and whether it is intended to be applied to a person, or object the Classifier will again, to a certain extent if not entirely, show whether it is to be rendered in English by the Possessive *whose*, or *which*. The 嘅 ke' always follows the Classifier, the Classifier however, as above, always changing according to the object spoken about, as:—

邊個嘅 ₍Pin ko' ke'? This may be *whose*? or the Neuter according to the context, &c.
邊張嘅 ₍Pin ₍chöng ke'? The Classifier here at once shows this cannot be *whose*. The Classifier is one that is only applied to inanimate objects. It must therefore be rendered by the Neuter in English.

Remark.—In other words it may be said that *who*, *which*, or *what* are expressed in Chinese by 邊 ₍pin, and that the Classifier, which is always present and which must always be the appropriate one, shows how it is to be rendered into English, there being no ambiguity in Chinese, as the word 邊 ₍pin is common to both Genders.

XCIV. The Plural of *who*, *what*, and *which* is formed by adding 哋 ₍ti to the 邊 ₍pin, as:—邊哋 ₍pin ₍ti. No Classifier is necessary in the Plural, irrespective of whether persons, animals, or inanimate objects are spoken of, as:—

邊哋人 ₍Pin ₍ti ₍yan? *Which men?*
邊哋做嚟呢 ₍Pin ₍ti tso² ₍lai ni? *Who (plural) did it?*
邊哋禽獸係呢 ₍Pin ₍ti ₍k'am shau' hai² ni? *Which animals are the ones?*

XCV. Before Nouns the names of things, which are capable of subdivision without losing their distinctive character, the plural form is used in Chinese where in

PRONOUNS.

English the subject in question would not be looked upon from a grammatical point of view as an aggregate of small particles each having a singular character of its own, as it is in Chinese, as:—

邊啲糖係呢 ₂Pín ₂ti ₂t'ong hai² ₂ni? *Which sugar is it?*
你糴邊啲米 ²Nei tek₂ ₂pín ₂tí ⁵mai? *Which rice did you buy?*
乜人嚟 Mat₂ 'yan* ₂lai? *Who comes?*
乜野呢 Mat₂ ⁵ye ₂ni? *What is it?*

XCVI. Another word is used to represent *who, what,* or *which,* viz.:—乜 mat₂, but when it refers to any inanimate object the Noun, 野 ⁵ye, *thing* always follows it. When it relates to a human being the Noun, 人 ₂yan, *man,* or the Pronoun, 誰 'shui* invariably follows it. No Classifier is ever used with it, as:—

乜誰做呢 Mat₂ 'shui* tsò² ₂ni? *Who did it?*

XCVII. The Possessive, when 乜 mat₂ is used, is formed by affixing the sign of the Possessive, 嘅 ke'. This is always placed after the Nouns, 人 ₂yan, *man,* or 野 ⁵ye, *thing,* or the Pronoun 誰 'shui*, *who* as the case may be, as:—

乜人嘅 Mat₂ 'yan* ke'   ⎫
乜誰嘅 Mat₂ 'shui* ke'   ⎬ *Whose?*
乜野嘅呢 Mat₂ ⁵ye ke' ₂ni? *What does it belong it?*

Remark.—The 乜 mat₂ in conversation is often slurred over in pronounciation so that it sounds like mi (mih). It then takes (having no longer a final *k*, and therefore not coming into the Lower Entering Series, or 入 Yap₂ Tones) the Upper Even Tone, or 上平 shöng² ₂p'ing.

XCVIII. The Plural has the same form as the Singular.

Remark.—These three forms might be literally rendered, as:—

乜人 Mat₂ 'yan*? *What man?* i.e., *Who,* or *Which?*
乜誰 Mat₂ 'shui*? *What who?* i.e., *Which,* or *Who?*
乜野 Mat₂ ⁵ye? *What thing?* i.e., *Which?*

Note.—Though the objection is not so great with 乜 mat₂ as in the case of 邊 ₂pín to the dictionary way of putting these forms, on account of their use being limited to the designation of men and inanimate objects, it is as well that the learner should remember what the component parts of these phrases mean. He should then be able to speak intelligibly and correctly. The dictionaries are not full enough in their definitions under these words.

PRONOUNS.

RELATIVES.

XCIX. The Relative can scarcely be said to be expressed in Chinese. The sentences in which the Relative Pronoun occurs in English are generally expressed in Chinese, as follows, the Relative being understood, as:—

我就係見呢個人 ^{s}ngo tsau^2 hai^2 ,kin^s ,ni ko^s ,yan, *this is the man whom I saw.*

個間屋跌倒個間屋呢 ko^s ,kán uk$_o$, tít$_o$ 'tò ko^s ,kán uk$_o$, ,ni, *the house which fell down.*

話我知咽個行去咯 wa^2 ^{s}ngo ,chí 'ko ko^s ,háng+ hui^s lok$_o$, *he who told me walked away.*

我騎咽隻馬跌倒咯 ^{s}ngo ,k‘éi 'ko chek$_o$ ^{s}ma tít$_o$ 'tò lo^s, *the horse that I rode fell down.*

我就係講呢個人咯 ^{s}ngo tsau^2 hai^2 'kong ,ni ko^s ,yan lok$_o$, *this is the man that I spoke of.*

呢個人就係幫我嘅 ,ni ko^s ,yan tsau^2 hai^2 ,pong ^{s}ngo ke^s, *this is the man that helped me.*

佢借我個部書, 佢唔曾俾翻我咯 ^{s}k‘ui tse^2 ^{s}ngo ko^s pò^2 ,shü, ^{s}k‘ui ,m ,ts‘aug 'péi ,fán ^{s}ngo lok$_o$, *he has not returned me the book, which he borrowed from me.*

係佢做嘅 hai^2 ^{s}k‘ui tsò^2 ke^s, *it was he who did it.*

係佢嚟呢處嘅 hai^2 ^{s}k‘ui lai^2 ,ni shü^s ko^s, *it was he who came here.*

Note.—嘅 ke^s it will be noticed is about the nearest approach to the sign of the Relative.

ADJECTIVE PRONOUNS.

DEMONSTRATIVE PRONOUNS.

C. 呢 ,ni, *this* and 個 ko^s, or 咽 'ko, *that.* See previous remarks on these.

CI. The Plural *these,* and *those* are 呢啲 ,ni ,tí, and 個啲 ko^s ,tí.

CII. 呢啲 ,ni ,tí and 個啲 ko^s ,tí are, however, often used in Chinese where the Singular form is used in English, viz:—before Nouns, such as weather, sand, dust, flour, gunpowder, powders, wheat, grain, rice, &c., the names of liquids and names of similar objects consisting of an aggregate of infinitesimal particles, or in other words before Nouns representing objects which are capable of subdivision without losing their distinctive character, as:—

呢啲藥散 ,ni ,tí yök$_2$ 'sán, *this power* (medicine).
個啲水 ko^s ,tí 'shui, *that water.*

ADJECTIVE PRONOUNS.

Note.—呢 ,ní is used at the end of explanatory phrases, or clauses, and seems sometimes to have the power of intensifying the Demonstrative, or to have the meaning of the English word "there," as:—

個人,個高個呢,係咯 ko' ,yan, ko' ,kò ko' ,ní, hai² lok₀, *that man, that tall one (there), is the one.*

INTERROGATIVES.

CIII. *Which*, and *what* are represented by 邊 ,pín. The Classifier appropriate to the Noun must always be used after 邊 ,pín.

Note.—Some of the Dictionaries and Phrase Books are again in error here, giving 邊個 ,pín ko', as *which*. The remarks made previously with regard to 呢 ,ní and 個 ko' apply here as well with regard to 邊 ,pín.

CIV. *What* is also rendered by 乜 mat, alone, or by 乜野 mat, ʼye, as:—

你話乜 (or 乜野) ʼNéi wá² mat, (or mat, ʼye)? *What do you say?*
個年有乜事呢 Ko' ,nín ʼyau mat, sz² ,ní? *What events happened that year?*

CV. *Whosoever, whosesoever, whoever,* &c. may be expressed in Chinese by the use of several different phrases to convey the meaning of the English, as:—

邊個 (or 是但邊個) 做都要辦佢咯 ,pín ko' (or shí² tán² ,pín ko') tsò² ,tò yíú² pán² ʼk'úi lok₀, *whoever does t s wil be punished.*
但凡你地釋放佢罪嘅,佢 罪必被釋放 tán² ,fán ʼnéi téi² shik, foung³ ʼk'úi tsui² ke³, ʼk'úi ko' tsui² pit, péi² shik, fong', *whosoever sins ye remit they are remitted unto them.*

CVI. The interrogative 乜 Mat,? *What?* is placed after the rest of the sentence instead of before it as in English when a Verb is used; but the construction of the sentence is the same as in English (subject to Note 1) when a Noun is used with it, as:—

乜野事 Mat, ʼye sz²? *What is the matter?*
講乜野 ʼKong mat, ʼye? *What are you saying?*
乜野人 Mat, ʼyo ,yan? *What kind of man?*
乜野工夫 Mat, ʼyo ,kung ,fú? *What work?*
讀乜野書 Tuk, mat, ʼyo ,shü? *What book are you reading aloud?*
睇乜野 Tʻai mat, ʼyo? *What are you looking at?*

ADJECTIVE PRONOUNS.

Note 1.—The verb is generally omitted in such sentences. It sometimes has the force of conveying more emphasis to the sentence when brought in, but not always, as:—

也野船 Mat, ʻye ˳shün? *What vessel is it?*
係也野船 Hai² mat, ʻye ˳shün? *What vessel is that?*

Note 2.—In Colloquial the 也 mat, is very often changed into ˳mi in pronunciation.

Note 3.—也 mat, is only used before 人 ˳yan man, and 佳 ʻshui*, and not with a Classifier as 邊 ˳pín is used.

CVII. The impersonal *there* and *it* are left out in the interrogative form, as:—

有冇 ʻyau ʻmó? *Is there, or not?*

RELATIVES AND INTERROGATIVES.

CVIII. Relative and Interrogative Pronouns must be rendered according to the sense of the word, viz., *which of the two*, &c., as the case may be, as:—

呢兩個仔,邊個遵依爺親嘅旨意呢, Ní ʻlöng koʼ ˳tsai, ˳pín koʼ ˳tsun ˳yí fít² ˳tsʻan keʼ ʻchʻí yí ˳ni? *Whether of them twain did the will of his father?*

DISTRIBUTIVES AND INDEFINITES.

CIX. The Distributive and Indefinite Pronouns, *each, either, neither, any, other*, may be expressed in Chinese by the following words, or combinations, as:—

Each, 每 ʻmúi, as:—每個到咯 ʻmúi koʼ tòʼ lok˳, *each one was there.*

Note 1.—Such unnecessary words as *any* are often left out in a Chinese sentence, as:—

有冇 ʻYau ʻmó? *Are there any?*

Note 2.—The Classifier (care must be taken that it is an appropriate one) must be used with 每 ʻmúi in most cases, the exceptions to the use of the Classifier being when 每 ʻmúi is used before Nouns of Time and Place.

Either 是但 shí² táu², or 是但邊個 shí² tán² ˳píu koʼ, as:—是但邊個都好 shí² tán² ˳pín koʼ ˳tò ʻhò, *either will do.*
Either, —— or, 或 wák˳ —— 或 wák˳, as:—或呢哟, 或啊哟 wák˳ ˳ní ˳tí, wák˳ ʻko ˳tí, *either these, or those.*

Neither, 兩個都唔 (or 冇) ʻlöng koʼ ˳tò ˳m (or ʻmó), as:—
兩個都冇打佢 ʻlöng koʼ ˳tò ʻmó tá ʻkʻúi, *neither of them struck him.*
兩位都冇做 ʻlöng ʻwaí* ˳tò ʻmó tsò², *neither of them did it.*

ADJECTIVE PRONOUNS.

Any is understood, or it may be expressed by 啲 ₄ti *a little, some*, as:—

個啲菓于咁吤我唔食咯 ko⁾ ₄tí ʻkwo ʻtsz kòm⁾ ₄yai ʻngo ₄m shik₂ lok₀, *that fruit is so bad I will not eat any.*

樹上有橙,你有食啲冇呀 shü² shöng² ʻyau ʻch'áng*, ʻnéi ʻyau shik₂ ₄tí ʻmò á⁾? *There were some oranges on the tree, did you eat any?*

檯上有銀,你有揸啲 (or 多少) 冇呢 T'oi* shöng² ʻyau ʻngan*, ʻnéi ʻyau ₄ning ₄tí (or ₄to ʻshíú) ʻmò ₄ni? *There was money on the table, did you take any?*

Other, and Another are expressed by 第二 tai² yí², or 別 pít₂. Some of the dictionaries are again in error, giving 別個 pít₂ ko⁾ as *other*. Remarks which have previously been made with regard to similar words apply with equal force to 別 pít₂. It is used both with an appropriate Classifier, and alone like 呢 ₄ni.

The other's 別 (Classifier here if used) 嘅 pít₂ [C.] ke⁾; others', 別啲嘅 pít₂ ₄tí ke⁾.

啲 ₄tí is used to denote plurality with 別 pít₂ in the same manner as with 呢 ₄ni. 嘅 ke⁾ is used with 別 pít₂ to shew possession, as represented by the English, *other's*, or *others'*. When a Classifier is used with it, 嘅 ke⁾ is placed after the Classifier, as:—

別個嘅 pít₂ ko⁾ ke⁾, *the other's.*

Each other may be expressed as follows, viz:—

兩家相愛 ʻlöng ₄ká ₄söng oi⁾, *they love each other.*

佢哋兩個憎惡,好似你憎我,我憎你噉嘅 ʻk'ui téi² ʻlöng ko⁾ ₄tsang wú⁾, ʻhó ʻt'sz ʻnéi ₄tsang ʻngo, ʻngo ₄tsang ʻnéi ʻkòm ke⁾, *they hated one another* (i.e. they two hated, as if you hated me and I hated you).

CX. *Self* is expressed by 自己 tsz² ʻkéi with the Personal Pronouns, as:—

Myself, 我自己 ʻngo tsz² ʻkéi, (*I myself*).
Yourself, 你自己 ʻnéi tsz² ʻkéi, (*you yourself*).
Himself, herself, or itself, 佢自己 ʻk'ui tsz² ʻkéi, (*he himself, she herself, or it itself*).
Ourselves, 我哋自己 ʻngo téi² tsz² ʻkéi, (*we ourselves*).
Yourselves, 你哋自己 ʻnéi téi² tsz² ʻkéi, (*you yourselves*).
Themselves, 佢哋自己 ʻk'ui téi² tsz² ʻkéi, (*they themselves*).

Note.—自己 tsz² ʻkéi is often used alone without the Personal Pronoun when the sense is sufficiently clear without the Pronoun, as:—

係自己做嘅 hai² tsz² ʻkéi tsò² ke⁾, *I did it myself.*

係佢自己做嘅嗎? 係自己做嘅咯 Hai² ʻk'ui tsz² ʻkéi tsò² ke⁾ má⁾? Hai² tsz² ʻkéi tsò² ke⁾ lok₀. *Did he do it himself? Yes, he did it himself.*

ADJECTIVE PRONOUNS AND VERBS. 77

ADJECTIVE PRONOUNS.

A man's own self, 一個人自己 yat, ko' ˌyan tsz² ˈkéi.
Men's own selves, or people themselves, 人哋自己 ˌyan téi² tsz² ˈkéi.

CXI. *Self* is also often expressed by 本身 ʻpún ˌshan (own body), as:—
係你本身做咩 Hai² ˤnéi ʻpún ˌshan tsò² ˌme? *Did you do it yourself?*
Myself, himself, &c., are formed in the same way with 本身 ʻpún ˌshan as with 自己 tsz² ˤkéi, as given above.

CXII. *Self* would be used in English where the Chinese often make use of the following and similar expressions, as:—

親眼 ˌts'an ˤngán; 親耳 ˌts'an ˤyí; 親手 ˌts'an ˈshau, &c., as:—
你親耳聽見咩 ˤNéi ˌts'an ˤyí ˌt'engˈ kín' ˌme? *Did you hear it yourself?* (i.e. with your own ears).
你親眼見佢咩 ˤNéi ˌts'an ˤngán kín' ˤk'ui ˌme? *Did you see him yourself?* (i.e. with your own eyes).
嗱, 係你親身做唔係呢 Ná², hai² ˤnéi ˌts'an ˌshan tsò² ˌm hai² ˌni? *Now, did you do it yourself?* (i.e. with your own body).
係, 乜唔係呀, 係我親手做嘅咯 Hai², mat, ˌm hai² á'? Hai² ˤngo ˌts'an ˈshau tsò² ke' lok˳, *yes, why not? I did it myself*, (i.e. with my own hands).

Note.—That the 自己 tsz² ˤkéi *self*, i.e. myself, yourself, &c., always immediately follows the Personal Pronoun, and is not placed at the end of the sentence as sometimes in English. He *sold it himself*, such a construction in Chinese if literally followed might be thought to mean that the man sold himself—in fact it would be unintelligible. The proper construction in Chinese is, *he himself sold it*, as:—

佢自記賣嘅咯 ˤk'ui tsz² ˤkéi mái² ke' lok˳, *he himself sold it.*

VERBS.

CXIII. The Active and Passive Voices are distinguished as follows:—

個貓捉老鼠 ko' ˌmáu chuk˳ ˤló ˈshü, *the cat catches rats.*
個老鼠被貓捉倒咯 ko' ˤló ˈshü pei² ˌmáu chuk˳ ˤtó lok˳, *the rat is caught by the cat.*

CXIV. The Passive Voice is but seldom used in comparison with the Active; therefore the learner must use it but sparingly, preferring the Active Voice to it, and should generally turn all Verbs in the Passive Voice in English into the Active in Chinese.

VERBS.

CXV. Other Verbs are sometimes used in combination with the principal Verb in some cases when it is of importance to give prominence to the ideas conveyed by the use of Moods and Tenses in English, subject to what follows.

CXVI. There are no special modes of expression that will serve to differentiate the Infinitive, Indicative, or Imperative except the positions of the words in the sentence, or the context, or obvious meaning, as:—

我嚟 ʰngo ˬlai, *I come.*
叫佢嚟 kiú³ ʰk'ui ˬlai, *tell him to come.*
做好人 tsò² ʰhò ˬyan, *be a good man.*
做好人你算係好難啩 tsò² ʰhò ˬyan ʰnéi sün³ hai² ʰhò ˬnán kwá³, *you probably think it is very hard to be a good man.*
俾咽部書我 ʰpéi ʰko pò² ˬshü ʰngo, *give me that book.*

CXVII. With regard to the Subjunctive, the Conjunction, and/or sense will show that a Chinese Verb is to be rendered in English in the Subjunctive Mood, as:—

佢或喺處我就見佢 ʰk'ui wák̬ ʰhai shü³, ʰngo tsau² kín³ ʰk'ui, *if he were here, I should see him,* or *if he is there, I shall see him,* or *if he had been there, I should have seen him.*

CXVIII. The Conjunction is however often understood and the dependent member of the sentence will then show that the Verb must be put into the Subjunctive Mood in English, as:—

佢做,我唔中意咯 ʰk'ui tsò², ʰngo ˬm ˬchuug yí³ lok̬, *if he does it, I shall not be pleased.*

Note.—The voice often rests on and after the Verb when in the Subjunctive. The beginner will do no harm by always thus pausing on such a Verb, especially when no Conjunction is expressed. It serves to call attention, and has a tendency to bring the meaning out more clearly. In fact there are a number of little niceties of this kind in Chinese, the use of which assist materially in elucidating the meaning where according to our ideas the want of Grammatical forms obscures the sense.

The student will probably notice when a Chinese has anything to say about any matter, that he prefers to tell what we consider a very long narrative instead of condensing what he says. Remember, before condemning him for being an interminable gossip and long-winded, that if he begins, as he prefers to, at the commencement and gives you the events as they occurred in their natural sequence, then nearly all obscurity from the want of Tenses, &c. is done away with, and all the minutiæ being entered into at length the whole matter according to his ideas is made plain. The best plan is to let him go on his own way.

VERBS.

Cut him short in his narrative, and after several ineffectual protests on his part, after great difficulty, and after the use of an enormous amount of tautology, quite contrary to the spirit of the Chinese language, you may arrive finally at his story in disjointed fragments, which you have to piece together as best you can, or what is more likely he has been utterly unable to tell you what he wants and you can but guess at his meaning. We forget how easy it is in our own language with its fulness of grammatical form, as compared with the Chinese, to express what we have to say shortly.

CXIX. More reliance must, however, be placed on the obvious meaning, if it is possible to have any certainty on that subject in such cases, as Chinese sentences may often be put either into the Indicative or Subjunctive in English, as:—

佢話我聽我就打佢 ^{s}k'ui wá^{2} $_{c}$ngo $_{c}$t'engt, $_{c}$ngo tsau^{2} ^{c}tá ^{s}k'ui, *he told me, and I struck him,* or *if he tells me, I will strike him.* In such a case it is necessary to know whether any striking has taken place. If not, it would probably best convey the meaning to put the sentence in the Subjunctive. Very often in a case of doubt simply asking:—*Did you strike him?* 你有打佢冇吖 ^{s}Néi ^{s}yau ^{c}tá ^{s}k'ui ^{s}mò $_{c}$á? will solve the difficulty; for the reply will be very likely something like the following 冇. 佢 係話我知. 我就打佢咯 ^{s}mò, ^{s}k'ui hai^{2} wá^{2} $_{c}$ngo $_{c}$chí, $_{c}$ngo tsau^{2} ^{c}tá ^{s}k'ui lok$_{o}$, *no, if he tells me, then I will strike him.* This sentence is of course capable of being construed into other Tenses in English.

Note.—或 wák$_{?}$ of course would bring out the sense of the Subjunctive more clearly; but unfortunately in Chinese, as in many other languages, one must take the sentences as one finds them, and as the people speak them. If one should try to speak Chinese according to English idioms, as many foreigners do more or less, it would produce such a gibberish compared to Chinese, as pidgin English is compared to correct English.

CXX. Certain combinations can be used to express the ideas conveyed in English by the use of Participles, as:—

Imperfect, 我見個細伎仔打緊隻狗 $_{c}$ngo kín$^{?}$ ko$^{?}$ sai$^{?}$ $_{c}$man ^{c}tsai ^{c}tá ^{c}kan chek$_{o}$ ^{c}kau, *I saw the child beating a dog.*
The Perfect may be put into Chinese in some such manner as the following:—佢走去 因爲個人嚇親佢 ^{s}k'ui ^{c}tsau hui$^{?}$ $_{c}$yan wai^{2} ko$^{?}$ $_{c}$yan hák$_{o}$ $_{c}$ts'an ^{s}k'ui, *frightened by the man he ran away.* Of course this Chinese sentence may be translated in several different ways into Eng'ish.
Acting Perfect Participle, 已經打阻)咯 ^{s}yí $_{c}$king ^{c}tá (^{c}cho) lok$_{o}$, *having struck.*
Active Perfect Participle of continued action, 已經打緊咯 ^{s}yí $_{c}$king ^{c}tá ^{c}kan lok$_{o}$, *having been striking.*

VERBS.

Passive Indefinite Participle, 已經被人打緊咯 ₅yí ₍kíng pói² ₅yan ʻtá ʻkan lok₀, *being struck.*

Passive Perfect Participle, 已經被人打(阻)咯 ₅yí ₍kíng pói² ₅yan ʻtá (ʻcho) lok₀, *having been struck.*

Note.—It is necessary to introduce the object or thing which has struck, or which has performed the action.

Avoid, however, as much as possible the use of such complicated constructions: change them to simpler ones such as, *the man struck me and then———.*

GERUNDS.

CXXI. Such forms as, "I like reading," may be rendered in Cantonese by such sentences, as:—

我中意讀野 ₅ngo ₍chung yí² tuk₍ ₅ye, *I like to read things.*
佢中意讀書 ₍k'ui ₍chung yí² tuk₍ ₅shü, *he is fond of studying.*
佢想得好名聲 ₍k'ui ʻsöng tak₍ ʻhó ₅ming ₍shing, *he is desirous of being distinguished.*
我已經成朝寫字, 所以見疲 ₅ngo ₅yí ₍king ₅sheng† ₍chíu ʻse tsz², ʻsho ₅yí kín³ kwui², *after having been writing the whole morning, I am tired* (i.e. I have been &c., therefore, &c.)

TENSE.

CXXII. The Verb by itself may represent an action as taking place in the Present, Past, or Future time, as:—

我打你 ₅ngo ʻtá ʻndí, { *I strike you.* / *I struck you.* / *I will strike you.* }

CXXIII. Where the context, or sense does not show the time during which the action is performed, and where it is essential that such time should be most clearly expressed, certain words, or Particles, or Adverbs of time are introduced into the Chinese sentence and atone in some measure for the want of inflexion, as follows:—

1. To show present time, or continued action 緊 ʻkan, or Adverbs denoting present time, such as 而家 ₅yí ₍ká, *now,* 現時 yín² ₅shí, *at the present time,* and similar phrases denoting present time are used, as:—

現時有 yín² ₅shí ʻyau, *there is* (at present).
我而家去 ₅ngo ₅yí ₍ká hui², *I am going* (now).

VERBS.

2. To show past time, or completed action such words, or Particles, as, 勻 ₛwan, 曉 ₍hiú, 完 ₍yün, 咀 'cho, 了 ʽliú, 倒 ʽtò, 黎 ₍lai, or Adverbs, or Adverbial phrases of past time are used with the Verb, such as 個陣時 ko' chan² ₛshí, *at that time,* 昨日 tsok₂ yat₂ *yesterday,* &c., &c., as:—

揾嚟咯 ʽwan ₍lai lok₀, *I have looked for it.*
唔見曉咯 ₍m kin' ₍hiú lok₀, *it is lost.*
讀過 tuk₂ kwo³, *I have read it.*
整勻嘅咯 ʽchíng ₛwan sü' lok₀, ⎫
做曉 tsò² ₍hiú, ⎬ *it is finished.*
做完 tsò² ₛyün, ⎭

3. To show future time Adverbs, or Adverbial phrases of future time are added to the Verb to qualify it, and bring out into prominence the idea of future time; for it is to be remembered that time—all time—is already inherent, as it were, in the Chinese Verb; the object of these auxiliary words is to bring out into view so plainly the particular phase of time meant, that there shall be no mistake about it. 然後 ₍yin hau², 將來 ₍tsöng ₍loi, &c., &c., &c., are such Adverbs of futurity, as:—

我將來去 ʽngo ₍tsöng ₍loi hui³, *I shall go* (by and by).
我然後做 ʽngo ₍yin hau² tsò², *I shall do it afterwards* (i.e. after the present time).

CXXIV. The mere changing in some cases of the tone of the Verb into the Third Rising Tone is sufficient to show that the action is completed.

我話你知 ʽngo wá² ʽnéi ₍chi, *I tell you* (or *I said to you* —).

我話咯 ʽngo 'wá* lok₀, *I have said it.*

講成唔會呢 ʽKong ₛshéng* ₍m ₛts'ang ₍ní? *Is the matter settled?*

成咯 ₛshéng* lok₀, *it is settled.*

你幾時到呢 ʽNéi ʽkéi ₛshí tò' ₍ní? *When did you arrive?*

十點鐘到咯 shap₂ ʽtím ₍chung 'tò* lok₀, *I arrived at ten o'clock.*

Remark.—When the word is already in the Upper Rising Tone, the emphasis, which is sometimes thrown on it to mark the Past Tense prolongs the tone—in short the voice rises during a longer space of time in uttering the word, as for example in 曉 ʽhiú, *to understand.* That is to say it is changed from the Upper, or First Rising Tone to the Third Rising Tone. And this likewise would be the case with a word, which might happen to be in the Lower Rising Tone.

VERBS.

CXXV. In the Lower Entering Tone the word, in such cases, is uttered in what must be called for want of a better name an Entering Rising Tone, as:—

讀書未呀 Tuk$_2$,shü mèi^2 á'? *Have you read (your) book yet?* (or *learned your lesson?*)

讀咯 'tuk* lok$_o$, *I have.*

NUMBER AND PERSON.

CXXVI. There is no means of expressing the modifications of the English Verb in Chinese in regard to Number and Person, &c. subject to what follows, as:—

佢愛 'k'ui oi³, *he (she, or it) loves,* or *they love.*

CXXVII. If great clearness is to be expressed, as to Voice, Mood, or Tense, &c., &c., in a Chinese Verb, it is possible, though not usual, to convey the meaning in English into the Chinese sentence in the following, or some similar manner, which at the best, must, in many respects, strike one as a lame expedient; for to convey with any distinctness the ideas shown with such ease in many languages into Cantonese it is necessary, as stated above, to employ different Adverbial phrases of time, and Particles.

The following paradigm will give the learner an idea how to form combinations in Chinese to express time when it is absolutely necessary that it should be expressed; but the Chinese eschew such particularity as much as possible. The Examples given below, it must be remembered, are but expedients, and must, necessarily, often be imperfect. Expedients can only be used when no forms exist. No amount of expedients can free such a language from a certain amount of ambiguity. At the same time it must be remembered, that our own language is not altogether free from ambiguity—in fact no language is:—e.g. *I found him out.* And our own language is also wanting in expressions, or terms which in Chinese, and some other languages are simply expressed without the verbiage necessary, in such instances in English. For instance we have no word in English for the Chinese word 送 sung³, but must paraphrase it as 'something to eat with the rice'; the Scotch, however, in this instance have an equivalent in the word 'kitchen.' Again our terminology for degrees of relationship is not so complete, nor so clearly expressed as it is in Chinese, and some other languages. Nor have we any terms in use for the day preceding the day (or night, or morning, or evening) before yesterday, and the day (or night, or morning, or evening) following the day after to-morrow, such as the Chinese have.

VERBS.

CXXVIII. 打 ʻTÁ, *TO SMITE,* OR *TO STRIKE.*

ACTIVE VOICE,

INFINITIVE MOOD.

Indefinite Tense, [*To*] *smite,* 打 ʻtá.
Imperfect Tense, [*To*] *be smiting,* 打緊 ʻtá ʻkan.
Perfect Tense, [*To*] *have smitten,* 個陣時打咗 ko' chan² ₅shí ʻtá ʻcho.
Perfect of continued action, [*To*] *have been smiting,* 個時已經打緊 ko' ₅shí ⁵yí ₍king ʻtá ʻkan.

PARTICIPLES.

Imperfect, *smiting.* 打緊 ʻtá ʻkan.
Perfect, *having smitten,* 已經打咗 ⁵yí ₍king ʻtá ʻcho.
Perfect of continued action, *having been smiting,* 個陣時已經打緊 ko' chan² ₅shí ⁵yí ₍king ʻtá ʻkan.

INDICATIVE MOOD.

Present Indefinite Tense, *I, &c. smite,* 我, &c. 打 ⁵ngo, &c. ʻtá.
Present Imperfect Tense, *I, &c. am smiting,* 我, &c. 打緊 ⁵ngo, &c. ʻtá ʻkan.
Present Perfect, *I, &c. have smitten,* 我, &c. 打咗 ⁵ngo, &c. ʻtá ʻcho.
Present Perfect of continued action, *I, &c. have been smiting,* 我, &c. 就係打嚟 ⁵ngo, &c. tsau² hai² ʻtá ₍lai.

Past Indefinite Tense, *I, &c. smote,* 我, &c. 打咗 ⁵ngo, &c. ʻtá ʻcho.
Past Imperfect, *I, &c. was smiting,* 我, &c. 個時打緊 ⁵ngo, &c. ko' ₅shí ʻtá ʻkan.
Past Perfect, *I, &c. had smitten,* 我, &c. 唔時就係打咗 ⁵ngo, &c. ʻko ₅shí tsan² hai² ʻtá ʻcho.
Past Perfect of continued action, *I, &c. had been smiting,* 我, &c. 個陣時已經係打緊 ⁵ngo, &c. ko' chan² ₅shí ⁵yí ₍king hai² ʻtá ʻkan.

Future Indefinite Tense, *I, &c. shall smite,* 我, &c. 將來打 ⁵ngo, &c. ₍tsōng ₍loi ʻtá.
Future Imperfect Tense, *I, &c. shall be smiting,* 我, &c. 後來打緊 ⁵ngo, &c. hau² ₍loi ʻtá ʻkan.

VERBS.

Future Perfect Tense, *I, &c. shall have been smiting*, 將來咽陣時到, 我, &c. 已經打咀咯 ˏtsöng ˏloi ko' chan² 'shi* to', ˏngo, &c. ˢyi ˏking 'tá 'cho lo'.

Future Perfect of continued action, *I, &c. shall have been smiting*, 將來咽陣時到, 我, &c. 已經係打緊 ˏtsong ˏloi ko' chan⁶ 'shi* to', ˢngo, &c. ˡyi ˏking hai² 'tá 'kan.

IMPERATIVE MOOD.

Smite, 打 'tá.

CXXIX. For the Subjunctive Mood use 或 wăk₂, or 若 yök₂, or these with 係 hai², or similar words before the Tenses of the Indicative as given above, either immediately following the Pronouns, or use such words without any Nominatives expressed at all, as:—

佢或嚟 ˢk'ui wăk₂ ˏlai, *he may come*.
我若嚟，你唔使去 ˢngo yök₂ ˏlai, ˢnéi ˏm 'shai hui', *if I should come, you need not go*.

CXXX. The Impersonal form of the Verb, *there is*, or *there are* is not used in Chinese. Its equivalent is simply 有 ˢyau, *have* and 冇 ˢmó, *not have*, or *none*, *nothing*.

CXXXI. In the cases where in English the impersonal *it* is used, in Chinese the Verb in some case precedes the Noun, as:—

落雨 lok₂ ˢyü, *it rains*.
落雪 lok₂ süt₀, *it snows*.
落大雨 lok₂ tái² ˢyü, *it rains heavily*.

CXXXII. In other cases the Chinese prefer to use the simple and more natural form where the Noun is expressed, and the Verb follows it, as:—

風吹 ˏfung ˏch'ui, *the wind blows*.

CXXXIII. For the Passive Voice use 被 péi² before the Verb in its different Tenses as given above, the person or agent being expressed, if in no other way by the impersonal, 人 ˏyan, *someone*.

CXXXIV. Where emphasis is expressed in English by *do*, it may be rendered in Chinese by 實 shat₂, or 眞正 ˏchan ching', &c., as:—

我眞正愛你 ˢngo ˏchan ching' oi' ˢnéi, *I do (really) love you*.

VERBS.

CXXXV. A number of auxiliary words, particles in some cases, Verbs and other parts of speech in other cases, are used with Chinese Verbs at certain times, and have the effect of rendering clearer the meaning of the Verb, as regards the time of being and action. They also limit and define the nature of the being, or action expressed by the Verb (see Paradigm of Verb); but if rendered into English literally these words have the contrary effect to what they have in Chinese. Many of these words are given, and the manner of their use exemplified elsewhere in this book.

CXXXVI. Interrogative sentences are formed in several ways.

1. By simply giving a rising intonation to the word, or last word in the sentence very much the same as in English, as:—

係 'Hai*? *Yes?*
佢係嚟 'K'ui hai² 'lai*? *Has he come?*

2. By the simple addition of an Interrogative Particle at the end of the word, or sentence, either taking the place of the Affirmative Final Particle, where such is used, or in some cases forming a suffix to it. Practice and a careful attention to good speakers will teach the proper use of these, as:—

係咩 Hai² ,me? *Yes?*
係囉咩 Hai² lo' ,me? *Is it so?*

3. A most common form is the Interrogative-Negative.

係唔係 Hai² ,m hai²? *Is it so, or not?*
有冇 'Yau 'mò? *Is there any, or not?*

4. It often happens that Nos. 2 and 3 are combined, as:—

係唔係呢 Hai² ,m hai² ,ni? *Is it so, or not?*

Note.—It will be seen that unlike the English the Subject of the Verb precedes the Verb in the Interrogative sentence as well as in the Affirmative, and the Verb therefore follows instead of preceding it as in English. There are no auxiliaries to usher in an Interrogative sentence in Chinese. If there are any words to show that it is Interrogative they close the sentence, as:—

個人係今朝嚟囉咩 Ko' ,yan hai² ,kam ,chiú ,lai lo' ,me? *Oh! Did the man come this morning?*
佢係食乜野呢 'K'ui hai² shik, mat, 'ye ,ni? *What does he (or she, or it) eat?*
係咁多嚟囉咩 Hai² kom' ,to ,lai lo' ,me? *Were there so many as that came?* or *Was that the number that came?* lit. *'Twas so many came eh?*

VERBS.

Exception.—What at first sight might appear an exception is in sentences, such as, 係我做咩 Hai² ˚ngo tsò² ˌme? *Did I do it?* but it will be seen that it is no exception to the affirmative form of this sentence, as, 係我做咯 Hai² ˚ngo tsò² lok₀, *It was I who did it.* The *it* is not represented in Chinese, and so in sentences where it is used in English it is omitted in Chinese and the subject to the first Verb has to be supplied when turning the Chinese into English.

CXXXVII. In answering questions, the Chinese language is less elliptical than the English, as in Chinese it is often necessary to repeat the words employed in the Interrogative. The Chinese is more like French in this respect, as it is not considered polite to simply say *yes*, or *no* in reply to a question, as:—

佢有嚟咩 ˚k'ui ˚yau ˌlai ˌme? *Did he come?*
佢有嚟 ˚k'ui ˚yau ˌlai, *he has come.*

CXXXVIII. The Interrogative-Negative is largely used in asking questions, and in such cases it often happens that 係 hai² or 有 ˚yau, or 唔係 ˌm hai² or 冇 ˚mò is repeated in the answer as well as the Verb used in asking the question (in this respect again like French), as:—

佢係出街,係唔係呢 ˚K'ui hai² ch'ut, ˌkái, hai² ˌm hai² ˌni? *Has he gone out, or not?*
係咯,係出街咯 hai² lok₀, hai² ch'ut, ˌkái lok₀, *yes, he has gone out.*
佢係走去,係唔係呢 ˚k'ui hai² ˚tsau hui³, hai² ˌm hai² ˌni? *Has he run away or not?*
係,佢係走去咯 hai², ˚k'ui hai² ˚tsau hui³ lok₀, *yes, he has run away.*

CXXXIX. When a pronoun is used in the question it is well to repeat it in the answer, or use another, as the sense, or the person of the speaker may require, as:—

係佢唔係吖 Hai² ˚k'ui ˌm hai² ˌá? *Is it he, or not?*
係佢咯, or 係吖, 係佢咯 hai² ˚k'ui lok₀, or hai² ˌá, hai² ˚k'ui lok₀, *it is he* (like French again.)

Remark.—Therefore when replying to a question, as a rule, take the question that has been asked you, and simply put it in an Affirmative, or Negative form, leaving out when it is an Interrogative-Negative question the Affirmative, or Negative part of the question, as the case may require.

CXL. The Negative precedes the Verb, as:—

唔知 ˌm ˌchí, *I do not know.*

VERBS.

CXLI. If the Negative follows the Verb it is interrogative, as:—

有做冇 ⁵Yau tsò² ⁵mò, *Did you do it, or not?*

Exception.—The Negative 唔 ₅m follows the Verb when it is desired to express simple negation in those cases where its preceding the Verb implies not simple negation, but an unwillingness to perform any action or deed, as:—

我做唔得 ⁵ngo tsò² ₅m tak₃, *I was not able to accomplish it,* or simply, *I did not do it.*
我做唔嚟 ⁵ngo tsò² ₅m ₅lai, *I could not do it,* or *I did not do it.*
我唔做 ⁵ngo ₅m tsò², *I will not do it.*

Note.—Inability is expressed by 唔會 ₅m ⁵wui, *not able.*

CXLII. The Negative is placed before a single Verb, and after the Nominative, if it is expressed, as:—

我唔愛咯 ⁵ngo ₅m oi³ lok₀, *I do not want it.*
唔做咯 ₅m tsò³ lok₀, *(I) will not do it.*

CXLIII. Where certain words are used as adjuncts to the Verbs, whether they are Verbs themselves, or other parts of speech, the Negative is either placed between the principal Verb and its auxiliary, or the Verb and its adjunct, as the case may be, or the Negative immediately precedes the two, as:—

我摸唔到 ⁵ngo ₍o ₅m tò³,
我唔摸得到 ⁵ngo ₅m ₍o tak₃ tò³, } *I cannot reach up to it.*
我摸唔得到 ⁵ngo ₍o ₅m tak₃ tò³,
我唔做得 ⁵ngo ₅m tsò² tak₃, } *I cannot do it.*
我做唔得 ⁵ngo tsò² ₅m tak₃,

CXLIV. The Negative follows an Adverbial Phrase of time, as:—

現時冇 yin² ₅shí ⁵mò, *none at present.*
而家冇 ₅yí ₍ká ⁵mò, *none at present.*
呢陣時冇咯 ₍ni ch'an² ʽshí* ⁵mò lok₀, *none at this time.*

CXLV. The simple Affirmative and Negative, *yes* and *no,* are generally represented in Chinese by the words 有 ⁵yau *there is,* or the Verb *to have,* or 係 hai² *it is,* and 冇 ⁵mò *there is not,* or *not to have,* or 唔係 ₅m hai² *it is not* respectively, as:—

有冇 ⁵yau ⁵mò, *Is there any?*
有 ⁵yau, *there is some.*
係噉唔係 Hai² ⁵kom ₅m hai²? *It is so, or not?*
唔係噉 ₅m hai² ⁵kom, *it is not so.*

VERBS.

Note.—It might be said, that the words 有 ʽyau, 係 hai², and 冇 ʽmò, 唔係 ₅m hai² are so largely used in making statements, and asking questions in Chinese, that in accordance with Remark under CXXXIX, they often come into the reply in Chinese where in English a simple, *yes*, or *no* would suffice. In some cases they simply represent the English Verbs *have*, *did*, *to be*, &c., and the Negative employed together with these Verbs.

CXLVI. The words 係吖 hai² ₀á are often used with the meaning only of *well*, *very well*, or as a simple sign that the statement that has been made has been heard, without implying assent in any way whatever.

Note.—The most marked use, which I have noticed of this 係 hai² in this sense is in murder, or other criminal cases, when in rebuttal of a statement by an accusing witness, the prisoner will sometimes reply, 係吖，但係我冇做到嚟吖 hai² ₀á, tán² hai² ₅ngo ʽmò tsò³ tò³ ₅lai ₀á, *yes* (or *well*); *but I did not do it.* The idea seems to be this—Oh yes, I have heard what he says, *or very well, that is his statement*; but the fact remains that I did not do anything of the kind at all. It must be noted what an important part the final plays in this meaning.

Remark.—It must be remembered that the Verb is not always used in Chinese where it would appear in English, upon the principle, probably, that what can be understood from the sense need not be expressed in words, as:—

佢有做冇呢？我點知到佢呀？ ʽK'ui ʽyau tsò³ ʽmò ₀ni? ʽNgo ʽtím ₀chí tò³ ʽk'ui á³? *Did he do it or not? How do I know (whether) he (did or not?)*

CXLVII. 係咩 hai² ₀me often represents the exclamations which are so often used in English conversation, such as:—

佢夥計翻黎咯 ʽk'ui ʽfo kéi³ ʽfán ₅lai lok₀, *his partner has returned.*
係咩 hai² ₀me? *Has he?*
我唔自在 ʽngo ₅m tsz² tsoi², *I am unwell.*
係咩 hai² ₀me? *Are you?*

Remark.—These exclamations generally imply astonishment, or disbelief.

CXLVIII. Nothing is 冇野 ʽmò ʽye, or 冇乜野 ʽmò mat₀ ʽye, as:—

冇乜事呀 ʽmò mat₀ sz² á³, *nothing is the matter.*
冇野呀 ʽmò ʽye á³, *nothing.*

Note.—冇乜 ʽmò mat₀, though it means nothing is sometimes used in the sense of *nothing much*, or *nothing particular.* In some cases its use seems somewhat similar to the use of *nothing* in English at times, as for instance, *What is the matter with you? Oh! nothing,* is sometimes said in reply, when there is really something the matter, but it is either of so

VERBS.

unimportant a character, or the speaker does not care to make any fuss about it, so he says, *nothing*.

CXLIX. No one is 冇人 ‚mò ‚yan, or 冇邊個 ‚mò ‚pín ko', as:—
冇人話 ‚mò ‚yan wá², *no one says so.*
冇邊個噉做 ‚mò ‚pín ko' 'kom tsò², *no one (or nobody) does so.*

CL. Do not is expressed by 咪 ‚mai, 唔好 ‚m 'hò, as:—
咪做 ‚mai tsò², or 唔好做 ‚m 'hò tsò², *Do not do it.*
咪掟 ‚mai ‚tau, *Do not touch it.*
咪咁多事 ‚mai kom' ‚to sz², *Do not be so troublesome.*

Remark.—There is a distinction between the two, but it is often lost sight of, and the two are used interchangeably. 咪 ‚mai means *do not*; a simple prohibition, while 唔好 ‚m 'hò has some sense in it of that it is not well to do so, and so means originally that it is not well to do it, as 我勸你,唔好做 ‚ngo hün' ‚néi, ‚m 'hò tsò², *I advise you not to do it.*

CLI. Verbs are often left out in Chinese Sentences.

1. The Verb is often understood in a Chinese sentence when it would be expressed in English, as:—
麵包酸 Mín² ‚pán ‚sün, *the bread is sour.*

2. The Verb is often understood in sentences composed of a subject and some quality predicated concerning it. In such cases the copula is understood, as:—
個船長 ko' ‚shün ‚ch'öng, *the ship is long.*
個人高大 ko' ‚yan ‚kò tái², *the man is tall.*

3. In sentences expressive of admiration, surprise, or wonder, or in sentences beginning with Interjections the Verb is often understood, as:—
嗳也,咁架勢 Ái ‚yá, kom' ká' shai', *Dear me, how handsome!*
啋,也你咁衰 Ts'oi, mat, 'néi kom' ‚shui? *Tush! why are you so stupid?*
吤,咪噉吓 Hai, ‚mai 'kom á, *Look here! do not do so.*
眞正好喇 Chan ching' 'hò ‚lá, *it is really good.*

CLII. The Subject always precedes the Verb: that of which something is predicated, that which is predicated of it.

Exception.—Sometimes in questions the Personal Pronoun follows the Verb, as:—
係我嚟咩 Hai² ‚ngo ‚lai ‚me? *Was it I who came?*

VERBS.

Note.—It will be seen though that this can scarcely be called an exception, and does not invalidate the rule as it, it translated according to its meaning and literally according to the construction, would resolve itself (or it might be rendered into) the following English :— *It was I came, eh ?*

CLIII. When two Verbs are used to state what in English would only require one the object is placed between the two, as in English, as :—

俾我去 ᶜpéi ˢngo hui², *let me go.*

CLIV. No Preposition is required before the Verb in the Infinitive in Chinese. Position and sense show that it is to be rendered by an Infinitive in English, as :—

佢話佢想打我 ˢk'ui wá² ˢk'ui ˢsöng ᶜtá ˢngo, *he said, he wished to strike me.*

CLV. In a sentence the Indirect Object follows the Direct when it is governed by 過 kwoʼ, which may be rendered in English by *to*, the sign of the Dative, as :—

俾個部書過我 ᶜpéi koʼ pò² ˌshü kwoʼ ˌngo, *give that book to me.*

But it may either precede or follow when 過 kwoʼ is not used, though it is better to follow, as :—

俾部書佢 ᶜpéi pò² ˌshü ˢk'ui, *give him a book.*

CLVI. In quoting what one has said the forms "said he" "said she" &c. are never used in Chinese, the Subject always precedes the Verb, as :—

佢話 ˢk'ui wá², *he said.*

Note.—The use of the Final 喎 ˌwá is more akin to the 'he said' of the English, as :—

佢打我喎 ˢk'ui ᶜta ˢngo ˌwá, *he said he would strike me.*

CLVII. That Chinese Verbs are as idiomatic in their use as English or French or other Verbs the following list of words or phrases in which 打 ᶜtá *to strike*, occur will show. This list is not exhaustive, as so common and so varied is the use of this word that new forms are constantly appearing.

1. It is used in the simple form 打 ᶜtá with the meaning of to strike, to beat, to hit, and is the common rallying cry in faction fights, street quarrels, &c., as :—

打火 ᶜtá ᶜfo, *to strike a light.*
打佢 ᶜtá ˢk'ui, *beat him.*

Note.—It is to be noted that a Chinese often says 佢打我 ˢk'ui ᶜtá ˢngo, and the same of similar acts of assault, when upon further investigation it is found that though an assault may have been committed in a strictly legal sense of the term that actually

VERBS.

no blow has fallen upon the person of the speaker. Care must therefore be taken not to render such phrases literally until it be found whether there was a threatened assault, or an actual one.

2. As striking takes a prominent part in war &c. it is used in the following combinations (in a quarrel).

打交 ʻtá ͵kau, *to fight* (in a quarrel).
打仗 ʻtá chöng², *to fight* (in battle).
打贏 ʻtá ͵yeng†, *to conquer; to win.*
打輸 ʻtá ͵shü. *to be defeated.*
打甪 ʻtá lut, *to get off; to rescue.* (It necessarily implies to get off by the use of blows).

3. With the idea of striking it is used in combination with the article which is habitually struck to indicate the name of the striker, that is, the man who earns his livelihood by continually striking such an object, as:—

打鐵佬 ʻtá tʻit, ʻlò, *blacksmith.*
打銅佬 ʻtá ͵tung ʻlò, *coppersmith.*
打鼓嘅 ʻtá ʻkwú ké², *drummer.*
打石佬 ʻtá shek, ʻlò, *stone-cutter.*

4. It is used in the names of actions in which striking is habitually used, as:—

打灰沙 ʻtá ͵fui ͵shá, *to chunam.*
打灰路 ʻtá ͵fui lò², *to caulk.*

5. It has the meaning of "by" when used with a Noun representing the way by which, or on which the progression takes place, as:—

打路去 ʻtá lò² hui², *to go by road, or by land.*
打水路去 ʻtá ʻshui lò² hui², *to go by water.*
打山去, or 打山路去 ʻtá ͵shán hui², or ʻtá ͵shán lò² hui², *to go by way of the hills, or to go by a mountain road.*
打窻出去 ʻtá ͵chʻöng chʻut, hui², *to go out by the window.*
打船去 ʻtá ͵shün hui², *to go by ship.*
打艇去 ʻtá ʻtʻeng hui², *to go by boat.*
打車去 ʻtá ͵chʻé hui², *to go by carriage, or any wheeled vehicle.*

6. It is used to express certain actions of the elements, as:—

打雷响 ʻtá ͵lui ʻhöng, *the sound of thunder.*
打風 ʻtá ͵fung, *to blow.*
打大風 ʻtá tái² ͵fung, or ʻtá ͵fung kau, *to blow a strong wind.*

VERBS.

打大雨 'tá tái² ,yü, *to rain heavily.*
個哋水打過嚟 ko⁰ ,ti 'shui 'tá kwo° ,lui, *the water beat over.*
打雷死 'tá ,lui ‚sz, *to be killed by a thunderbolt.*

7. It is used in combination, or in words to represent sudden and violent actions, as:—

打石炮 'tá shek‚ p'au°, *to blast.*
打盲 'tá ,máng, *to be struck blind* (i.e. to become blind from the effect of a blow, or a thunderbolt).
打跛 'tá ‚pai, *to become lame from the effect of a blow.*
打官府 'tá ,kwún 'fú, *to go up to Court; to yo to law.*
打跌 'tá tít‚, *to be struck down.*
跌打 tít‚ 'tá, *accident.* (See next sentence).
跌打丸 tít‚ 'tá ,yün, *accident pills* (i.e. to cure the effects of accidents).
打落水 'tá lok‚ 'shui, *to be thrown down into the water.*
打落地 'tá lok‚ tái², *to be thrown down on to the ground.*
打死 'tá ‚sz, *to be killed* (primarily by a blow, or in battle).

Note.—打死 'tá ‚sz, necessary implies that the death has resulted from a striking of some sort, or from a shot from a fire-arm.

8. It is used to express a number of other actions, as:—

打掃 'tá sò°, *to sweep.*
打水 'tá 'shui, *to draw water.*
打釘 'tá ‚teng†, *to drive in a nail.*
打花面 'tá ,fá min², *to paint for acting.*
打韆鞦 'tá ts'ín ‚ts'au, *to slue right round.*
打落 'tá lok‚, *to knock down.*
打沉 'tá ,ch'am, *to be sunk; to sink.*
打探 'tá t'ám°, *to pay a visit of inspection, or surprise.*
打赤身 'tá ch'ik‚ ‚shan, *to be naked.*
打發人去 'tá fát‚ ,yan hui°, *to send any one away anywhere* (as on a message).
打死繩 'tá ‚sz lit‚, *to tie a dead knot.*
打包 'tá ‚páu, *to do up in matting* (as a bale of goods).
打理 'tá ⁵léi, *to attend to anything.*

9. It means to buy in the phrases.

打米 'tá 'mai, *to buy rice.*
打伙食 'tá ⁵fo shik‚, *to buy provisions.*

VERBS.

10. It is used to express a profession, or occupation, as:—

打伙記 ʻtá ʻfo kéiʼ, *an inmate of a brothel.*

打雜 ʻtá tsápʼ₂, *a general assistant in a shop, or a coal trimmer on a steamer.*

打本 (嘅) ʻtá ʻpún (keʼ), *a capitalist, anyone who provides money for any undertaking, or work by some one else.*

11. It has the sense of *to play* in the following combinations, as:—

打骨牌 ʻtá kwatʼ₃ ʻpʻáiʼ, *to play at dominoes.*

打紙牌 ʻtá ʻchí ʻpʻáiʼ, *to play at cards.*

12. It is used for the action of fire-arms, as:—

開鎗打佢 hoi ₃tsʻōng ʻtá ʻkʻui, *shoot him.*

去打雀 huiʼ ʻtá tsökₒ, *to go shooting* (birds).

13. It implies addition, as:—

五個打七個 ʻng koʼ ʻtá tsʻatʼ₃ koʼ, *five added to seven.*

CLVIII. Some idiomatic uses of 行 ₃hángt, *to walk.*

1. It represents bodily, or physical motion, as:—

行船 ₃hángt ₃shūn, *to proceed, or start on a voyage, or to be employed on board ship.*

行街 ₃hángt ₃kái, is used in the sense of *taking a walk*, or *to go out*.

佢就致行出街呢 ʻkʻúi tsauʼ chíʼ ₃hángt chʻutʼ₃ ₃kái ₃che, *he has only just gone out.*

嚟行街喇 ₃lai ₃hángt ₃kái ₃lá, *come have a walk.*

2. It is also used in combination with the name of the object in connection with which certain men take that physical motion which is necessary for them to undergo to perform their daily toil, as:—

行船嘅 ₃hángt ₃shūn keʼ, *a sailor.*

行街嘅 ₃hángt ₃kai keʼ, *a man who attends to the outside business of the shop, or firm.*

3. It represents actions, or conduct in the phrases—

行刑 ₃hángt ₃ying, *to punish.*

行爲 ₃hángt ₃wai, *conduct.*

行禮 ₃hángt ʻlai, *to perform a ceremony.*

行清 ₃hángt ₃tsʻing, *to worship at the tombs.*

CLIX. On the uses of 起 ʻhéi which means *to rise; to stand up.*

1. It means in some combinations "to raise," as:—

抽起 ₃chʻáu ʻhéi, *to raise.*

起身 ʻhéi ₃shan, *to get up* (lit. *to raise the body*).

VERBS.

2. In combination with some words it means to start, to begin, as:—

起首 ʻhéi ʻshau, *to begin*.

起脚(行) ʻhéi kök₀ (ˌhángt), *to start on a journey*.

3. Used with 頭 ˌt'au it means beginning, as:—

起頭 ʻhéi ʻt'au*, *beginning*.

4. Used with 做 tsò² it means to build in a generic sense and is used with respect to the building of any edifice, as:—

起做 ʻhéi tsò², *to build*.

Note.—起做嘅 ʻhéi tsò² koʼ, is *a builder*, and 接盤起做嘅 tsip₀ ˌp'ún ʻhéi tsò² koʼ, is *a builder and contractor*. The natural order of the two callings is preserved in this sentence. We say a builder and contractor; but in so saying we reverse the order of things, as a man must first take a contract before he can begin to build, unless it be argued that the man first followed the business of a builder, and then added on to it that of a contractor. 起屋 ʻhéi uk₅, and 起舖 ʻhéi pòʼ are also used with regard to building houses: the first is used about houses, and the second about shops. These two must not be confused. In Cantonese Colloquial houses, and shops are kept quite distinct. A building, the lower story of which is used as a shop, or mercantile office (for there are no distinctions between the two except when the latter is a large concern and then it may be called a 行 ˌhong) is called a 舖 p'òʼ and not an 屋 uk₅, which is a house in which there is no shop.

5. Used after the Verb 做 tsò² it means completed, as:—

做起(嚟) tsò² ʻhéi (ˌlai), *it is done*.

CLX. 開 ˌhoi has a number of different meanings.

1. It means simply and commonly "to open," as:—

開野 ˌhoi ʼye, *to open anything*.

開張 ˌhoi ˌchöng, *to open a new shop*.

2. It is used with other words to represent the commencement of many actions and deeds, as:—

開身 ˌhoi ˌshan, *to start* (on a voyage).

開價 ˌhoi kàʼ, *the first stated price*, i.e. the price at the beginning of a bargain, lit. the opening price.

3. It has to be rendered into English sometimes by "off" or "out," &c., as:—

開船 ˌhoi ˌshün, *to go off to a vessel*.

開去 ˌhoi huiʼ, *to go off* (to anything).

(行)開嚟 (ˌhángt) ˌhoi ˌlai, *come nearer* (to the speaker).

Note.—開頭 ˌhoi ˌt'au, means, *outside*, *off there*, &c.

VERBS.

CLXI. 上 ʿshöng does not only mean to "go up."

1. It also means to enter in a book, as:—

上簿 ʿshöng ʿpò*, *to enter in a book.*
上數 ʿshöng shoʾ, *to enter accounts.*

Remark.—Compare our phrase to enter up accounts and other similar expressions.

2. It has the sense in the Chinese of, *going up* in the following phrases; but the genius of our language requires it to be otherwise rendered in English, as:—

上船 ʿshöng ˌshün, *to go on board a vessel,* i.e. to go up on to a vessel.
上學 ʿshöng hok₂, *to go to school, to begin to study,* i.e. to go up to study.
上岸 ʿshöng ngon², }
上街 ʿshöng ˌkái, } *to go ashore.*

Remark.—The difference between these two is that there must be a street, or streets when the latter is used, i.e. the one must go up on to a street, or streets, and not simply up on to the land; and a street, or streets necessarily implies a hamlet, village, town, or city.

3. The Chinese habitually say when speaking about going to the capital of the Empire, or the capital of a province "to go up" just as we say, "to go up to London," &c., as:—

上城 ʿshöng ˌshengt, *to go up to Canton,* i.e. the city.
上京 ʿshöng ˌking, *to go up to the capital* (of the Empire, Peking).

CLXII. On some uses of the word 落 lok₂.

1. It is used in the sense of descending, falling, &c., as:—

落嚟 lok₂ ˌlai, *come down,* i.e. descending come.

Note.—It must often be rendered in English by down as above, as:—

跌落 tit₀ lok₂, *to fall down.*

2. It is used in the sense of putting down, as:—

落本(錢) lok₂ ʿpún (ˌtsʾín), *to advance,* or *pay in,* or *pay up, capital,* i.e. to put down capital into any business or concern.
落定(銀) lok₂ ˌtengt (ʿngan*) *to pay (down) bargain money.*

3. It is often used where in English an impersonal form of expression would be used, as:—

落雪 lok₂ süt₀, *it snows.*
落雨 lok₂ ʿyü, *it rains.*

VERBS.

4. It must be translated in some instances by "begin," as:—

落手 lok, 'shau, *to begin* (any manual labour), i.e. to put to the hand.

落筆 lok, pat, *to begin writing, to commence writing a book, &c.*

5. In one, or two phrases it must be rendered, *to go on board,* as:—

落船 lok, ,shün, *to go on board a vessel.*

6. Again it must be sometimes rendered by "put in" or "mix," as:—

落沙 lok, ,shá, *to mix sand* (with anything).

CLXIII. It will be found that there is quite an idiomatic use of 嚟 ,lai and 去 hui' in some sentences.

1. When going or coming are spoken of, they are used with reference to the position of the speaker, and are equivalent to "come" and "go," as:—

上嚟 'shöng ,lai, *come up.*
上去 'shöng hui', *go up.*
落嚟 lok, ,lai, *come down.*
落去 lok, hui', *go down.*

2. But it is to be remembered that 嚟 ,lai when following Verbs is often used as a denoter, or sign that the action the preceding Verb refers to has been accomplished, as:—

佢做嚟咯 'k'ni tsò, ,lai lok₀, *he has done it.*

3. In answer to a call 嚟咯 ,lai lok₀, means, (I am) *coming.* 嚟 ,lai *to come* when used in phrases the equivalent of the English, *come in, come out, come back again, come up,* follows the word, which shows whether the action is one of exit, or entrance, of ascent, or descent. In other words the word which takes the place of, or represents rather, the Preposition in English precedes the Verb 嚟 ,lai, *to come,* &c., as:—

入嚟 yap, ,lai, *come in* (lit. in come, or entering come).
出嚟 ch'ut, ,lai, *come out* (lit. out come).
上嚟 'shöng ,lai, *come up* (lit. up come).
落嚟 lok, ,lai, *come down* (lit. down come).

Note.—The same holds good as to 去 hui', *to go.*

CLXIV. Idiomatic uses of 坐 'ts'o*† *to sit, to sit down.*

1. It is in common use in the sense of visiting; paying a visit; going to see anyone, as:—

(有) 得閒嚟坐 ('yau) tak, ,hán ,lai 'ts'o*†, *when you have time come, and see us,* (lit. come sit).

VERBS.

你時時見佢咩 係，我日日都入去坐嘅 ʻNei ₌shí ₌shí kín² ʻkʻui ₍mè? Hai², ²ngo yat₂ yat₂ yap₂ hui² ʻtsʻo*† ke², *Did you constantly see him?* *Yes, I went in every day to visit* (lit. to sit).

2. It is often used with the sense of *to ride*, or where we would use a Preposition, such as, "in," or "by," or "on," or where the sense would be plain enough in English without the use of any Preposition.

坐馬車 ʻtsʻo*† ₌má ₍chʻe, *to ride in a carriage.*
坐船去 ʻtsʻo*† ₍shün hui², *to go by vessel.*
坐艇嚟 ʻtsʻo*† tʻeng† ₌lai, *to come by boat.*
坐轎 ʻtsʻo*† ʻkíú*, *to ride in a sedan chair.*
坐車仔 ʻtsʻo*† ₍chʻe ʻtsai, *to ride in a jinrickshaw.*

Note.—To ride on animals is more commonly and better expressed by 騎 ₌kʻe, as:—

騎馬 ₌kʻe ʻmá, *to ride on horseback* 騎騾 ₌kʻe ₍lui, *to ride on a mule.* It is not wrong however to use 坐 ʻtsʻo*†, as:—

坐馬 ʻtsʻo*† ʻmá, *to ride on horseback.*
坐駱駝 ʻtsʻo*† lok₀ ₌tʻo, *to ride a camel.*

3. It is also used where in English the Verb "to be" and the Preposition "in" would be used, as:—

坐監 ʻtsʻo*† ₍kám, *to be in gaol.*
大人坐堂咯 Tai² ₌Yan ʻtsʻo*† ₌tʻong lok₀, *His Lordship is in Court.*

CLXV. Notice that with the word 死 ʻsz, *to die* (whether by natural, or unnatural means) the means, or method, or cause by, or from which, the person has died, or been killed is, more especially in the latter case, mentioned in Chinese, as:—

病死 peng² ʻsz, *to die from disease.*
整死 ʻching ʻsz, *to put to death* (used in a general sense).
打死 ʻtá ʻsz, *to kill, to slay.*

Note.—This is also used in a general sense to a certain extent, that is to say when speaking of death in battle, or by the hands, or by the elements; but not when applied to death by drowning, falling, &c., &c. Therefore it will be seen that though a dictionary may put, as some standard ones do put, under the heading "to kill" 殺 shát₀ ʻsz, 殺死 shát₀ ʻsz, 整死 ʻching ʻsz, it must be understood that they cannot be used indiscriminately, but have different shades of meaning.

跌死 tit₀ ʻsz, *to be killed by a fall.*
浸死 tsam² ʻsz, *to drown; to be drowned.*

VERBS.

Remark.—Compare English present illiterate phrase, *drowned dead.*

害死 hoi' 'sz, *to put to death by foul means.*
刏死 kat, 'sz, *to stab to death, or to kill by stabbing.*
斬死 'chám 'sz, *to execute, to stab so as to cause death.*
焗死 kuk, 'sz, *to put to death by suffocation.*
嚇死 hák₀ 'sz, *to frighten to death.*

Note.—This last is used in the same exaggerated way that the similar phrase is used in English, as:—

佢嚇死我 'k'ui hák₀ 'sz 'ngo, *he frightened me to death.*

CLXVI. The Chinese are very fond of euphemisms to soften the idea of death, so repugnant to many ears, as:—

1.—過身 kwo' ,shan,

Note 1.—The Buddhist idea of metempsychosis may be here referred to. In that case it would mean *to pass into another body.*

2.—過世 kwo' shai', *to pass into another life, or world.*
3.—唔在 ₅m tsoi², *not present, not here.*

Remark.—Compare the Hebrew *he was not* with this last phrase.

Note 2.—An emperor's death is spoken of as 崩 ,pang.

CLXVII. The Chinese generally use, like the French, the Verb to have 有 'yau when stating the size or weight of any object, or the age of any person, or thing, followed by the words 高 ,ko, *high,* 長 ,ch'öng, *long,* 深 ,sham, *deep,* 闊 fut₀, *broad,* 重 'ch'ung³, *heavy,* 年 ,nín, *years,* &c., &c., &c., as the case may be, as :—

有幾高 'Yau 'kéi ,kò? *How high is it?*
佢今年有幾大 'K'ui ,kam ,nín 'yau 'kéi tái²? *How old is he?*

Note 1.—All the above and similar sentences may be as well, and sometimes better rendered, by putting the 有 'yau at the beginning of the sentence, as :—

有幾高呢 'Yau 'kéi ,ko ,ni? *How high is it?*

Note 2.—The 有 'yau may also be omitted, as:—

佢三寸高過我 'k'ui ,sam ts'ün' ,kò kwo' 'ngo, *he is three inches taller than I.*

Note 3.—It will be seen that articles possess weight, &c. in China instead of being simply so heavy.

VERBS.

CLXVIII. 有 ‚yau is also used in place of the English Verb, *to be*, when speaking of the hour, as:—

有幾點鐘呢 ‚Yau ‘kéi ‘tim ‚chung ‚ui? *What time is it?*

CLXIX. 出 ch‘ut, *to go out*, and 行 ‚hángt, *to walk*, used with 街 ‚kái *street*, had better, as a rule, not be rendered literally, as:—

出街 ch‘ut, ‚kái, simply means *out*, and is similar to the French *en ville*, as:—
佢出街 ‘k‘ui ch‘ut, ‚kái, *he has gone out*.
行街 ‚hángt ‚kái, *to take a walk* (lit. to go out into the street), as:—
亞三呢 Á’ ‚Sám ‚ni? *Where is A Sám?*
佢啱啱行出街咯 ‘k‘ui ‚ngám ‚ngám ‚hángt ch‘ut, ‚kái lok₀, *he has just gone out*.

Note.—To bring the idea of being *on* the street into prominence, it is necessary to make use of some other words, as:—

個乞兒係邊處 Ko’ hat, ‚yi* ‘hai ‚pín shü²? *Where is the beggar?*
佢係街上 ‘k‘ui ‘hai ‚kái shöng², *he is on the street*. This last being more like the French *a la villa*.

CLXX. The term for *to marry* when applied to a man is different to that used when a woman is spoken about, as:—

1. To take a wife, or marry a wife, is 娶 ts‘ui², or 取 ‘ts‘ui.

2. The girls also of a family are said to have 出門 ch‘ut, ‚mún, when they marry, i.e. to go out of the door.

3. To marry a husband is 嫁 ká’.

Caution.—These terms must not be used the one for the other.

4. Other terms are also used, as, 取心抱 ‘ts‘ui ‚sam ‘p‘ò generally pronounced ‘t‘sò ‚san ‘p‘ò, *to take a daughter-in-law*, i.e. to get one's son married.

CLXXI. There are distinctions to be observed in the use of 抵 ‘tai, *to be worth*.

1. In speaking of articles, say, 值 (得) chik₂ (tak₂), or 抵 (得) ‘tai (tak₂).

2. But 抵 ‘tai cannot be used in speaking of individuals. A phrase that may be used in such a case is, 佢有大把錢 ‘k‘ui ‘yau tái² ‘pá ‘tsín*, *he has a lot of money* (lit. a great handful).

Note 1.—大把 tái² ‘pá may also be rendered by *much, a great deal*.

Note 2.—There are also other uses of 抵 ‘tai, such for instance as in 抵手 ‘tai ‘shan, *clever*, and in 唔抵得 ‚m ‘tsi tak,, *I cannot bear it*, or *I cannot stand it*.

VERBS.

CLXXII. Difference between 識 shik,, and 知 ,chí.

1. 知 'chí means "to know a fact; to be aware of; to be sensible of."

你知呢啲事幹唔知呀 'Néi ,chí ,ni ,tí sz² kon³ ,m ,chí á³? *Do you know about these matters?*

你知係噉唔係呀 'Néi ,chí hai² 'kom ,m hai² á³? *Do you know that it is so, or not?*

你知佢有嚟冇呀 'Néi ,chí 'k'ui 'yau ,lai 'mò á³? *Do you know whether he came, or not?*

你知邊個打你唔知呀 'Néi ,chí ,pín ko³ 'tá 'néi ,m ,chí á³? *Do you know who struck you?*

識 Shik, means, or implies, mental knowledge, science, acquaintance, and may generally be expressed by "to understand; to know how to do anything" (i.e. to be able); "to be acquainted with."

我識讀 'ngo shik, tuk,, *I can read it.*
我識字 'ngo shik, tsz², *I can read, and write.*
我識做 'ngo shik, tsò², *I know how to do it.*
我識佢 'ngo shik, 'k'ui, *I know him* (i.e. *am acquainted with*, not merely *know* him by having simply seen him once, or twice).

Note.—To know anyone from having seen him, as say a thief from having seen him in your house, would be 見過 kín' kwo³.

CLXXIII. 買 'mái, *to buy,* 賣 mái², *to sell.* The difference between the two words consists in the tones. 買 'mái, *to buy,* is in the lower rising tone, or 下上 há² shöng². 賣 mái², *to sell,* is in the lower entering, or 下入 há² yap,. Either 出 Ch'ut,, or 俾 'péi is often used with 賣 mái², *to sell,* and 入 yap,, *to enter,* is also often used with 買 'mái.

Remark.—It will be well for the beginner to get into the habit of using these words at first with 買 'mái, and 賣 mái², and thus cover any mistake he may make about the tone of the word, or at all events to fall back on them, if he is in any difficulty in making himself understood. He may also employ them in asking a question, if he is not sure that he has understood what has been said, as:—

係賣出咯 hai² mái² ch'ut, lok,, *it was sold.*
我賣俾佢 'ngo mái² 'péi 'k'ui, *I sold it to him.*
係買入嘅 hai² 'mái yap, ko³, *it was bought.*
你係話買入係唔係呀 'Néi hai² wá² 'mái yap, hai² ,m hai² á³? *Did you say bought, or not?*

ADVERBS.

CLXXIV. Adverbs are compared in the same manner as Adjectives.

Note.—In fact many Chinese Adjectives and Adverbs are one and the same. The distinctions of parts of speech are not marked with the clearness that exists to a great extent in English. Chinese parts of speech are more like some few English words that may be classed under different parts of speech according to the use they are put to, as:—

快馬 fái² ʿmá, *a quick horse.*
快啲嚟 fái² ˏti ˏlai, *come quickly.*
佢嚟得快 ʿk'ui ˏlai tak, fái², *he has come quickly.*

ADVERBS OF TIME.

CLXXV. Adverbs and Adverbial Phrases of Time sometimes either precede, or follow the Verb, or often commence a sentence, instead of ending it as in English, as:—

聽日嚟 ˏt'ing yat, ˏlai, *come to-morrow.*
而家去 ˏyí ˏká hoi², *go now.*
嗰陣時叫咯 ʿko chan² ˏshí kiú² lok², *(he) called out at that time.*
今日好天 ˏkam yat, ʿhò ˏt'ín, *it is good weather to-day.*

Note 1.— 聽日 ˏt'ing yat, to-morrow, must not always be taken in a literal sense, it often means simply some indefinite time in the future, as:—

聽日嚟見我喇 ˏt'ing yat, ˏlai kín² ʿngo ˏlá, *come see me again.*

Note 2.—The *to* which appears in the English construction of to-day, to-night, is represented in Chinese by 今 ˏkam *this*, or *the present*, as 今日 ˏkam yat, *to-day*, and 今晚 ˏkam ʿmán, *to-night.*

Remark.—In colloquial the *y* of 日 yat, after 今 ˏkam is changed into m.

Note 3.—Note the difference which may exist in meaning due to the Adverbial Phrase of time occupying a different position in a sentence, as:—

嗰時個人嚟 ʿko ˏshí ko² ˏyan ˏlai, *the man came at that time.*
個人嚟嗰時 ko² ˏyan ˏlai ʿko ˏshí, *the time that the man came.*
我細嗰個陣時 ʿNgo sai² ʿko ko² chan² ˏshí, *when, or at the time I was small.*
個陣時我細個 ko² chan² ˏshí ʿngo sai² ko², *at that time I was small.*

CLXXVI. When the Nominative of the Verb is expressed whether it be a Noun or Pronoun, it, with its qualifying words, in many cases either precedes the Adverb, or Adverbial Phrase of Time, or not, as:—

我今晚嚟咯, or 今晚我嚟咯 ʿngo ˏkam ʿmán ˏlai lok₀, or ˏkam ʿmán ʿngo ˏlai lok₀, *I shall come to-night.*

ADVERBS.

CLXXVII. The Adverb, or Adverbial Phrase sometimes follows both Subject Nominative and Verb, as in English, as:—

我嚟咯，今晚 ^{c}ngo $_{c}$lai lok$_{o}$, $_{c}$kam ^{c}mán, *I shall come to-night.*

Note.—But it is added more as an after-thought in such a case. The best form for the Beginner to get into the habit of using will be the one in which it immediately follows the Subject of the sentence.

CLXXVIII. In some cases the Adverb, or Adverbial Phrase must occupy a certain place in the phrase, or sentence, and no elasticity is allowed, as to its position, as:—

我就嚟咯 ^{c}ngo tsau^{2} $_{c}$lai lok$_{o}$, *I am just coming.*

ADVERBS OF PLACE.

CLXXIX. Adverbs of Place, or Chinese words which may be translated in English by Adverbs of Place, when used with simple Verbs follow the Verb as in English, as:—

擠呢處 $_{c}$chai $_{c}$ni shü$_{,}$ *place it here.*
搬去嗰處 $_{c}$pún hai^{o} ^{c}ko shü^{o}, *move it there.*
嚟呢處 $_{c}$lai $_{c}$ni shü^{o}, *come here.*

CLXXX. When there is an Object in the sentence Adverbs of Place often precede the Verb, or when the Verb *to be* is used they precede the Verb, as:—

呢處有好多嘢 $_{c}$ni shü^{o} ^{c}yau ^{c}hó $_{c}$to ^{c}ye, *there are many things here.*
呢處係有咯 $_{c}$ni shü^{o} hai^{2} ^{c}yau lok$_{o}$, *there are some here.*

CLXXXI. When Adverbs of Place are used with 係 ^{c}hai they generally precede the Verb, as:—

我喺呢處打個人 ^{c}ngo ^{c}hai $_{c}$ni shü^{o} ^{c}tá ko^{o} $_{c}$yan, *I struck the man here,* (at this place).

Note 1.—The Dictionaries are again wrong in saying that *here* is 呢處 $_{c}$ni shü^{o}, and *there,* 個處 ko^{o} shü^{o}. These two phrases are undoubtedly the phrases which are often used when we would say *here,* or *there*; but in reality they mean *this place,* and *that place,* and they are not the only phrases which are used in Chinese where in English one would say *here,* or *there.* It is therefore far better, while at the same time they may be best rendered many times in English by *here,* or *there,* to remember their construction, viz:— that 呢 $_{c}$ni, and 個 ko^{o} are respectively *this,* and *that,* and that any other word which

ADVERBS.

represents the English word *spot*, or *place* is used with either of them according to whether one wishes to say *here*, or *there*, as:—

呢處 ni shü', *this place*, English *here*.
呢笪 ni tát₀, *this spot*, English *here*.
呢定 'ni 'teng*†, *this spot*, English *here*.
個處 ko' shü', *that place*, English *there*.
個笪 ko' tát₀, *that spot*, English *there*.
個定 ko' 'teng*, *that spot*, English *there*.

Note 2.—*Where* is likewise rendered into Chinese by a number of different phrases, which are similar as regards the manner of their construction to those above. To represent where 邊 ₀pín, *which*, is used, and then any of the other words which represent *spot*, or *place*, such as, 處 shü', 笪 tát₀, 定 'teng*†, 位 'wai*, 吓 ˢhá, as:—

係邊處 'Hai ₀pín shü'? *Where is it, or at what place is it?*

Remark.—No Verb is required, or can be used in such sentences. Notice that *where is* is transposed in Chinese into *is where*.

CLXXXII. The Adverb often occupies a different position in a Chinese sentence to that it occupies in an English one. When an Adverb is used in connection with a Verb to amplify its means, it is placed before the Verb instead of after it as in English. Note the following transposition of ideas according to our mode of thought. To the Chinese it is, however, the natural mode of expressing oneself, and ours the unnatural, as:—

English.		Chinese.		
Come back.		Back come,	翻嚟	₀fán ₀lai.
Come up.		Up come,	上嚟	ˢshöng² ₀lai.
Come down.		Down come,	落嚟	lok₂ ₀lai.
Come out.		Out come,	出嚟	ch'ut₂ ₀lai.
Go back.		Back go,	翻去	₀fán hui'.
Go up.		Up go,	上去	ˢshöng hui'.
Go down.		Down go,	落去	lok₂ hui'.
Go out.		Out go,	出去	ch'ut₂ hui'.
Down stairs.		Floor down,	樓下	₀lau há².
Up stairs.		Floor up,	樓上	₀lau shöng².

ADVERBS OF MANNER.

CLXXXIII. Adverbs of Manner may be placed in many cases in different positions in a sentence, as the following examples will show, their position in the

ADVERBS.

sentence sometimes producing a slight difference in the meaning, as:—

佢寫得快 ‛k'ui ‛se tak, fái², *he can write quickly.*
佢寫快都得 ‛k'ui ‛se fái² ‚tò tak,,
佢快都寫得 ‛k'ui fái² ‚tò ‛se tak,, } *he can write quickly.*
快都寫得嘅 fái² ‚tò ‛se tak, ke², *it can be written quickly.*

Note.—The insertion of the Negative even in the sentence does not alter the readiness of the Adverb of Manner to appear in any part of the sentence, as:—

佢唔寫得快 ‛k'ui ‚m ‛se tak, fái²,
佢快唔寫得嘅 ‛k'ui fái² ‚m ‛se tak, ke², } *he can not write quickly.*
佢寫快就唔得嘅 ‛k'ui ‛se fái² tsau² ‚m tak, ke²,

CLXXXIV. 都 ‚tò used in the sense of "as well," "also" is used before the Verb, as:—

兩個都喺處 ‛löng kọ² ‚tò ‛hai shü², *the two were there also, or as well.*

Note.—It appears after the Verb also in other senses.

CLXXXV. 噉 ‛kom, or 敢樣 ‛kom ‛yöng*, *so,* or *in this manner* precede the Verb, they qualify, as:—

佢噉樣走嘅 ‛k'ui ‛kom ‛yöng* ‛tsau ke², *he ran like this.*

CLXXXVI. When, however, an Auxiliary as 係 hai² is used, 噉 ‛kom, or 噉樣 ‛kom ‛yöng* come between the Auxiliary and the Verb, as:—

佢係噉走 ‛k'ui hai² ‛kom ‛tsau, *he did so run.*

CLXXXVII. Too, 過頭 kwo² ‚t'au and 得嚟 tak, tsai² follow the Adjective they qualify contrary to the usage in English, as:—

多過頭 ‚to kwo² ‚t'au, *there are too many.*
少得嚟 ‛shíu tak, tsai², *there are too few.*

CLXXXVIII. More is often represented in Chinese by 重 chung², as:—

重有得嚟 chung² ‛yau tak, ¸lni, *there is more to come.*
重有啲(添) chung² ‛yau ‚ti (‚t'ím), *there is a little more.*
重有 chung² ‛yau, *there is more.*

CLXXXIX. The Adverb *to* used after many English Verbs is represented in Chinese at times by 過 kwo², as:—

俾過我 ‛péi kwo² ‛ngo, *give it to me.*

ADVERBS AND PREPOSITIONS.   105

ADVERBS.

CXC. The Negative is introduced into the middle of the phrases, 若然 yŏk₂ ₍yin, *if*, and 自然 tsz² ₍yin, *of course, consequently*, as:—

若不然 yŏk₂ pat₂ ₍yin, *if not*.
自不然 tsz² pat₂ ₍yin. See Remark.

Remark.—This last is very seldom used in a negative sense. Strange to say it is almost always used in a strongly positive sense.

CXCI. The phrases 誰知 ₍shui ₍chí, and 誰不知 ₍shui pat₂ ₍chí, though in the one phrase a Negative, 不 pat₂, *not*, is employed, and in the other it is not, have both the same meaning, the idea of which may perhaps be as well represented in English by the following, as by anything else, viz: *but unexpectedly, but who would have thought it.*

Remark 1.—See Remark under CXC.
Remark 2.—The phrases 仍然 ₍ying ₍yin, *still*, and 雖然 ₍sui ₍yin, *although* are never used with the Negative.

CXCII. When a word which represents the Adverb in English is used with two Verbs in Chinese it is placed between the two, as:—

Without Adverb.

揞去 ₍ning hui³, *take away*, i.e. lit. take go.
揞嚟 ₍ning ₍lai, *to bring here*, i.e. lit. bring come.

With Adverb.

揞出去 ₍ning ch'ut₂ hui³, *take out*.
揞入嚟 ₍ning yap₂ ₍lai, *bring in*.

PREPOSITIONS.

CXCIII. Many Prepositions precede the Verb in Chinese, even when there may be two Verbs in the sentence, though in the latter case they may be placed with equal correctness between the two. Those which may be used either before, or after the Verb oftener precede than follow it, as:—

同我去 ₍t'ung ⁵ngo hui³, *go with me*.
孖我去做 ₍má ⁵ngo hui³ tsò², *go with me and do it*, or *go, and do it for me*.
你同埋我去做 ⁵néi ₍t'ung ₍mái ⁵ngo hui³ tsò², *go with me, and do it*.
去同我做 hui³ ₍t'ung ⁵ngo tsò², *go and do it for me*, or *come with me, and do it*.
我在呢間屋住有十多年咯 ⁵ngo tsoi² ₍ni ₍kán uk₂ chü² ⁵yau shap₂ ₍to ₍nín lok₀, *I have lived in this house ten years, and more*.

PREPOSITIONS.

我打裏頭個條路入 ⁵ngo ꜀tá ⁵lui ꜀t'au ko³ ꜀t'íú lò² yap₂, *I entered by the inside road.*

你去就打山邊個條路行 ⁵néi hui³ tsau² ꜀tá ꜀shán ꜀pín ko³ ꜀t'íú lò² ꜀hángt, *when you go, go by the road on the hill side.*

CXCIV. Some Prepositions always precede the Verb, as:—

我打路去 ⁵ngo ꜀tá lò² hui³, *I went by road.*
我打啊便過 ⁵ngo ꜀tá ꜀ko pín² kwo³, *I passed by that way.*
佢當我面前做 ⁵k'úi ꜀tong ⁵ngo mín² ꜀ts'ín tsò³, *he did it in my presence.*

CXCV. Prepositions which are used with Verbs to modify, or extend their meaning are sometimes placed after the Objects, and not immediately after the Verbs, as in English, while at other times they immediately follow the Verbs, as in English, as:—

樟個樽翻嚟 ꜀ning ko³ ꜀tsun ꜀fán ꜀lai,
樟翻個樽(嚟) ꜀ning ꜀fán ko³ ꜀tsun (꜀lai), } *bring back the bottle.*

CXCVI. If the Personal Pronoun is expressed in the sentence, it comes first, and then the Prepositional Phrase followed by the Verb:—see sentences above.

Exception.—因爲 ꜀yan wai², however, either follows, or precedes the Pronoun.

CXCVII. The Preposition is often not expressed, but understood, as:—

留番過我食 ꜀lau ꜀fán kwo³ ⁵ngo shik₂, *keep it for me to eat,* becomes 留番我食 ⁵lau ꜀fán ⁵ngo shik₂.

CXCVIII. Prepositional phrases follow Adverbial phrases, as:—

我聽晚喺呢處瞓 ⁵ngo ꜀t'ing ⁵mán ꜀hai ꜀ni shü³ fan³, *I shall sleep here (at this place) to-morrow night.*

POSTPOSITIONS.

CXCIX. Some words which are Prepositions in English follow the Noun in Chinese, as:—

門裏 ꜀mún ⁵lui, *within the door.*
門外 ꜀mún ngoi², *outside the door.*
身上 ꜀shan shöng², *on the person.*
心中 ꜀sam ꜀chung, *in the heart.*
面前 mín² ꜀ts'ín, *before the face.*

PREPOSITIONS.

屋後 uk, hau², behind the house.
手下 ʻshau há², under the hand, or under the command of.
尾內 uk, noi², within the house.

CC. Notice that the above words are capable of transposition, and have a different meaning when so transposed to those given above, as:—

裏門 ʻlui ₌mún, an inside door.
外門 ngoi² ₌mún, an outside door.
上身 shöng² ₌shan, the upper part of the body.
中心 ₌chung ₌sam, the very centre.
前面 ₌ts'in miu², before, or opposite.
後屋 hau² uk, houses at the back.
下手 há² ʻshau, to move the hand down; to begin anything.
內屋 noi² uk, houses within an enclosure, (seldom used.)

CCI. *After.*—After is placed after its governed words in Chinese instead of before as in English, as:—

從此之後 ₌ts'uug ʻtsz ₌chí hau², after these things.
佢落嚟之後 ʻk'ui lok, ₌lai ₌chí hau², after he came down.
從今以後 ₌ts'ung ₌kam ʻyí hau², from this time henceforth.
講完之後 ʻkoug ₌yün ₌chí hau², after finishing talking.

CCII. *After* is sometimes placed after the Subject of the sentence, and before the Verb, as:—

佢後來嚟嘅 ʻk'ui hau² ₌loi ₌lai ke², he came afterwards.

CCIII. The English Preposition "at" is not used in Chinese before time, as:—

六點嚟 luk, ʻtím ₌lai, come at six o'clock.

CCIV. "By" when used to show the manner, or route, or method by which a journey has been, or is to be taken, is represented by 打 ʻtá, as:—

打路去 ʻtá lò² bui³, to go by road (i.e. by land).
打水路去 ʻtá ʻshui lò² bui³, to go by water.
打個處過 ʻtá ko³ shú³ kwo³, to go by that way, or place.

CCV. "By" when used in English after a Comparative before a Noun of Number, Measure, or Weight, or a Number relating to age is not used in Chinese,

PREPOSITIONS.

the word 有 ⁵yau being quite sufficient, as:—

佢高過你有一寸 ⁵k'ui ₂kò kwo³ ⁵néi ⁵yau yat₂ ts'ün³, *he is taller than you by one inch.*

貴有一半 kwai³ ⁵yau yat₂ pún³, *it was dearer by one half.*

你重過我有一斤 ⁵Néi ⁵ch'ung* kwo³ ⁵ngo ⁵yau yat₂ ₂kan, *you are heavier than I by one catty.*

佢細過我有三年 ⁵k'ui sai³ kwo³ ⁵ngo ⁵yau ₂sam ₂nín, *he is younger than I by three years.*

CCVI. In a Chinese Sentence when the dimensions of an object are given the Preposition "by" is rendered often by 打 'tá, *to strike,* being an idiomatic use of that Verb, as:—

五尺(長)打三尺(闊) ⁵ng ch'ek₀ (₂ch'öng) 'tá ₂sám ch'ek₀ (fút₀), *five feet by three feet.*

CCVII. "Of" is not expressed before the name of a month, as in English, as:—

英二月三號 ₂Ying yí³ yüt₂ ₂sám hò², *the 3rd. of February* (lit. English second month, and third day).

CCVIII. "Of" is also not used after weights and measures, as in English, as:—

十斤魚 shap₂ ₂kan 'yü*, *ten catties (of) fish.*

兩尺半綠髮 ⁵löng ch'ek₀ pún³ ₂sz fát₀, *two and a half feet of silk stuffs.*

Note.—In Chinese accounts the position of these words would be altered, viz: 魚十斤 'yü* shap₂ ₂kan, *fish, 10 catties,* &c.

CCIX. 同 ₂t'ung means *for,* and *from,* as well as *with,* as:—

我同佢買 ⁵ngo ₂t'ung ⁵k'ui ⁵mái, *I bought it from him.*

我同佢賣 ⁵ngo ₂t'ung ⁵k'ui mai³, *I sold it for him.*

我同佢去 ⁵ngo ₂t'ung ⁵k'ui hui³, *I went with him.*

CCX. There is no need to use a Preposition with the Verb 坐 'ts'o*, *to sit,* though it can be, and is sometimes used, as:—

坐 'ts'o*, *to sit,* or *sit down,* or *to sit on.*

Remark.—It will be seen that the Verb 坐 'ts'o* represents all these ideas. Note also the following:—

坐落 'ts'o* lok₂, *to sit down.*

坐在 'ts'o* tsoi⁶, *to sit on.*

PREPOSITIONS.

坐住 'ts'o* chü², *to be sitting on*, or *to be sitting*.
坐上個處 'ts'o* ˊshöng ko' shü', *sit up there*.

CCXI. The Preposition is sometimes left out, as:—

你呢 ˊNéi ˎni? *Where were you?*

Remark.—This is somewhat like the English, *And you?* which sometimes occurs.

Note.—Note, however, that it is polite to repeat in answer to a question the question itself as an answer; but without, of course, its interrogative adjuncts.

CCXII. The word "for," or phrases "in order to" or "in order for" are sometimes represented by 嚟 ˎlai.

佢起間屋嚟俾佢住 ˊk'ui ˋhéi ˎkán uk, ˎlai 'péi ˊk'ui chü², *he built a house for him to live in.*

佢上去嚟帮佢嘅 ˊk'ui ˊshöng hui' ˎlai ˎpong ˊk'ui ke', *he went up in order to assist*, or *help him*.

CCXIII. 過 kwo' occupies sometimes the position of *to*, and has that meaning when used with a Noun, or Pronoun governed by a Verb, as:—

俾過我 'péi kwo' ˊngo, *give it to me*.

CCXIV. 過 kwo' can, however, often be understood, the principle of position shewing that the Noun, or Pronoun must be in a Dative Case.

Remark.—That is to say if 我 ˊngo follows such a Verb as 俾 'péi, anyone can see that it must mean *to me*. Ergo it is unnecessary to put in the 過 kwo'.

CCXV. 到 tò' is used before Nouns and Pronouns in the sense of *to arrive at*, or *reach to*, &c., as:—

佢昨日到城 ˊk'ui tsok, yat, tò' ˎshengt, *he arrived at Canton yesterday*.
佢唔摸得到 ˊk'ui ˎm ˋò tak, tò', *he could not reach to it*.

CONJUNCTIONS.

CCXVI. With regard to Conjunctions the beginner in Cantonese colloquial must try and do away with all his preconceived notions of joining sentences together, and speak as a rule in short simple sentences, as far as possible, unconnected by Conjunctions.

CCXVII. The use of a word to express "and" in English is not always necessary by any means in Chinese, the juxtaposition of several words in a sentence

CONJUNCTIONS.

implying often that there is a connection. A slight break in the voice between the different words thus connected will serve to draw attention to the fact that the words are joined together, as:—

我, 你, 佢, (都) 去街咯 ⁵ngo, ⁵néi, ⁵k'ui, (ᵢtò) hui³ ᵢkái lok。, *I, you (and) he (all) went out.*

CCXVIII. To prevent misapprehension when a number of names of people, or things are thus joined together in a seemingly unconnected way, it is common to insert after them words such as 喊嚟哈 hám ᵢpá ᵢláng, *all*, 喊 hám, *all*, 都 ᵢtò, *and*, or *also* &c., and thus group them together, and show that they are connected, as:—

事頭, 事頭婆, 細佬仔喊嚟哈去澳門 sz² 't'au*, sz² ᵢt'au ᵢp'o, sai³ ᵢman 'tsai, ᵢhám ᵢpá ᵢláng hui³ Ò³-ᵢmûn, *the master, mistress (and) children have all gone to Macao.*

CCXIX. For the same reason 同 ᵢt'ung, *with*, is used where in English "and" would be employed, as:—

English.—*He and I went.* Chinese.—我同佢去 ⁵ngo ᵢt'ung ⁵k'ui hui³, *he went with me.*

CCXX. With names of persons and things it is also common to introduce a Numeral in the sentence immediately after the Nouns, which in English would simply be connected by "and," as:—

English.—*John, Thomas, Mary and I read the book.* Chinese.—我, 亞一, 亞八, 亞連, 四個(人)讀個部書 ⁵ngó, A' yat,, A' pát,, A' ᵢlín, sz' ko³ (ᵢyan), tuk₂ ku³ pò⁶ ᵢshü, *I, A yat, A pat, A lin, four (persons) read that book.*

CCXXI. Instead of a Conjunction being used the Verb is often repeated before, or after, several Nouns whether they are Nominatives to the Verbs, or Objects, or in the Dative Case.

俾水, 俾雪, 俾個玻璃杯過我 ⁵péi ⁵shui, ⁵péi ⁵sut。, ⁵péi ko³ ᵢpo-ᵢléi (or ᵢléi)-ᵢpúi kwo³ ⁵ngo, *give water, give ice, give a tumbler to me.*
我俾你俾佢咯 ⁵ngo ⁵péi ⁵néi ⁵péi ⁵k'ui lo³, *I give it to you, and him.*

Note.—This last sentence is ambiguous, and rather bad Chinese, and may mean, *I give it to you to give to him.* A Numeral introduced into the sentence will free it from this ambiguity and put in in good style as in No. CXX, as:—

我俾你兩個人咯 ⁵ngo ⁵péi ⁵néi ⁵löng ko³ ᵢyan lok。, *I give it to you two.*

CONJUNCTIONS.

CCXXII. And is sometimes represented in Chinese by 零 ‚leng† when used with numerals, as :—

一百零一十 yat‚ pák₀ ‚leng† yat‚ shap₂, *one hundred and ten.*

CCXXIII. But 零 ‚leng is more often used to denote that a denomination has been left out, and when twice repeated that two denominations have been left out. In fact it often takes the place of the nought in the Arabic numerals, as :—

一兩零一分 yat‚ 'löng ‚leng† yat‚ ‚fan, *one tael and one fun.*
一十五兩零零一 yat‚ shap₂ 'ng 'löng ‚leng† ‚leng† yat‚, *fifteen taels and one li.*

CCXXIV. And is not required in a Chinese sentence when the different dimensions of an object are given, as :—

五寸長三寸闊 'ng ts'ün' ch'öng ‚sam ts'ün' fút‚, *five inches long (and) three inches broad.*

CCXXV. "And" is often left out between Numerals as in German, as :—

一百一十九 yat‚ pák₀ yat‚ shap₂ 'kau, *one hundred and nineteen.*

INTERJECTIONS, EXCLAMATORY PARTICLES AND THEIR TONAL VARIANTS.

CCXXVI. The following are some of the words used in Cantonese for Interjections.

吖 ‚Á! *Ah!*
呀 Á²! *Ah!*
唉 ‚Ai! *Oh!*
挨 ‚Ái! *Alas!*
嗌 Ái²! *Ah!*
嚊 ‚Ch'ai! *Tush! Bosh! Tut!*
嗻 ‚Ch'e! ,, ,, ,,
呲 ‚Ch'ʻe²! ,, ,, ,,
嗤 ‚Ch'ʻi! ,, ,, ,,
踩 ‚Ch'oi! *also pronounced ts'oi!* (used by women) *Tush! Bosh!*
唉 E²! *Now!*
嗄 ‚Ha! *Ha! Indeed! Oh!*
吓 'Há! *What!*
吓' Há'! *Ah!*
嚱 ‚He! *Tut!* (don't be afraid)

呵 ‚Ho! *What!*
呵 'Ho! *Indeed! Oh!*
荷 Ho²! *Indeed!* —
嗥 'Hò! *Ho!*
耗 Hò'! *Ho!*
嚯 ‚Hò! *Pooh!*
吁 ‚Hui! *Tut! Hulloa!* (This must be pronounced shortly.)
吁 ‚Hui! *or* Hui²! *Ah!* (This must be lengthened out in pronunciation).
咪聲 'Mai ‚sheng! *Chut!*
乜噉呀 Mat‚ 'kom é'! *What!*
那 Ná²! *There!* 那那 ná² ná²! *Now! Now!*
嘛 Ne²! *There now!*
啊 O²! *Oh!*

CONJUNCTIONS.

唏 ˏHe! *What!*
嘆 ˏHai! *Here!*
嚛 ˏHái! *Oh! What a bother you are!*
喊 Hái²! *Alas!*
Hng²! *Dear me! Fiddlesticks!*

弊 Pai²! *Alas!*
ˏP'í! *Tush* (used by women.)
喂 ˏWoi! *Hulloa there!*
喂 Woi²! *Hulloa!*

FINALS.

CCXXVII. Though the Final Particles so freely used in Chinese have in most cases no exact meaning as separate words, yet they often throw a strong emphasis upon the sentence, and express in the clearest manner whether it is Interrogative or Affirmative—whether the speaker is simply assenting to some proposition that is stated, or expressing surprise at it—whether a simple statement is being made, or whether it is being stated in the most positive manner, and with all the emphasis possible—or whether the speaker is not very sure of what he says, and with this uncertainty asks in an indirect manner whether it is so, or not. It will thus be seen that such words as these express different feelings, and modulations of intensity of such feelings, and bring out different shades of meaning as they are used singly, or in combination (very much as stops are used in an organ to modulate, and intensify the sound of the music.) It will be seen that such words as these are very difficult, or impossible even of translation into English where accent and emphasis alone do their work to a great extent.

A proper use of these Finals will bring out one of the niceties of the language. There is a great beauty in all these variations of meaning of a sentence, which is often lost when little attention is paid to them. Certain English scholars of Chinese, who have devoted nearly all their attention to the fossilised book-language, and despise, in their comparative ignorance of it, the living language—the colloquial—lose sight of all these, and many other beauties in the Cantonese colloquial.

It is curious, and most interesting to notice how small and insignificant a word at the end of a sentence will change the meaning of the whole sentence, like the rudder at the stern of the ship governing the motions of the whole vessel.

CCXXVIII. List of Finals, and their Tonal Variants.

1. ˏÁ, 吖, interrogative, emphatic, or merely euphonic.
2. Á², 呀, emphatic, or merely euphonic.
3. Á², 呀, emphatic, more so than the last.
4. ˏChá, 嗻, cautionary, or restraining.
5. 'Chá, 嗻, stronger, or more urgent than the last.

FINALS.

6. Chà', 咋, cautionary, or restraining, or delaying, but rarely implying doubt.
7. ₍Che, 呮, or 嗻, implying limitation.
8. Chè', 啫, implying limitation, &c.
9. ʻChà, 啫, implying limitation, but stronger than the last.
10. ₍Chí, 吱, emphatic.
11. ʻCho, or ʻchö, 咀 emphatic.
12. ₍E, 唉, interrogative.
13. ₍Ká, 咖 }
14. Ká', 嘎 } emphatic-affirmative.
15. Ke', 嚱, somewhat similar to the last, or simply euphonic.
16. Ko', 个, same as last.
17. ₍Kwa, 啩, implying doubt, or some degree of probability; there is also an expectancy of a reply sometimes expressed in it,—a reply which will solve the doubt, or intensify the probability.
18. Kwá', 啩, the same as last.
19. ₍Kwo, 喎 }
20. Kwo', 喎 } the same as last.
21. ₍Lá, 喇, emphatic, or simply euphonic.
22. Lá', 獵, implying certainty, or simply euphonic.
23. Lak,, 拉, emphatic.
24. ₍Le, 哩, affirmative.
25. ʻLe, 哩, same as last.
26. Le', 唎, imperative, or emphatically affirmative.

27. ₍Le, 哩,
28. ʻLe, 哩,
29. Le², 唎',

{ The best way to indicate the difference between these two series of Les may be best illustrated by supposing a traveller was telling a tale the truth of which he could see was doubted by his auditors. He might use any of the second series of Finals in replying to any question put to him in which he could plainly see there was doubt felt by the questioner; but supposing his tale concluded and corroborative evidence proving that his marvels were truths, then the former series would be employed by him, their use giving a slight trace of jubilant triumph, which, if expressed in English colloquial, might be, "There you see that's just what it is." }

30. ₍Lo, 羅, affirmative, or emphatic.
31. Lo', 羅', same as last.
32. Lok₀, 咯, the same as last, but intensified in its sense.
33. ʻMá, 嗎, simply interrogative, or interrogative combined with surprise.
34. ʻMá, 嗎, interrogative and expecting an affirmative reply.

FINALS.

35. Má³, 嗎, interrogative: asking certainly as to any matter.
36. ₅Má, 嘛, same as last, or the meaning might be expressed by "(*I told you so before*), *now isn't it so?*"
37. ⁵Má, 嗎, interrogative, and expecting an affirmative reply.
38. Má², 嗎, affirmatively-interrogative.
39. ₅Me, 咩, interrogative, or expressing some surprise as well, as—"Is it so?"
40. ₅Mo, 麼, ⎫
41. ⁵Mo, 麼, ⎬ interrogative, implying doubt.
42. Mo³, 麼³, ⎭
43. ₅Mo, 麼, ⎫
44. ⁵Mo, 麼, ⎬ simply interrogative, used after hearing anything said, having the sense of, "Oh! that's what it is, is it?"
45. Mo², 麼², ⎭
46. ₅Ná, 那, ⎫ emphatically demonstrative.
47. Ná², 那, ⎭
48. ₅Ne, 哪, ⎫
49. ⁵Ne, 哪, ⎪
50. Ne³, 哪, ⎬ emphatically demonstrative, used when one might say in English, "There now, what I said was true you see."
51. ⁵Ne, 哪, ⎪
52. Ne², 哪, ⎭
53. ₅Ne, *or more commonly* ₅ni, 呢, ⎫ interrogative, or emphatically demonstrative.
54. ₀Ne, *or* ₀ni, 呢, ⎭
55. ₅O, 啊, ⎫
56. O³, 啊, ⎬ strongly emphatically affirmative. The first is rarely used.
57. O², 啊, ⎭
58. Po³, 鼻, interrogative.
59. Péi², 鼻³, affirmative.
60. Po³, 播, very emphatic, used often after the final 羅 lo³.
61. Wá³, 話, ⎫
62. ⁵Wá, 話, ⎬ denoting that the statement preceding it has been made by some one before.
63. Wá², 話, ⎭
64. Wo³, 啊, ⎫
65. ₅Wo, 啊, ⎬ same as above.
66. Wo², 啊, ⎭
67. ₅Yá, 吔, ⎫ affirmative.
68. Yá³, 吔, ⎭
69. ₅Yá, 吔, ⎫
70. ⁵Yá, 吔, ⎬ expressing slight surprise.
71. Yá², 吔, ⎭

FINALS.

72. Yák₁, 喫,
73. Yák₀, 喫, } affirmative.
74. Yák₂, 喫,
75. Yo',
76. Yo², } expressive of surprise.

Note.—Considerably more than half of the above Finals and their Variants do not appear in any dictionary.

CCXXIX. No definite rule can be laid down as to when Finals are to be used, or omitted. See CCXXX.

CCXXX. Use finals at the end of a third, or perhaps nearly a half of the phrases and sentences (as well as after the same proportion of the single words) that you use.

CCXXXI. Remember that it is of great importance to use appropriate ones. The above list will show that they have a peculiar and often particular force and meaning, which is worse than lost if wrong ones are made use of.

CCXXXII. If the same final is put into a 上平 shöng² ₂ping and 上去 shöng² hui', the former has generally more emphasis of meaning than the latter.

CCXXXIII. The following combinations of 係 hai² and 唔係 ₂m hai² the equivalents for *yes* and *no* in Chinese and a number of different Finals will give some idea of the shades of meanings that a judicious use of those little words will admit. A few of them it will be seen are synonymous, but it must be remembered that it is well nigh impossible to give an exact rendering of the little shades of difference that exist in their use in Chinese; and the same particle used in different connections is capable of giving different meanings.

Of course the learner will understand that the English words that appear below, opposite the Chinese, do not all appear in the Chinese, but where a certain state of feeling is given expression to in English in certain words, the same feeling would probably cause the Chinese words that are opposite the English to be uttered. It is thus rather a free translation without which it would be impossible to convey anything of the sense of these little enclitic particles.

1. 係 Hai² | *Yes*, (affirmative).
2. 㗎 'Hai? | *Yes?* (judicative of great surprise.)
3. 係哩 Hai² ₂lo | *Yes*, (you are right it is so.)
4. 係啊 Hai² o' | *Yes*, (indeed it is so.)
5. 係嚜 Hai² ₂no | *Yes*, (didn't I say it was so, *or* I told you so.)

FINALS.

6. 係咩 Hai² ͵me? — Yes? (yes? Oh! is it so?)
7. 係嗎 Hai² ͵má? — Yes? ('tis so, isn't it?)
8. 係嗎' Hai² má'? — Yes? (it is indeed so, is it not?)
9. 係廰 Hai² mò'? — Yes? (the same.)
10. 係吖 Hai² ͵á — Yes, ('tis so)
11. 係呀 Hai² á' — Yes, (it is so indeed.)
12. 係卦 Hai² ͵kwá — It's so I think.
13. 係卦 Hai² kwá' — I think, yes—I think it so, is it not?
14. 係囉 Hai² ͵lo — Yes, all right.
15. 係咯 Hai² lok₀ — Yes, that's it.
16. 係囉' 嗎' Hai² lo' má'? — It's so, is it not, eh?
17. 係囉咩 Hai² lo' ͵me? — Oh! it's so, is it indeed?
18. 係囉' Hai² lo' — Yes, 'tis so.
19. 係囉卦 Hai² lo' kwá' — 'Tis so I think.
20. 係囉卦 Hai² lo' ͵kwá — It's so, isn't it?
21. 係唉 Hai² ͵e — Indeed it's so?
22. 係唔係呢 Hai² ͵m hai² ͵ni? — There, isn't it so now?
23. 係唔係嘅 Hai² ͵m hai² ͵ne? — Is it so, or not? or simply Is it so?
24. 係唔係呀 Hai² ͵m hai² á'? — Is it so, or not? or simply Is it so?
25. 係唔係吖 Hai² ͵m hai² ͵á? — There, didn't I tell you it was so.
26. 係唔係啊 Hai² ͵m hai² o'? — Do tell me is it so, or not?

Remark.—The above list is not exhaustive.

ON THE USE OF SOME OF THE FINALS.

CCXXXIV. 吖 ͵á, is generally spoken in a short sharp manner, while the voice often at times lingers on 呀 á'. The more emphatic 吖 ͵á is meant to be, the shorter and sharper must be its pronunciation, while the converse is the case with regard to 呀 á'.

CCXXXV. When to use 吖 ͵á and 呀 á'. 1. 吖 ͵á is used when say the proposition enunciated is disputed, as for instance if one were to say, "*You* may say it was not hot yesterday, but it *was* very hot." 2. 呀 á' is used when a simple statement is made, not in opposition to any expressed opinion such as given in No. 1 above, or it is used when a strongly confirmatory statement is made. 呀 á' is used Interrogatively, but 吖 ͵á never.

CCXXXVI. The Final 咋 chá' is often the final in phrases commencing with 咪 'mai, 唔好 ͵m 'hò, &c. It often expresses what in English would be shown by the words "wait a bit," "yet a while," and "yet."

FINALS.

CCXXXVII. The Final 嘞 kwá' can be used alone, or with the emphatic Finals 喇 ,lá, 囉 lo', 咯 lok。, but not with others. When so used it qualifies this emphatic meaning, introducing an element of uncertainty, and possibly occasionally a half interrogative meaning is thrown in as well. This Final cannot be used with Interrogative Finals, such as 吖 ,á, 呀 á', 嗎 má', 咩 ,me, 麼 mo' and 呢 ,ni. The Finals given above comprise all with which it can be used.

CCXXXVIII. Some Affirmative and Interrogative Finals can be used together, the Interrogative coming last.

CCXXXIX. The Final 嘴 po' is used alone, or with 囉 lo', or 咯 lok。. See also CXXXVI, Nos. 2, and 4, CXLVI, and CXLVII.

A FEW SIMPLE DIRECTIONS FOR THE GUIDANCE OF THE BEGINNER.

CCXL. When there are several Subject Nominatives to a Verb, or several Verbs to a Subject Nominative in English, distribute them in Chinese into short sentences with one Subject alone to one Verb; and put them separately if you are asking questions, getting an answer to the first before putting the second, and so on.

CCXLI. Avoid dependent clauses as much as possible. Reduce every sentence, that is not the most simple in its construction, to its original elements, and put each as a simple sentence as above.

CCXLII. Do not put several contingencies to a Chinese at one and the same time. Put one at a time, if they must be put; but above all things avoid contingencies, or supposititious cases as much as possible. Some Chinese cannot understand them at all.

Remark.—As the Chinese takes his food all minced up, or chopped into pieces, so he takes his mental pabulum in small doses and cannot understand a long sentence. If he assents seemingly to what you say, supposing you will persist in putting a long inquiry to him, formed of several component sentences and contingent clauses, you will doubtless find he has not grasped the whole in its entirety. He may assent or dissent, as the European supposes, to what has been said, when at the same time the whole complicated sentence that the foreigner has constructed with the greatest amount of ingenuity has gone in at one ear and out at the other without having made any impression of the sense on his mind. He has perhaps seized hold of the last clause in the sentence, and answered it without any regard to what precedes it.

SIMPLE DIRECTIONS.

CCXLIII. Omit in long sentences all subsidiary words where possible:—such as 嘅 ke' (often the sign of the possessive), 哋 téi² (the sign of the Plural), 哋 ˏti, &c., &c.

  Remark.—These little words are often omitted with advantage in short phrases even.

CCXLIV. Unless it is wished to draw special attention to the fact that what happened was in a Past Tense, or has just been completed, omit, as a general rule, signs of such past time. The same holds good of Future time. In fact in Chinese the Tenses need but little looking after: they generally take care of themselves.

  Note.—This rule holds especially good in long sentences where nearly everything is sacrificed to conciseness.

CCXLV. In an Interrogative sentence begin by saying what you have to say in Affirmative form, then put an Interrogative Final at the end of your sentence, or repeat your sentence in a Negative form after the Affirmative form. Never attempt to use Interrogative constructions as in English.

CCXLVI. As a rule when replying to a question take the question that has been asked you, and simply put it in an Affirmative or Negative form, leaving out when it is an Interrogative-Negative question the Negative or Affirmative part of the question, as the case may be.

FINAL DIRECTIONS.

CCXLVII. Aim at simplicity of construction.

CCXLVIII. Avoid all complicated sentences.

CCXLIX. Avoid abrupt answers to questions.

CCL. Listen attentively to all you hear.

CCLI. Pick out all the words that are new to you; find out their meanings from your dictionary, or if you do not find them in your dictionary, which is more than likely, go to what is a better source of information, the Chinese themselves; then when you know what they mean, use them yourself.

CCLII. Remember that imitation is a strong point in learning Chinese.

CCLIII. Do not be afraid to speak at all times in Chinese.

CCLIV. Remember that it is considered impolite for a Chinese to laugh at your mistakes, and consequently he will rarely do it; and if a Foreigner laughs at you remember that it is he that should feel ashamed with himself for laughing at you when he probably still makes many mistakes, and not you for making a mistake while the language is new to you.

FINAL DIRECTIONS.

CCLV. You cannot avoid making many mistakes at first.

CCLVI. Bungle on somehow at the very first rather than not speak at all.

CCLVII. Resolve that you shall speak Chinese, and you will do it.

CCLVIII. Ask those with whom you are in the habit of talking to tell you when you are wrong.

CCLIX. When you can speak a little, take a newspaper published in English—a local one is preferable—and tell your teacher the news in Chinese—beginning with the local items first, as this will interest him, and you will be able to learn a great many Chinese words in this way. At your first attempt you will find that it seems well nigh impossible to put the English into Chinese, therefore be content with merely giving your teacher a bare outline of the contents in your own words, eschewing the leaders at first, and after a while you will find that you have more confidence and a better command of words, then follow the newspaper more and more until finally you give every word in the newspaper articles as far as possible. Use your dictionary freely in this exercise.

CCLX. Learn as many synonymous words as possible.

CCLXI. Practise half a dozen different ways of saying the same thing in Chinese. You will then find when speaking that if you are not understood when saying anything, you will very likely be able to put it in another form which will be intelligible.

CCLXII. Talk over what seem to you to be your mistakes with your teacher, and find out if they are mistakes, and why they are mistakes, and what is the right word, or right phrase, or right construction to use instead of that you have used.

CCLXIII. Do not attempt to talk much with those who do not speak good Cantonese at first. You will only get confused if you do.

CCLXIV. Speak to your servants in Chinese and make them speak to you in Chinese. Listen to nothing from them in English, unless you find that you cannot understand what has been said in Chinese, then, and only then, as a last resort when you have used every other means to discover the meaning of the word. When you have got the English of it then let the Chinese be repeated to you again, and be prepared for it next time.

CCLXV. Above all things have patience and plod on even if you seem to be making no progress. A language that has taken the Chinese thousands of years to develop is not mastered by you in a day.

FINAL DIRECTIONS.

CCLXVI. Get a good teacher, and trust him rather than your dictionary, if the two differ, as differ they must if he is a good teacher.

CCLXVII. Get some colloquial books, such as:—

"The Peep of Day" in Cantonese Colloquial.
"The New Testament" in Cantonese Colloquial.
"The Pilgrim's Progress" in Cantonese Colloquial.
"The Holy War" in Cantonese Colloquial.
"The Shing Yü Hau" in Cantonese Colloquial.
"The Bible History" in Cantonese Colloquial.
"Come to Jesus" in Cantonese Colloquial.
Parts of the "Old Testament" in Cantonese Colloquial, such as:—
"The Book of Genesis."
"The Book of Ruth."
"The Book of Psalms," &c., &c., &c.

And let your teacher read them over to you until you can read them yourself, then read them with him. You will find this course of reading of great assistance. The purely native colloquial books you will find at first of little use compared with those named above. When you can talk pretty well you may turn to them as well.

CCLXVIII. If you are free to follow your own course of study, then leave the book language alone until you are well grounded in colloquial. You can find sufficient variety by reading the books named above, and by writing. The latter will be of great assistance in aiding the memory with new words learned.

Of course if you are wiser than Dame Nature, who insists that Chinese youngsters shall learn to speak Colloquial before they learn the book language, then you will attempt the learning of two languages at the same time—two languages, be it remembered, that are at the same time so similar and yet so dissimilar that it is well nigh impossible to attempt to study the two at the same time without doing great injury and injustice to one or other, or both. The colloquial generally suffers, and the consequence, owing in a great measure to this initial mistake, is that we can boast of but few good speakers of Chinese. Therefore, if possible, have nothing to do with the book language until you have attained a very good knowledge of colloquial—say until you have worked over it (that is to say if you have been working hard and well) for a year, or eighteen months.

CCLXIX. Do not be discouraged, however, from what has been said just above, and do not suppose that you cannot speak Chinese until you have been at work for months over it. You can begin to speak almost as soon as you begin to learn, and

FINAL DIRECTIONS.

in half, or a quarter of the time mentioned above you ought to be able to enter easily into conversation with those about you, if you have worked with a will, and at nothing else but colloquial.

CCLXX. Remember that the tones are of great importance, but at the same time do not make them bugbears. Try to learn them well, and then do not keep hesitating when you talk, as some have done, over nearly every word, while you think of the proper tone to put it in. You must first learn the tone of the word thoroughly, then you will utter it in the proper tone almost mechanically.

CCLXXI. Remember that the idioms are of as equal importance as the tones, or of even, if that were possible, paramount importance.

CCLXXII. Mix with the Chinese as much as you can. Be very inquisitive and very communicative.

CCLXXIII. Be careful in the use of the so-called Classifiers. They cannot be used indiscriminately. Only use appropriate ones.

CCLXXIV. Remember that though the colloquial and so-called book language are very distinct in many respects, different words being often used for the same thing, yet that there is a neutral ground, as it were, between the two, and that Chinese native scholars are also often inclined to use what are really book words and phrases in common conversation. Therefore when the learner is sufficiently familiar with good, simple, pure colloquial so as to be able to carry on a conversation of some length in it, his attention should be turned to some of these book words and phrases, so as not to be at a loss when conversing with scholars. At the same time let him not get into the habit of using such words and phrases habitually when simpler forms will as clearly express his meaning. If he desires to have a good vigorous knowledge of the language, let him cultivate the colloquial element, as in English he would the Anglo-Saxon element.

CCLXXV. As to dictionaries, the beginner should get the Author's *Cantonese Made Easy Vocabulary*, which will be of use though not containing so many words as Dr. Chalmers' English-Cantonese Dictionary. For Cantonese-English ones, if he is prepared to spend time and money on the learning of the language, he should either get Dr. Williams' Tonic Dictionary, or the latest one, Dr. Eitel's Cantonese Dictionary. Both are Cantonese-English Dictionaries.

CCLXXVI. As to companion books to study along with the present book, some of the Author's other works will be found of great assistance, such for instance as, "How to Speak Cantonese," and "Readings in Cantonese Colloquial."

FINAL DIRECTIONS.

CCLXXVII. Remember that the dictionaries are by no means free from mistakes. As to pronunciation trust to good Cantonese speakers rather than to books; the same holds good of tones; it holds good also to a certain extent with regard to definitions. Let it be remembered that English-Chinese, or Chinese-English Dictionary making is but in its infancy.

CCLXXVIII. Festina lente.

FINIS.

APPENDIX.

Excursus 1.

CHINESE GRAMMAR.

As the Chinese ideas of Grammar as applied to their own language may conduce to a fuller understanding of the structure of Chinese sentences, and the parts that the different words play in the construction of such sentences, a short account of it is here given. Owing to the peculiarities of the Chinese language it is much simpler than English Grammar.

In the first place words are divided into 實字 shat$_2$ tsz^2, i.e. real, or full, or significant words, and 虛字 ꜀hui tsz^2, empty words, or particles.

The former "have a sense of their own independent of their use in any particular sentence." The latter "are employed only for grammatical purposes, to express relations between words, to connect sentences and clauses, and to complete the sentence, so that it may be clear in meaning and elegant in form."

The next division the Chinese employ is that of 死字 ꜂sz tsz^2, dead words, and 活字 wút$_2$ tsz^2, living words. The former are Nouns; the latter are Verbs.

These are the grand divisions which the Chinese employ; and in many respects they appear to be better adapted for their language—a language in which a word may be used as a Noun, an Adjective, or a Verb—than our English complex grammatical distinctions.

Excursus 2.

THE DIFFERENCES BETWEEN THE BOOK LANGUAGE AND CANTONESE COLLOQUIAL.

It it well that the Learner should understand clearly the differences between the book and colloquial languages.

To begin with to state the difference broadly, the one may be said to be a dead language while the other is a living one. The one is essentially the language of books, of documents, and letters—the written language; while the other is the language of friendship, of commerce, of intercourse—the speech of the people—the spoken language.

APPENDIX.

The book language is handed down from a remote antiquity, and the closer it assimilates (in its classical form at least) to the canons of antiquity, the finer it is considered to be. It is a crystallised form of the language; its genius is against expansion; while the colloquial is a present day language, and like all modern spoken languages has a continual growing, advancing, radical element of slang, and new words, and phrases opposed to the conservative element of the book language, which is too dignified to descend to slang, and adopts new words in a solemn and dignified manner. The book language is concise, terse, and sententious; the colloquial, though the same terms may be used when comparing it with modern European languages, is diffuse when compared with the book language.

The book language is not understood without years of study, and even then the more obscure the diction of its classical form, the more hidden its meaning, the more is it prized and thought highly of; the colloquial is understood by all from infancy to old age, whether educated, or uneducated.

The colloquial may be divided into a lower, or simpler colloquial, and a higher colloquial, or one approximating more to the book language in its use, to a greater or less extent, of certain words, which are not simple colloquial words. The latter Dr. Eitel has termed in his dictionary, "mixed," and it is not a bad term for them, as it is a definition as well. The simple colloquial is used by everyone, and is understood by everyone, the distinction between it and the higher colloquial consisting in the addition to the simple colloquial, which forms the basis or groundwork of all speech in China, of a number of what might be termed "dictionary words," that is to put it in a general way words, which a Chinese child, or woman would not understand. The more a man has dipped into books, or the more he wishes to differentiate himself from the common herd, so much the more he uses these words. It will therefore be seen that to learn Cantonese Colloquial thoroughly well it is advisable to learn first the simpler colloquial, which forms the basis of the spoken language, adding on a higher and higher superstructure, if time and circumstances permit, in the way of a knowledge and use of "mixed" words, i.e. certain words, strictly book language words, but which custom and habit have sanctioned the use of in speech when those using them and those hearing them are sufficiently educated either in books, or in the use of these words, to render their use intelligible.

It will be seen that with a good knowledge of the simple colloquial one can go anywhere and be understood by anyone from the highest to the lowest, who speak the dialect in its purity. It will be noticed that only *certain* words belong to this "mixed" class, and are capable of being used in the method explained above. It would never do to begin talking in the book language—it is simply for books and writing—anymore than it would do for, say, a Frenchman to acquire his knowledge of English from Chaucer, or even Beowulf, and then air his Anglo-Saxon and old English in modern London.

The book language has also several styles, the high classical almost as obscure to the unaided student as a nebula to an amateur astronomer without a proper telescope, and in some instances it is so obscure in its sense as to lead to the belief that the explanations offered are little better than guesses at the truth, in the same way that none of our telescopes are strong enough to resolve some of the distant star masses, or clusters of nebulous matter, and analogy and common sense are the only guides.

There is likewise a simple book language, which is the best to use if one wishes what he writes to be understood.

There is an official style, with all its set forms somewhat like ours, and forms of address.

There is a corresponding style, set and formal, abounding in allusions, which require years upon years of study to fully appreciate.

And a business style in which accounts and business are transacted.

Contracted forms of the characters are largely used in epistolary correspondence, as well as in the business entries in mercantile books, and the making out of accounts.

In writing there is also a running hand, and there is also a grass hand, the latter of which few Europeans trouble themselves about to any extent.

Excursus 3.

THE REASONS WHY EUROPEANS AS A RULE ARE SUCH POOR SPEAKERS OF CANTONESE.

I. The language is so different from any European Language.

1st. In grammatical construction.

(a). There being no Numbers, or Cases to Nouns and Adjectives, and no Moods, Tenses, Numbers, and Persons to Verbs.

> Note.—This though really simplifying the language causes it to appear more difficult at first, and makes it necessary for the learner to find different ways to mark, or denote these differences, because a foreign learner of Chinese has been accustomed hitherto to use all the complicated modes of expressing his meaning with which European languages abound. European children in China if allowed equal facilities for learning Chinese as for learning English take to the simpler language more readily, not having had any difficulties put in the way of its acquisition by having learned a more complex system of declension and inflection.

(b). In the apparently free and easy way in which a word does duty as a Noun, Adjective, Verb, or other part of speech as circumstances may demand.

> Note.—In English many words, though perhaps not so many as in Chinese, are of more than one part of speech, but being familiar with them it does not strike us as peculiar, and

furthermore our dictionaries state them to be of such or such a part of speech, whereas in most of the dictionaries hitherto published, for the use of those learning Chinese, no parts of speech are regularly given, and everything appears to be in confusion in that respect.

(c). The Prepositions and Conjunctions, which we have been accustomed to see in daily use do not appear in Chinese in many cases. In some cases such words are not needed in the latter language, and in other cases other particles utterly unfamiliar in their application or use abound, some of which are untranslatable into English. They therefore appear like unknown quantities with which we work in the dark.

2nd. The idioms of the language are so different. This is owing:—

(a). To the people being so differently conditioned that things do not appear the same to them as to us.

(b). To what is really often a more logical way of putting a matter, but we having been accustomed to an illogical way of putting the same thing from our infancy upwards prefer it to the simpler mode. Chinese is essentially a language for infants, for children, and for simplicity of thought, not only from its monosyllabic character, but from the natural sequence with which incidents are related. Of course this does not always hold good; but it is often the case in Chinese when it is not the case in English.

3rd. The words in the language do not always express exactly the same meaning in one language as they do in the other. This difficulty does not only arise when Chinese and English are compared, but applies to other languages as well. Such being the case it is not surprising that we should find a similar state of affairs when we come to compare English and Chinese.

(a). These differences are to be seen in the case of a certain Chinese word having only a limited meaning compared with a word in English which is supposed to represent it. Consequently some of the shades of meaning which the English word covers will have to be represented in Chinese by another word, or other words.

(b). The converse when a Chinese word embraces a far larger number of ideas than the corresponding English word with its limited meaning can cover.

(c). Complications also may arise, such for instance as the following:—when a certain Chinese word may be represented in English by one word, and also may have one or two of the meanings, which another English word expresses, but not all of them.

Note.—This, however, is very much the same as (a.)

(*d*). The converse of (*c.*)

>Note.—This is not surprising when it is remembered that there is scarcely a single English word which is perfectly synonymous with another word. So-called synonyms have generally some shade of difference of meaning.

(*e*). Two apparently synonymous words will often be used together, when at other times the one or the other will be used alone, and this usage or non-usage of them together in an arbitrary manner, as it appears to the learner.

>Note.—The difficulties under (*e.*) are increased by the most of the dictionaries and vocabularies not calling attention to this peculiar method of using words.

4th. It is most difficult to arrive at the correct pronunciation of the language.

(*a*). Because in some instances there is no possibility, or but little, of showing the correct pronunciation by the use of an English alphabet. In some cases there is no analogy in the pronunciation to that the learner has been accustomed to, and there is but little possibility of representing a sound, which does not exist in the English language when correctly pronounced.

>Note.—This is especially the case with the unaspirated consonants, k, p and t, which are pronounced with a strong aspiration in English as correctly spoken. The dictionaries and phrase books have helped to increase this difficulty by stating that k, p and t, are pronounced as in English, when such is not the case.—The way in which it is stated in such publications leads the learner to suppose that such is the correct pronunciation of k, p and t, when unaspirated, and it therefore would necessarily follow that when aspirated the letters k, p and t are, or should be, pronounced stronger than in English, whereas in truth the case is that k, p and t when aspirated in Cantonese correspond with the correct pronunciation of those consonants in English.

>Note.—These errors, as well as others, are due to the book-maker following in his pronunciation the errors of some predecessor. [In such a case it is most amusing to see with what dogmatic determination he will, when his error is pointed out to him, persist in saying that his representation of the sounds is the correct one.] The reasons of his following the errors of his predecessor are due to the following causes. In the first place he is as a general rule a miserable speaker of Cantonese, mispronouncing many of the words he tries to utter, and so having no correct standard he takes as his standard a previous book-maker, whom he believes to be correct in every particular in pronunciation, and another reason is that the book-maker often has for his teacher a man who does not speak pure Cantonese and the impure sounds come into his dictionary or book.

5th. The tones offer apparently a great difficulty to the beginner, and some always find them difficult.

>Note.—Doubtless the difficulty would be decreased in many cases if they were properly tackled at the first, and tackled with the idea that they must and can be mastered.

APPENDIX.

The difficulty is owing:—

(*a*). To there being nothing similar in European languages.

(*b*). To people from different parts of the country giving different tones to the same words.

(*c*). To different tones being given to certain words at certain times.

(*d*). To the majority of the dictionaries ignoring the patent fact that there are more than eight tones in Cantonese, a mistake which leads the learner into trying to fit every word into one or other of the tones to which it is supposed, and stated to belong, whereas in truth and in fact it belongs to another tone entirely ignored by the dictionary maker.*

6th. From the difficulties which stand in his way in trying to acquire the language from the little assistance he derives from his teacher.

(*a*). To begin with, his teacher probably knows no language but his own, which he has never had to learn in its entirety since his memory has been a sufficient recording power to reflect the whole of his past life in review before him. He has therefore no knowledge of the difficulties in the way of a learner, and does not therefore render that sympathetic assistance which looks out for the difficulties in the pupil's way and prepares him for them, or assists him out of them.

(*b*). The teacher, finding that the learner does not pronounce the words correctly after two or three trials, gives it up as a useless effort, and is content with mediocrity on the part of his pupil from an idea that that is all that is attainable.

(*c*). The teacher often has not the power, or ability to explain matters, so as to put them within the grasp of his pupil. His explanations are given in words often at the time unintelligible and unknown to his pupil, and his second or third attempts after the first have failed are probably just as bad.

These difficulties are not meant to discourage the learner from his arduous task, any more than the making of a chart is meant to discourage the captain from taking a voyage. It is to be hoped that the pointing of them out will enable the learner to overcome them more readily and successfully, than if he were not aware of them till he suddenly came upon them, or gradually learnt about them by experience.

---

* Dr. Eitel's dictionary is an exception, as he follows Mr. Parker's guidance to a large extent with regard to the tones, and Mr. Parker is evidently a competent guide in such matters. Dr. Chalmers' English-Cantonese Dictionary also gives many of the Third, or Colloquial Rising Tones. The Author's Vocabulary also contains these tones.

INDEX. 1

INDEX
TO SECOND, OR GRAMMATICAL, PART
OF
CANTONESE MADE EASY.

THE ROMAN NUMBERS REFER TO THE SECTIONS, AND THE FIGURES TO THE PAGES.

A

A' 啊 XXX, Note, 43.
Adjectives formed from Nouns, LXVIII, 62.
Adjectives, position of, LX, 59.
Adjectives, position of, with Classifier, XLIII-LII, 46-48.
Adjectives, Two, with Classifier, XLVI-XLIX, 46.
Adjective used attributively, LX, 59.
Adjective used predicatively, LX, 59.
Adverb, Comparison of, CLXXIV, 101.
Adverbs of Manner, CLXXXIII, 103.
Adverbs of Place, CLXXIX, 102.
Adverbs, Position of, CLXXV et. seq., 101 et. seq.
Adverbs of Time, CLXXV et. seq., 101 et. seq.
Adverbs used to denote Time instead of Tense, CXXIII et. seq., 80 et. seq.
After, CCI, CCII, 107.
And left out, CCXVII, CCXXIV, CCXXV, 110.
And, Other words used instead of, CCXVIII-CCXXII, 110.
Answer. Same words used in, as in question, CXXXVII, 86.
Any left out, CIX. Note 1, 75.
Article omitted, XXXIV, 44.
Article, No, used before half, XXXIV, 44.

Article used before Classifier of persons, XXXV, 44.
At not used before Time, CCIII, 107.
Auxiliary words used with Verbs, CXXXV, 85.

B

By, CCIV, CCV, 107.

C

Cardinal Numerals, Part 1, 3.
Case shown by position, XI, 38.
Case, No, in Chinese, X, 38.
Chi 之 sign of Possessive, XVIII, 39.
Chung² 重, LXII, 60.
Ch'ut, 出, Idiomatic use of, CLXIX, 99.
Classifier, Definition of, XXXVI-XXXIX, 44.
Classifier dropped in Plural, LII, LIII, 48.
Classifier, Every Noun has appropriate, XXXVIII, 44.
Classifiers, Genuine, XXXIX, 44.
Classifier used instead of Indefinite Article, LV, 49.
Classifier, Mistakes in use of, XXXVIII, 44.
Classifiers, List of, LVI et. seq., 49 et. seq.
Classifier, Position of, XL-LIV, 45.

Classifier used after Noun, XLI, XLII, 45.
Classifier used alone, LIV, 48.
Classifier used with 呢 ˏni, LI, 48.
Comparative formed by 啲 ˏti, LXI, 59.
Comparative formed with 上 shöng², LXVI, Remark, 60.
Comparative, 更 kang³ used for, LXII, 60.
Comparative of Adjectives, LXI-LXV, 59.
Comparative of Adverbs, CLXXIV, 101.
Comparative of Equality, LXIII, 60.
Comparative, Qualified, LXI, note, LXII, 60.
Comparative, Repeated, LXIV, LXV, 60.
Comparative, repeated, Use of 起 yüt₂ with, LXV, 60.
Compass, Points of, XXVI, 42.
Conjugation, No, in Chinese, I, 36.
Conjunction in Subjunctive often understood, CXVIII, 78.
Conjunctions, not used, CCXVI, 109.

D

Dates, LXXV et. seq., 64.
Dates, Inversion of, LXXV, 65.
Dates, 初 ˏch'o used with, LXXVI, 65.
Dates, 號 hò² used with, LXXVIII, 66.
Dative placed between two Verbs, XIII, 38.
Days of the week, LXXII, LXXIII, 67.
Declension of Personal Pronouns, XC, 69.
Demonstrative Adjective Pronoun with Classifier, XLV, XLVII, L, LII, LIII, 46.
Demonstrative Pronouns, C, et. seq., 73 et. seq.
Difference between "he scolded me," and "he said to me," XI, Note, 38.
Difference between 識 shik₁, and 知 ˏchí, CLXXII, 100.
Difference between "to buy," and "to sell," CLXXIII, 100.
Distributives and Indefinites, CIX, et. seq., 75 et. seq.

Distributive Numerals, LXXXIV, 67.
Distinctions in the use of 抵 ˏtai-"to be worth," CLXXI, 99.
Division of month into three, LXXVII, 65.

E

Emphasis, CXXXIV, 84.
Euphemisms used for death, CLVI, 98.
Expressions denoting time, LXXXVI, 68.

F

Finals, CCXXVII et. seq., 128 et. seq.
Finals, List of, CCXXVIII, 112 et. seq.
Future Tense, CXXII, CXXIII, No. 3, 80.

G

Gender, XIX et. seq., 39 et. seq.
Gender, context shows, XIX, 39.
Gender, not inherent to Chinese word, XXV, 41.
Gender, not necessary condition of Chinese word, XXV, 41.
Gender of names of animals, XXIII, 40.
Gender of names of birds, XXIII, 40.
Gender of names of human species, XX-XXII, XXIII, Note, 39.
Gender, often not used when necessary in English, XXV, 41.
Gender used to prevent confusion, XXV, 41.
Gerunds, CXXI, 80.

H

Half, XXXI, 43.
ˏHángt 行, Idiomatic uses of, CLVIII, CLXIX, 98, 99.
ˏHéi 起 Idiomatic uses of, CLIX, 98.
Hò² 號 used with dates, LXXVIII, 66.

INDEX.

ₑHoi 開, Idiomatic uses of, CLX, 94.
Hui' 去, Idiomatic uses of, CLXIII, 96.

I

Imperative (mood), CXVI, CXXVIII, 78, 84.
Impersonals, CVII, 75.
Indicative, CXVI, 78.
Inferior named before Superior, XXIII, Remark, 41.
Infinitive, CXVI, CXXVII, 78, 83.
Infinitive, No Preposition before, CLIV, 90.
"In order to," or "for," CCXII, 109.
Interrogation, In, sentence is same as in Affirmative, CXXXVI, No. 4, Note, 85.
Interrogatives, CIII et. seq., 74 et. seq.
Interrogative formed with rising intonation, CXXXVI, No. 1, 85.
Interrogative-Negative, CXXXVI, No. 8, CXXXVIII, 85.
Interrogative Particles, CXXXVI, No. 2, 85. See also List of Finals, CCXXVIII, 112 et. seq.
Interrogative Pronouns, XCII et seq., 71 et. seq.
Interrogative Sentences, CXXXVI-CXLI, 85.
Intonation, rising, Interrogative formed with, CXXXVI, No. 1, 85.

K

Ke' 嘅 sign of Possessive, XV, 38.
Ke' 嘅 understood, XVI, 39.
Ko' 個 used for Definite Article, XXXIII, 43.
Ko' 個 used without Classifier, LI, 48.
'Kom 噉, or 'kom 'yŏng* 噉樣, Position of, CLXXXV, CLXXXVI, 104.
'Kù 牯 used for Masculine, XXIII, 40.
ₑKung 公 used for Masculine, XXI, XXIII, 39, 40.
Kwo' 過 uses of, CCXIII, CCXIV, 109.
Kwo' ₑt'au 過頭 follows Adjective, CLXXXIX, 104.

L

ₑLai 嚟 used for "for," &c., CCXII, 109.
ₑLai 嚟, Idiomatic uses of CLXIII, 96.
Large half, XXXI, 43.
ₑLeng† 零, Uses of, CCXXII, CCXXIII, 111.
'Lò 佬 used for Masculine, XXII, 40.
Lok₂ 落, Uses of, CLXII, 95.
Long month, LXXXI, 66.

M

Marry, to, Different words used for, 'CLXX, 99.
Meaning shows Mood, CIX, 79.
Month divided into three, LXXVII, 65.
Month, Long, LXXXI, 66.
Month, Short, LXXXI, 66.
Moods, CXV, CXXVIII, 78, 83.
More, CLXXXVIII, 104.
More, or less, LXXIII, 64.

N

'Ná 嬭 applied to women, XXIII, Note, 40.
'Ná 嬭 used for Feminine, XXIII, 40.
ₑNám 男 used for Masculine Gender, XX, 39.
Negative following Verb, CXLI, 87.
Negative, Position of, CXL-CXLIV, 86, 87.
Negative precedes Verb, CXL, 86.
Negative used with if, of course, consequently, CXC, 105.
New and old, not old and new, LXIX, 62.
New Year's day, LXXX, 66.
New Year's eve, LXXIX, 66.
No, CXLV, 87.
No one, CXLIX, 89.
Not, Do, CL, 89.
Nothing, CXLVIII, 88.
Noun, same, either Masculine or Feminine, XIX, 39.
ₑNui 女 used for Feminine Gender, XX, 39.

Number in Verbs, CXXVI, *et. seq.*, 82 *et. seq.*
Numeral Adjectives, LXX *et. seq.*, 62 *et. seq.*
Numeral Adverbs, LXXXV, 67.
Numerals, Cardinal, Part I, 3.
Numeral often used when no plural would otherwise be shewn, IX, 37.
Numeral used for Article must have Classifier, XXXIII, Note, 43.
Numeral used with Classifier, XLVIII, XLIX, LIII, 47.

O

Object, Position of, XII, 38.
Object, Position of indirect, CLV, 90.
Object, Position of, with two Verbs, CLIII, 90.
Object taking precedence of other words, XIV, 38.
Object placed between two Verbs, XIII, 38.
Obvious meaning shews Case, XI, 38.
Of, CCVII, CCVIII, 108.
Ordinal Numerals, LXXIV, 64.

P

Pák, *yet* 伯爺, XXI, 40.
Participles, CXX, 29.
Particles, Interrogative, CXXXVI, No. 2, 85. See also List of Finals, CCXXVIII, 112.
Passive Voice, CXIII, CXIV, CXXXIII, 77.
Past Tense, CXXII, No. 2, CXXIV, 80, 81.
Past time shewn by changing the tone, CXXIV, CXXV, 81, 82.
Person in Verbs, CXXVI, *et. seq.*, 82 *et. seq.*
Personal Pronoun left out, LXXXVII, 68.
Personal Pronouns preceding Noun in Apposition, XVII, 39.
Personal Pronoun preceding Noun in Possessive, XVII, 39.

Phrase, A, used to express Plural, VIII, 37.
Plural formed by reduplication of Noun, VII, 37.
Plural of Demonstrative Pronoun, CI *et seq.*, 73.
Plural of Interrogative Pronoun, XCIV, XCVIII, 71.
Plural of Personal Pronoun, LXXXVIII, 68.
Plural shewn by general context, V, 36.
Plural shewn by qualifying words, V, 36.
Plural, Sign of, VI, 37.
Plural understood from sense, IV, 36.
P'o 婆 used for Feminine, XXI, XXII, 39, 40.
Position, everything in Chinese sentence, II, 36.
Position often shows the part of speech, II, 36.
Position of Object, XII, 38.
Position of Preposition, CXCIII *et seq.*, 105 *et. seq.*
Position of Subject, XII, 38.
Position takes place of Declension and Conjugation, II, 36.
Possessive Case, XV-XVIII, 38, 39.
Possessive Case of Interrogatives, XCIII, XCVII, 71.
Possessive of Personal Pronoun, LXXXIX, 69.
Postpositions, CXCIX, 106.
Predicatively, Adjective used, LX, 59.
Preposition, No, before Infinitive, CLIV, 90.
Preposition, Position of, CXCIII *et. seq.*, 105 *et. seq.*
Preposition understood, CXCVII, CCXI, 106.
Preposition with "to sit," CCX, 108.
Present Tense, CXXII, CXXIII, No. 1, 80.
Pronoun, Interrogative, XCII *et. seq.*, 71 *et. seq.*
Pronoun to be repeated in answer, CXXXIX, 86.

R

Reflective Pronoun and Noun, XCI, 70.
Relationship, terms for, Peculiar use of, XXVII, 42.
Relatives, XCIX, 73.
Rendering of Relatives and Interrogatives, CVIII, 75.

INDEX.

S

Self, CX *et. seq.*, 76 *et. seq.*
Self immediately follows Personal Pronoun, CXII, Note, 77.
Sense shews Gender, XIX, 39.
Sentences, Interrogative, CXXXVI-CXLI, 85.
Sentence same in Interrogative as in Affirmative, CXXXVI, No. 4, Note, 85.
ˢShöng 上, Uses of, CLXI, 95.
Short mouth, LXXXI, 66.
Sign of Plural, VI, 37.
Singular and Plural, No difference between, III, 36
ˌSin ˌShāng 先生, Use of, XXVIII, 43.
Sit, to, Preposition with, CCX, 108.
ˈSíu-púnʼ 小半, XXXI, 43.
Subject always precedes Verb, CLII, 89.
Subject, Position of, CLII, 89
Subjunctive, Conjunction in, often understood, CXVIII, 78; CXVII *et. seq.*, 78 *et. seq.*
Subjunctive Mood, CXXIX, 84.
Superior named before Inferior, XXIII, Remark, 41.
Superlative formed with chiʼ 至, LXVI, 60.
Superlative formed with kikˌ 極, LXVI, 60.
Superlative formed with shöng² 上, LXVI, 60.
Superlative formed with ʻting 頂, LXVI, 60.
Superlative of Adjectives, LXVI *et. seq.*, 60 *et. seq*
Surnames precede other names, XXX, 43.
ˢSz 死, Uses of, CLXV, 97.
ˌSz ˌnái 師奶, XXVIII, Note, 43.

T

ˈTá 打, Idiomatic uses of, CLVII, 90.
Túiˀ-púnʼ 大半, XXXI, 43.
Ták, tsaiˀ 得齋 follows Adjective, CLXXVII, 104.
ʻTang 等 IX, Note, 37.

Téi² 哋 sign of Plural, VI, 37.
Ten understood, LXX, Note, 63.
Tenses, CXV, CXXII *et. seq.*, 78, 80 *et. seq.*
Than with a Comparative, LXVII, 61.
Time, Ambiguity regarding, LXXI, 63.
Time, Phrases denoting, LXXII, 64.
Titles come after name, XXIX, 43.
To, CLXXXIX, 104.
ˌTò 都, Position of, CLXXXIV, 104.
Tòʼ 到, Use of, CCXV, 109.
Tones of Personal Pronoun, XCI, Note 2, 70.
ˈTsai 仔 in combination, XXIII, 41.
ˈTsai 仔 used as diminutive, XXIII, Note, 41.
ʼT-soʼ, Idiomatic uses of, CLXIV, 96.
ˌTung 同, Use of, CCIX, 108.

V

Verbs, Impersonal forms of, CXXX-CXXXII, 84.
Verbs left out, CLI, 89.
Verbs used in combination, CXV, 78.
Voice, Active, CXIII, CXXVIII, 77, 83, 84.

W

Well; Very well, CXLVI, 88.
When Nouns are rendered Masculine, or Feminine, XIX, 39.
Words denoting relationship placed after name, XXVII, 42.

Y

Ynt, — used instead of Article, XXXIII, 43.
ˢYau 有, Idiomatic uses of, CLXVII, CLXVIII, 98, 99.
ˌYe 爺 applied to males, XXIII, Note, 40.
Yes, CXLV, 87.
Younger named first, XXIII, Remark, 41.

OTHER WORKS BY THE SAME AUTHOR.

CANTONESE MADE EASY:

A Book of Single Sentences in the Cantonese Dialect with Free and Literal Translations and Directions for the Rendering of English Grammatical Forms into Chinese.

BY

J. DYER BALL, M.R.A.S., &c,

OF HER MAJESTY'S CIVIL SERVICE, HONGKONG.

Price, - - - - - - - - - - - - $2.00

THIS BOOK HAS BEEN INTRODUCED INTO THE HONGKONG CIVIL SERVICE EXAMINATION SCHEME.

EXTRACTS FROM NOTICES OF THE ABOVE WORK.

Mr. Ball has conferred a great boon on all beginners in Cantonese Colloquial. The good books on the subject are scarce and out of print; the books that do exist are compilations of pretentious rubbish, full of English idioms repeated *ad nauseam*. We have had an opportunity of examining Mr. Ball's work and we most cordially recommend it. Unlike his previous work on Hakka, it gives the tones, the pronunciation according to Sir William Jones' system, and the Chinese characters. * * We can say that as far as our examination has extended it is worthy of Mr. Ball's reputation as a 'master of Cantonese Colloquial.'—*China Review*, Vol. XI., p. 258.

This little work, bound in a stout paper wrapper, will be found to supply a want long felt by students of Cantonese. In the excellently worded explanatory preface very great stress is laid upon the acquisition of correct tones. * * * * After these remarks on tones a few lines are devoted to the grammar of the Chinese language; then follows an explanation of the final particles, or finals, the remarks on the use of which appear to be very sensible. * * * * The preface is followed by an introduction of some five pages in length containing exercises in tones and a lengthy syllabary, or directions for pronouncing Chinese sounds when represented by Roman letters. Then follow the numerals and a series of useful dialogues. * * * * In these dialogues a literal as well as free translation of the Chinese sentence is given. * * * * After the sentences comes a list of classifiers. * * * * Following the list of classifiers comes some original and really admirable work in the shape of cleverly written and exhaustive directions for rendering English grammatical forms into Chinese. * * * * We now come to the list of finals, or final particles, to the use of which the writer has evidently given very great attention, and we do not remember having previously seen anything like so exhaustive a list, or such sensible directions for the use of these finals. This is followed up by some final directions, and directions for the guidance of the beginner. * * * * In conclusion we may say that Mr. Ball's work, being the only one worth a second glance which is procurable, we strongly recommend it to students, not only beginners, but even somewhat advanced students, of Cantonese colloquial.—*Daily Press*, 7th September, 1883.

We say without hesitation that his work far surpasses that of Dennys, for example, in the matter of idiom, and that his command of words, and his perception of delicate shades of meaning are much above the average of European attainment in Canton colloquial. In these respects the volume before us makes a valuable addition to the existing aids to beginners; and might be found useful to some of the more 'venerable and learned Sinologists.' * * * * Mr. Ball's Notes on classifiers and grammar will be found very valuable.—*China Mail*, 10th September, 1883.

In the work now before us, compiled and edited by Mr. J. Dyer Ball, M.R.A.S., etc., who, from his long experience amongst the Cantonese and from his long study of their language, is eminently fitted for the task which he has imposed upon himself, we find an almost unlimited variety in a comparatively small compass—the work contains little more than 100 pages inclusive of preface and introduction—wherewith the beginner may be guided. * * * * Mr. Ball has endeavored to give such expressive volubility to his work as far as his studies, learning, researches and long experience in China have enabled him to do. * * * * Of the work itself, taken as a whole we can say that it is a most admirable compilation. * * * * For an advanced sinologue there are very many valuable hints given. * * * * We approve * * of Mr. Ball's basis of arrangement in the fifteen lessons, and really commend the book for an *advanced student* to whom the work will prove in a number of ways a valuable addition towards the tending of the improvement in his mode of construing Chinese phrases and sentences in the Cantonese. * * * The work is got up in a neat form and is well printed.—*Hongkong Telegraph*, 12th Sept., 1883.

Now that the Franco-Chinese question is occupying so much public attention there will doubtless be many cadets, missionary students, and philologists turning their thoughts towards the East, and in some instances they will be anxious to know what are the languages chiefly spoken, and where reliable text-books may be obtained. I am glad to be able at this emergency to call the attention of such enquirers to a new work, by Mr. J. Dyer Ball, which has just been published in Hongkong under the title of *Cantonese Made Easy*. The dialect of Canton is the most important of South China; and as it contains fewer provincialisms than almost any other Chinese dialect, and employs the classical characters entirely in writing, the knowledge of this sub-language, so to speak, is indispensable to any one who intends taking a position in the East. Mr. J. Dyer Ball has rendered good service in his timely publication. Born in China, of European parentage, favoured with exceptional advantages for the acquisition of the dialects of China, having a natural gift for this particular work, and being employed in Her Majesty's Civil Service as Interpreter for the Supreme Court, he has had every oppor-

ADVERTISEMENTS. III

tunity to gain an accurate knowledge of Cantonese. * * * The difficult questions relating to tones, classifiers, finals, &c., are treated with a masterly hand.—*Academy*, 12th January, 1884.

* * * For the sake of your readers in Oxford and elsewhere who may be studying philology, or preparing for cadetships and civil service in the East I call attention to a new work on the Chinese language. The book is entitled *Cantonese Made Easy* and has been prepared by Mr. J. Dyer Ball, M.R.A.S., Interpreter to the Supreme Court, Hongkong. Mr. Ball was born in China, and speaks the language like a native. He has spent his life chiefly in the East and I can add my testimony to that of numerous reviewers respecting the excellency of his book.—*Bunbury Guardian*, 10th January, 1884.

THE CANTONESE-MADE-EASY VOCABULARY.
Price: One Dollar.

A Small Dictionary in English and Cantonese, containing only Words and Phrases used in the Spoken Language, with Classifiers indicated for each Noun and Definitions of the Different Shades of Meaning, as well as Notes on the Different uses of Words where Ambiguity might otherwise arise.

The work should be very useful to students of the Cantonese Dialect.—*China Mail*, 26th July, 1886.

Mr. J. Dyer Ball, author of 'Easy Sentences in the Hakka Dialect,' 'Cantonese Made Easy,' &c., has just issued a companion work to these useful publications to students of Chinese. * * * The words and phrases appear to have been most carefully collected and arranged, and we doubt not that this little dictionary will adequately fulfil the aims of the compiler.—*Hongkong Telegraph*, 27th July, 1886.

The author originally intended to attach the vocabulary to his work 'Cantonese Made Easy;' he has somewhat enlarged its scope, not confining it to words contained in those lessons alone, but giving an exhaustive list of different shades of the English meaning, to save the beginner from falling into mistakes to which he would otherwise be liable. The vocabulary seems to have been most carefully compiled, and it cannot fail to prove most useful to students, especially beginners.—*Hongkong Daily Press*, 29th July, 1886.

We may state that we have here a very neatly got up vocabulary of the most common terms which a beginner is likely to stand in need of. * * * The rendering of the terms selected appear to be given in good idiomatic colloquial style. * * * As the author gives, for the English words selected by him, the corresponding Chinese characters together with their pronunciation and tones, the little book is sure to prove useful.—*China Review*, July and August, 1886.

This book will prove useful to persons desirous of learning the Cantonese dialect.—*Chinese Recorder and Missionary Journal*, Nov. 1886.

Here it will not be out of place to mention that everything possible is being done to lighten the labours of merchants, cadets, missionaries, and students, in their study of that difficult language, the Chinese. The author has just forwarded to us a copy of 'The Cantonese-Made-Easy Vocabulary' (printed in Hongkong, on sale at Messrs. Trübner and Co., London, 1 dollar), by J. Dyer Ball, Esq., M.R.A.S., &c. Mr. Ball is one of the most accomplished linguists in Hongkong, in consequence of which we find him occupying the important post of Interpreter in the Supreme Court; and no more able pen could be found for the work of simplifying and popularising the Chinese tongue.

There are many people in England as well as abroad to whom Mr. Ball's work will be a boon. If gives first the English words in alphabetical order, then the Chinese equivalents, and finally a transliteration of the Chinese words, so that those who do not understand the characters may still be able to tell at a glance what is the Cantonese equivalent of the word before them. Thus the word *Any* is stated to be an *adj.* and *adv.*, then follows the Chinese word, and finally its pronunciation *mat*, so that *mat* is the Chinese equivalent of *any*; *yan* stands for *man*, *kiu* is the verb *to call*, and so on. Numerous notes are added where there is any danger of the learner being misled by the ambiguity of terms, and altogether the book is a capital *Vade-mecum* for the young student.—*Retford and Gainsborough Times, Worksop and Newark Weekly News*, 24th Dec., 1886.

While dealing with China it will not be out of place to mention another work for which future learners of that curious language will be grateful. This is 'The Cantonese-Made-Easy Vocabulary' by J. Dyer Ball, M.R.A.S., of H. M. Civil Service, Hongkong. The author is one of the best foreign speakers of Chinese we have ever had the good fortune to meet.

Born and brought up in the East, he can converse as readily in Cantonese as in English, and is consequently a most reliable authority on such critical points as *Tone* and *Classifiers*, which are the bugbears of every beginner in Chinese. The volume will also be valuable to the philologist, even though he may know little or nothing of the Celestial tongue, since every Chinese character is represented by the equivalent sound in English letters.—*English paper*.

AN ENGLISH-CANTONESE POCKET VOCABULARY.

BY

J. DYER BALL, M.R.A.S., &c.

Price, Seventy-Five Cents.

Notices by the Press.

Mr. J. DYER BALL, the chief interpreter of the Supreme Court and the author of *Easy Sentences in the Hakka Dialect, Cantonese made Easy*, and *The Cantonese-Made-Easy Vocabulary*, has just issued *An English-Cantonese Vocabulary*. * * * * * It is meant * * for the use of strangers, tourists, or even residents, who, from want of time, are unable to master the intricacies of the language, but who, at the same time, feel a desire to pick up a few words, so as not to be in

the position of deaf mutes when entirely surrounded by natives. Those who have any knowledge of the subject will readily appreciate Mr. BALL'S object in compiling this limited vocabulary, the want for which has been felt, severely felt we might say, ever since the Colony was founded. To say the least of them, tonic marks are decidedly confusing unless they are seriously studied, and their entire absence from this vocabulary will alone prove a recommendation. Mr. BALL'S book makes no pretensions to oust those vocabularies which are already in existence; it merely makes an attempt to supply a demand hitherto unprovided for.   *   *   *   *   *   *
It is sufficiently copious to enable any one to make himself or herself understood in the ordinary transactions of everyday life; and it is just possible that it may awaken a desire in some persons to know more of the language. Mr. BALL has very wisely issued the book at a low price, 75 cents a copy, and its merit and cheapness should ensure an extensive sale.—*China Mail*, 22nd September, 1886.

Mr. J. DYER BALL'S 'English-Cantonese Pocket Vocabulary' is quite a novelty in its way, and is the first publication we have seen in which some knowledge of Chinese is rendered possible without the use of Chinese characters. The sounds of the Chinese words in this little work are represented by English spelling, in exactly the same fashion adopted in many rudimentary treatises on the French and other foreign languages.   *   *   *   The plan adopted by Mr. DYER BALL is very simple, and we think an effective one. He wished to provide a method by which travellers and others, who may not consider the acquisition of Cantonese a game worth the candle, without any very serious study, can acquire a sufficient acquaintance with the vernacular to be understood if unhappily isolated amongst non-English speaking Chinese. Mr. BALL has done his work in his customary careful and painstaking fashion, and we imagine this little book will command a ready sale.—*Hongkong Telegraph*, 23rd September, 1886.

We have received a copy of another of those useful aids to the acquisition of the Chinese colloquial for which Mr. DYER BALL is becoming noted. This last work is entitled 'An English-Cantonese Pocket Vocabulary.' It contains common words and phrases, printed without the Chinese characters or tonic marks, and the sounds of the Chinese words are represented by an English spelling as far as practicable, while the author in his preface gives some very simple directions how to overcome the difficulties of pronunciation. The little book is not intended for those who intend to make a serious study of Chinese; it is intended to enable the English resident or tourist to pick up a sufficient vocabulary to make known his wishes or wants to the natives, and to understand something of what is going on around him when surrounded by Chinese.   *   *   *
The pamphlet will supply a want and its study is likely to lead to further exploration in the same direction.—*Hongkong Daily Press*, 24th September, 1886.

The pamphlet is published for the benefit of tourists or residents who have no time to master the intricacies of the Cantonese dialect, and who are deterred from the task when they take up other books on the subject bristling with tonic and other diacritical marks. Mr. Ball labours therefore here, as in his other pamphlets, to make an intrinsically difficult subject easy. We think the book has its merits by its extreme simplicity and by the judicious selection of a stock of the most ordinary and popular words and phrases. The spelling * * * may prove handy enough for the purposes stated.—*China Review*, Nov. and Dec., 1886.

EASY SENTENCES IN THE HAKKA DIALECT,
WITH A VOCABULARY.
Price: $1.

EXTRACTS FROM NOTICES OF THE ABOVE WORK.

Easy Sentences in the Hakka Dialect is the title of a small work just published by Mr. J. Dyer Ball, Interpreter of the Supreme Court of Hongkong. It is, for the most part, as the author says in the introduction, an adaptation of Giles' *Handbook of the Swatow Dialect*, and will prove as useful to those entering on the study of Hakka as Mr. Giles' book has proved in the case of the dialect spoken at Swatow. An extensive vocabulary is appended.'—*Daily Press*, 28th October, 1881.

'Mr. J. Dyer Ball, the efficient interpreter of Chinese in the Supreme Court here, has published a neat little Handbook entitled *Easy Sentences in the Hakka Dialect, with a Vocabulary*. The author has taken the *Handbook of the Swatow Dialect* (by Mr. H. A. Giles) as a basis, and indeed Mr. Ball freely acknowledges that the help he received from that little book in his study of the Swatow Dialect suggested the *brochure* now given to the public. Unlike most books of the kind, there are no Chinese characters given for the 'Easy Sentences,' the collection of phrases being Romanized Phonetically so as to give to the beginner the equivalent sounds in Chinese. The sentences given appear to be well arranged, and cover as much ground as is ever likely to be required by those desirous of attaining to a rough colloquial knowledge of Hakka. Mr. Ball frankly tells all others to go to a teacher, and indeed he strongly advises even the learner to go hand in hand with the teacher in his uphill work from the very beginning.'—*China Mail*, 22nd October, 1881.

* * * A very handy little volume * * * In the preface to his useful pamphlet, Mr. Ball states that his work is for the most part a translation of Giles' *Handbook of the Swatow Dialect*. * * Chinese is admittedly a difficult study to Europeans, but, as Mr. Ball states, there is no reason why with a little trouble, they should not pick up sufficient conversational knowledge so as to be able to understand what goes on about them as well as to make themselves understood. For this purpose Mr. Ball's compilation will answer every requirement. The sentences are judiciously arranged, and the method of conveying a correct method of pronunciation is apparently very clear and simple. The book is very well printed, and as it is published at a very low price, will no doubt obtain an extensive circulation.' * * *—*Hongkong Telegraph*, 22nd October, 1881.

'*Easy Sentences in the Hakka Dialect, with a Vocabulary.* Translated by J. Dyer Ball, Hongkong, 1881. This title indicates the character of the book. It contains 57 pages and fourteen chapters besides the vocabulary. The subjects of the chapters are designated thus :—Lesson I. Domestic. II. to V. General. VI. Relationship. VII. Opposites. VIII. Monetary. IX., X. Commercial. XI. Medical. XII. Ecclesiastical. XIII. Nautical. XIV. Judicial. It thus contains a wide range of subjects. We cordially recommend it to all students of the Hakka Dialect.' * * * *Chinese Recorder and Missionary Journal*, Nov.-Dec., 1881.

THE ABOVE WORKS ARE ON SALE.

IN HONGKONG,
At Messrs. KELLY & WALSH'S, W. W. BREWER'S, and LANE, CRAWFORD & Co.'s, Queen's Road.

IN SHANGHAI,   **IN YOKOHAMA,**
At Messrs. KELLY & WALSH'S.   At Messrs. KELLY & WALSH'S.

IN LONDON,
At Messrs. TRÜBNER & Co.'s, 57 and 59 Ludgate Hill.

IN THE SANDWICH ISLANDS
Copies may be obtained on applying to Mr. F. DAMON, Honolulu, Hawaiian Islands.

www.ingramcontent.com/pod-product-compliance
Lightning Source LLC
Chambersburg PA
CBHW021733220426
43662CB00008B/828